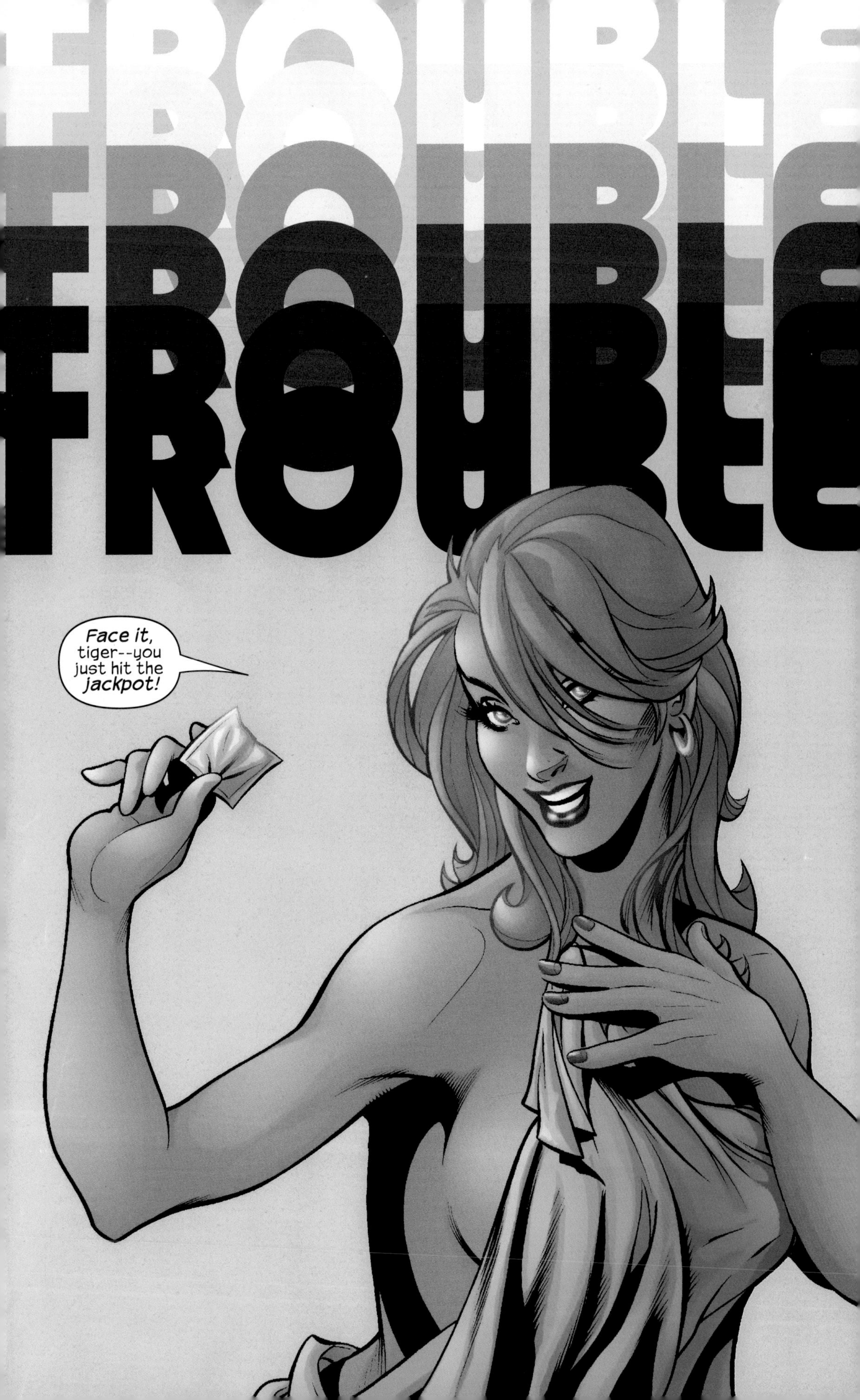
TROUBLE
Face it, tiger--you just hit the jackpot!

TRO

WRITER: **MARK MILLAR**
PENCILER: **TERRY DODSON**
INKER: **RACHEL DODSON**
COLORISTS: **MATT HOLLINGSWORTH** (ISSUES #1-3)
& **BRIAN REBER** (ISSUES #4-5)
LETTERER: **CHRIS ELIOPOULOS**
ASSISTANT EDITOR: **WARREN SIMONS**
EDITOR: **AXEL ALONSO**

COVER PHOTOS: **PHILIPPE BIALOBOS**
MAKE-UP: **GUILLERMO FERNANDEZ**
HAIR: **KRYSTOPH MARTEN** ART DIRECTION: **JOE QUESADA**
BIKINI TOPS: **DIPPERS CALIFORNIA** (ISSUE #1),
CRAFTWORK (ISSUE #2) & **WEATHERPROOF** (ISSUE #3)

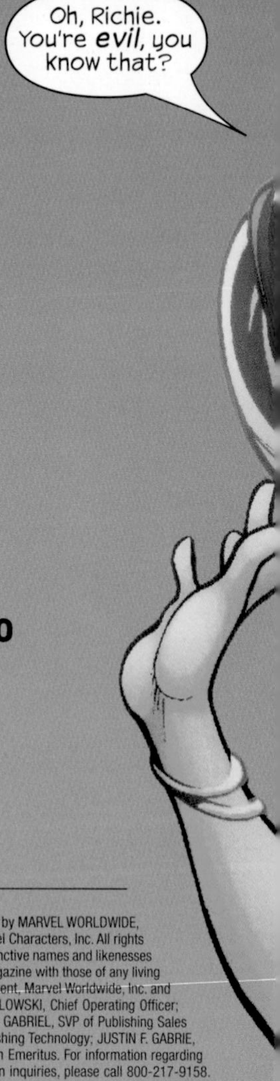
Oh, Richie. You're *evil*, you know that?

COLLECTION EDITOR: **JENNIFER GRÜNWALD**
EDITORIAL ASSISTANTS: **JAMES EMMETT** & **JOE HOCHSTEIN**
ASSISTANT EDITORS: **ALEX STARBUCK** & **NELSON RIBEIRO**
EDITOR, SPECIAL PROJECTS: **MARK D. BEAZLEY**
SENIOR EDITOR, SPECIAL PROJECTS: **JEFF YOUNGQUIST**
SENIOR VICE PRESIDENT OF SALES: **DAVID GABRIEL**
SVP OF BRAND PLANNING & COMMUNICATIONS: **MICHAEL PASCIULLO**
BOOK DESIGNER: **RODOLFO MURAGUCHI**

EDITOR IN CHIEF: **AXEL ALONSO**
CHIEF CREATIVE OFFICER: **JOE QUESADA**
PUBLISHER: **DAN BUCKLEY**
EXECUTIVE PRODUCER: **ALAN FINE**

TROUBLE BY MARK MILLAR. Contains material originally published in magazine form as TROUBLE #1-5. First printing 2011. ISBN# 978-0-7851-5086-2. Published by MARVEL WORLDWIDE, INC., a subsidiary of MARVEL ENTERTAINMENT, LLC. OFFICE OF PUBLICATION: 135 West 50th Street, New York, NY 10020. $19.99 per copy in the U.S. and $21.99 in Canada (GST #R127032852); Canadian Agreement #40668537. **Printed in the U.S.A**. ALAN FINE, EVP - Office of the President, Marvel Worldwide, Inc. and EVP & CMO Marvel Characters B.V.; DAN BUCKLEY, Publisher & President - Print, Animation & Digital Divisions; JOE QUESADA, Chief Creative Officer; JIM SOKOLOWSKI, Chief Operating Officer; DAVID BOGART, SVP of Business Affairs & Talent Management; TOM BREVOORT, SVP of Publishing; C.B. CEBULSKI, SVP of Creator & Content Development; DAVID GABRIEL, SVP of Publishing Sales & Circulation; MICHAEL PASCIULLO, SVP of Brand Planning & Communications; JIM O'KEEFE, VP of Operations & Logistics; DAN CARR, Executive Director of Publishing Technology; JUSTIN F. GABRIE, Director of Publishing & Editorial Operations; SUSAN CRESPI, Editorial Operations Manager; ALEX MORALES, Publishing Operations Manager; STAN LEE, Chairman Emeritus. For information regarding advertising in Marvel Comics or on Marvel.com, please contact John Dokes, SVP Integrated Sales and Marketing, at jdokes@marvel.com. For Marvel subscription inquiries, please call 800-217-9158. **Manufactured between 4/4/2011 and 5/2/2011 by R.R. DONNELLEY, INC., SALEM, VA, USA.**

10 9 8 7 6 5 4 3 2 1

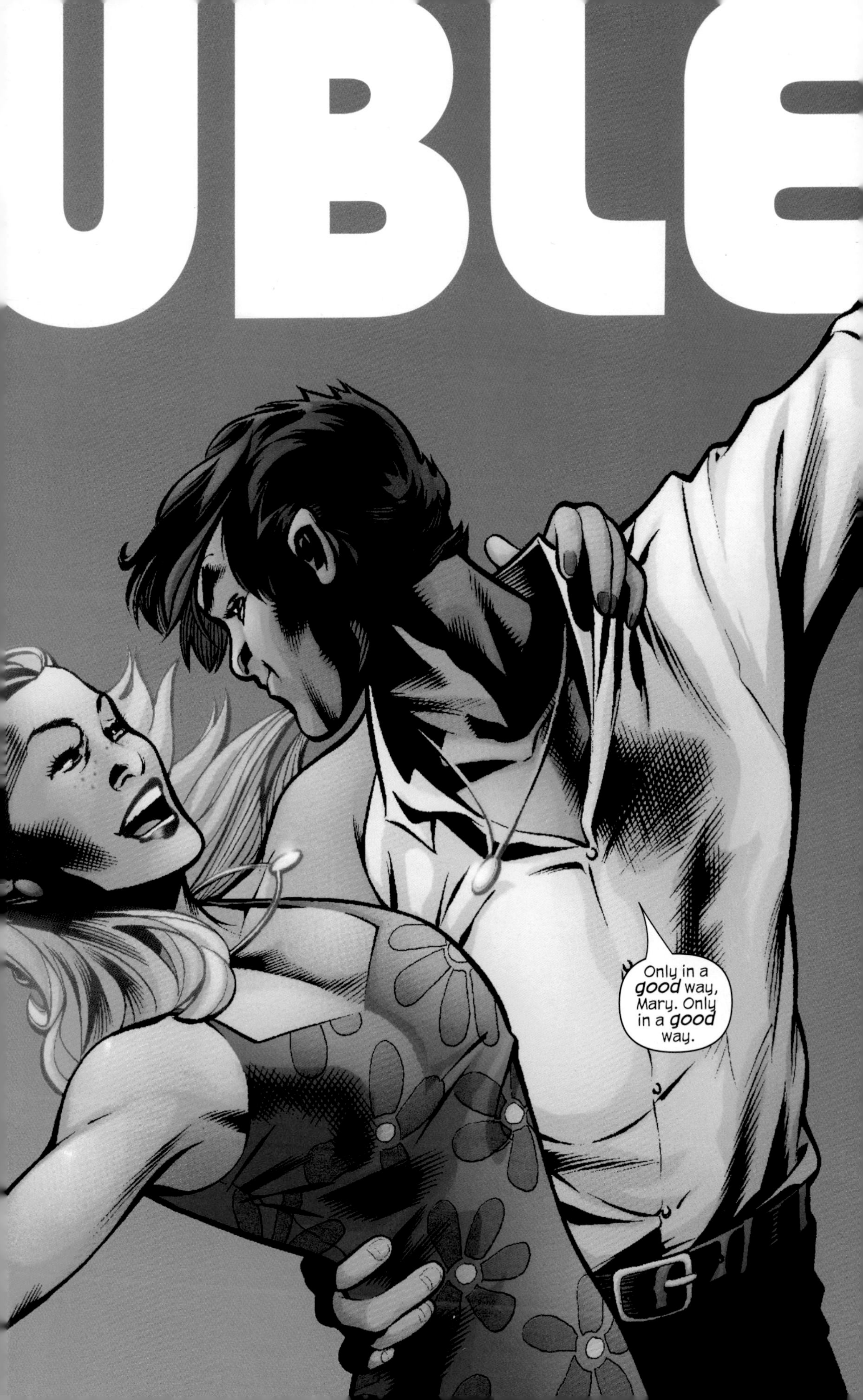
UBLE
Only in a good way, Mary. Only in a good way.

TROUBLE #1 2ND PRINTING VARIANT BY FRANK CHO & RICHARD ISANOVE

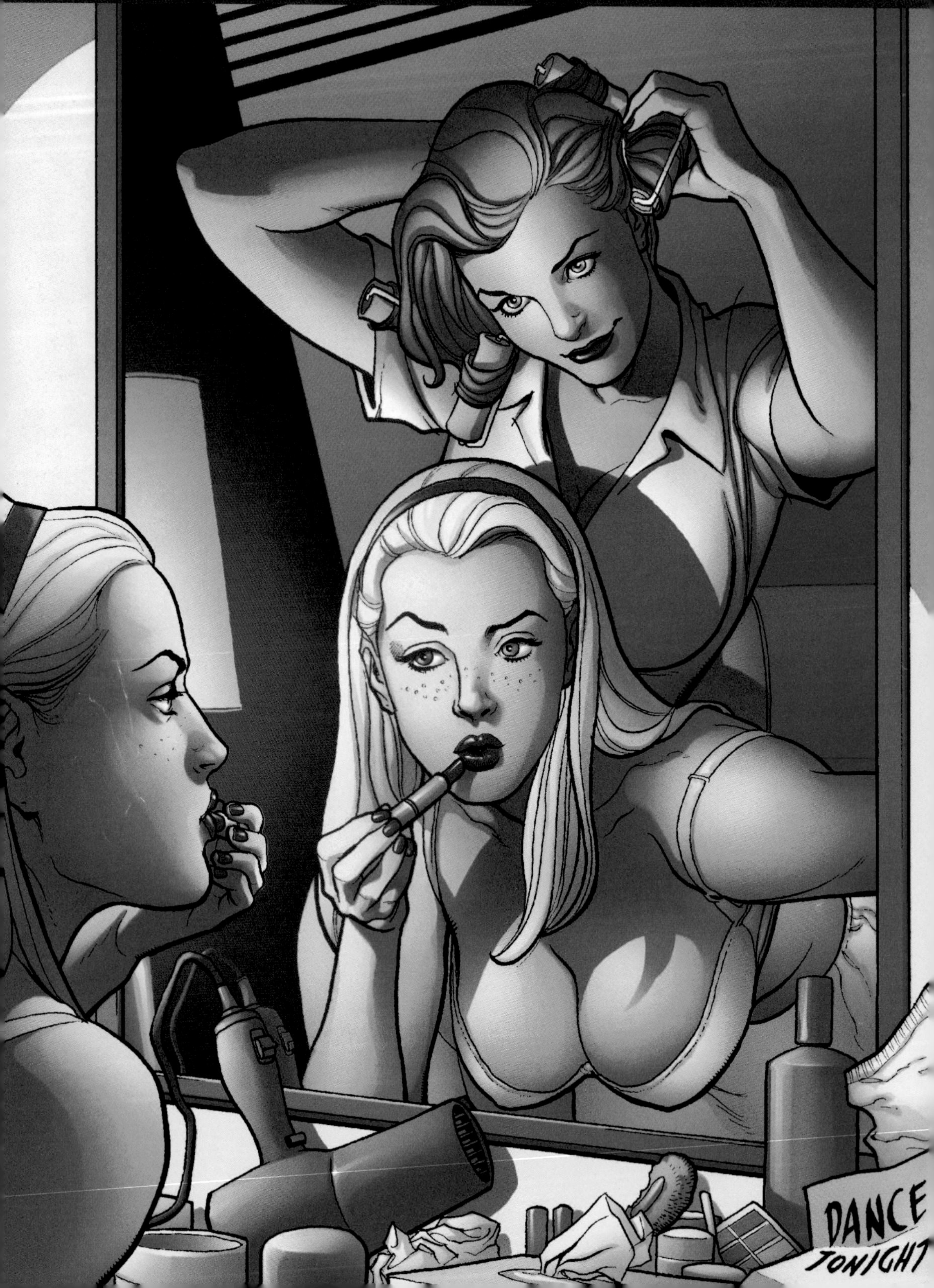
DANCE
TONIGHT

Trouble

part one of five

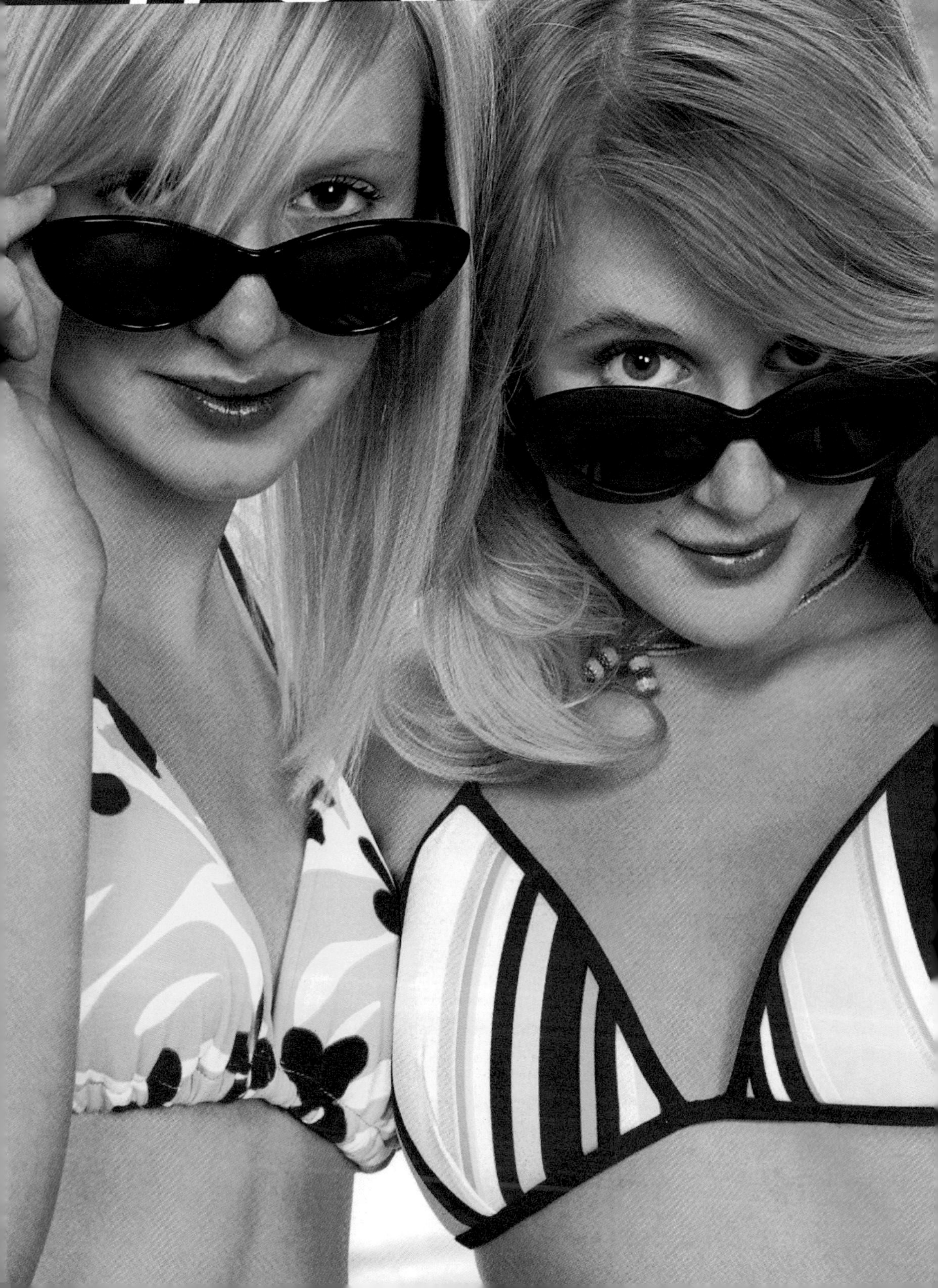

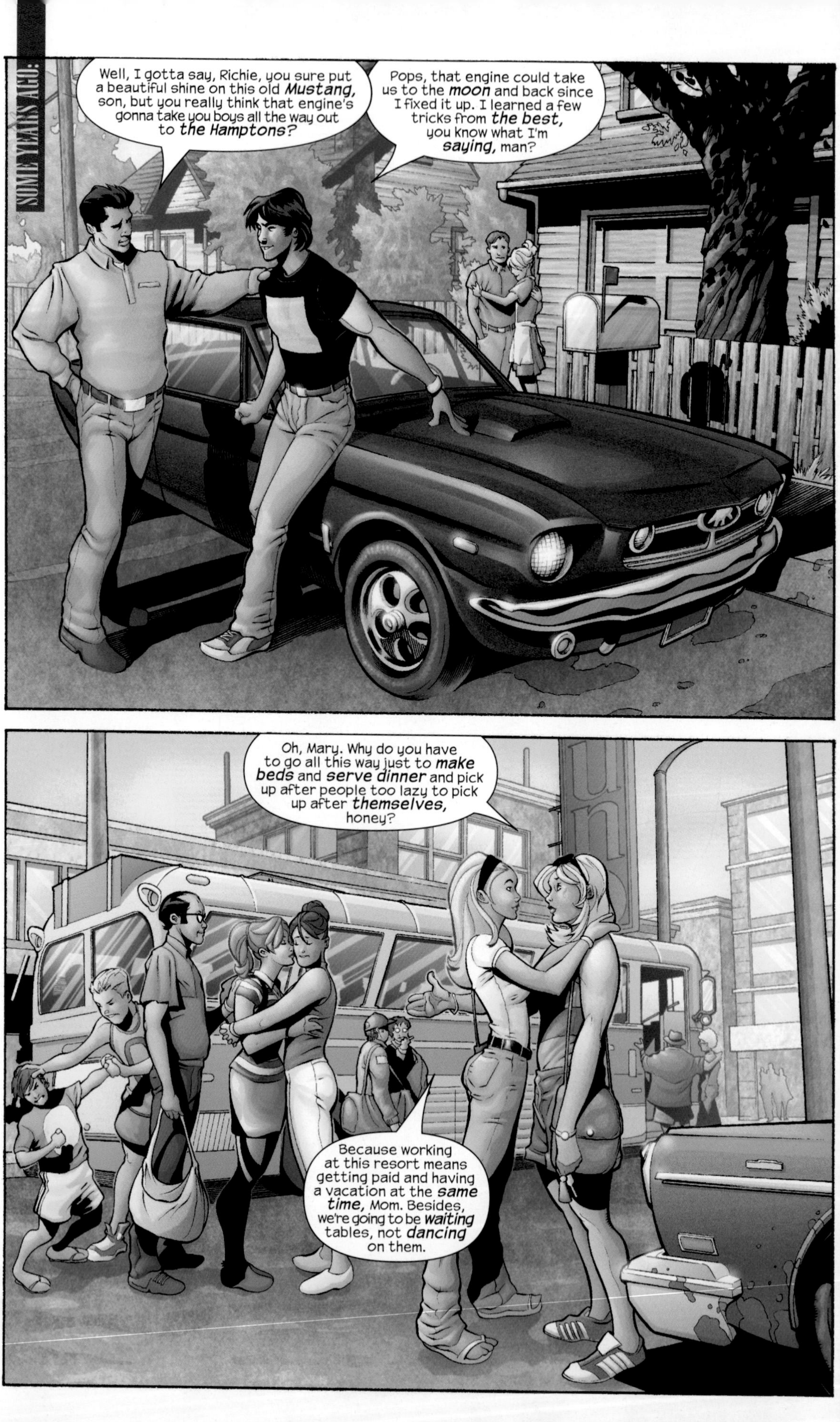
SOME YEARS AGO:
Well, I gotta say, Richie, you sure put a beautiful shine on this old Mustang, son, but you really think that engine's gonna take you boys all the way out to the Hamptons?
Pops, that engine could take us to the moon and back since I fixed it up. I learned a few tricks from the best, you know what I'm saying, man?
Oh, Mary. Why do you have to go all this way just to make beds and serve dinner and pick up after people too lazy to pick up after themselves, honey?
Because working at this resort means getting paid and having a vacation at the same time, Mom. Besides, we're going to be waiting tables, not dancing on them.

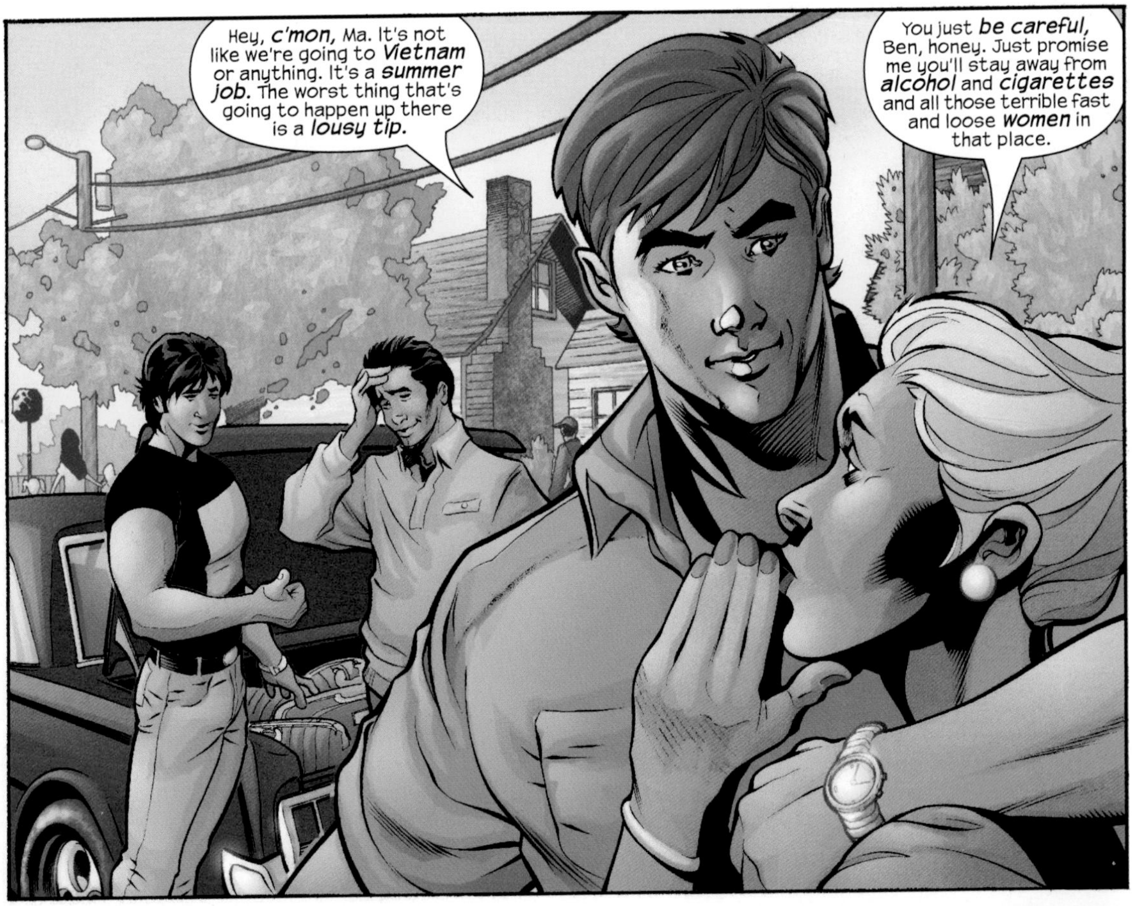
Hey, c'mon, Ma. It's not like we're going to Vietnam or anything. It's a summer job. The worst thing that's going to happen up there is a lousy tip.
You just be careful, Ben, honey. Just promise me you'll stay away from alcohol and cigarettes and all those terrible fast and loose women in that place.

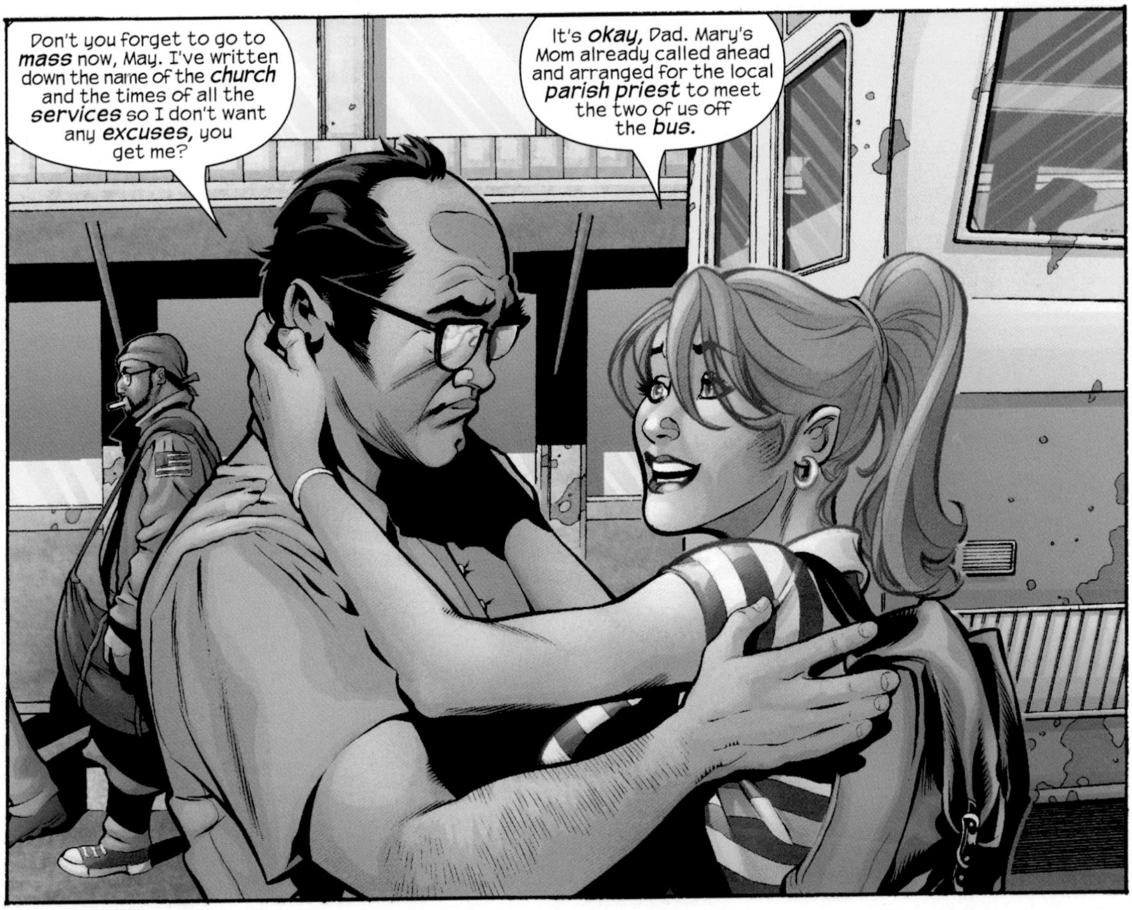
Don't you forget to go to mass now, May. I've written down the name of the church and the times of all the services so I don't want any excuses, you get me?
It's okay, Dad. Mary's Mom already called ahead and arranged for the local parish priest to meet the two of us off the bus.

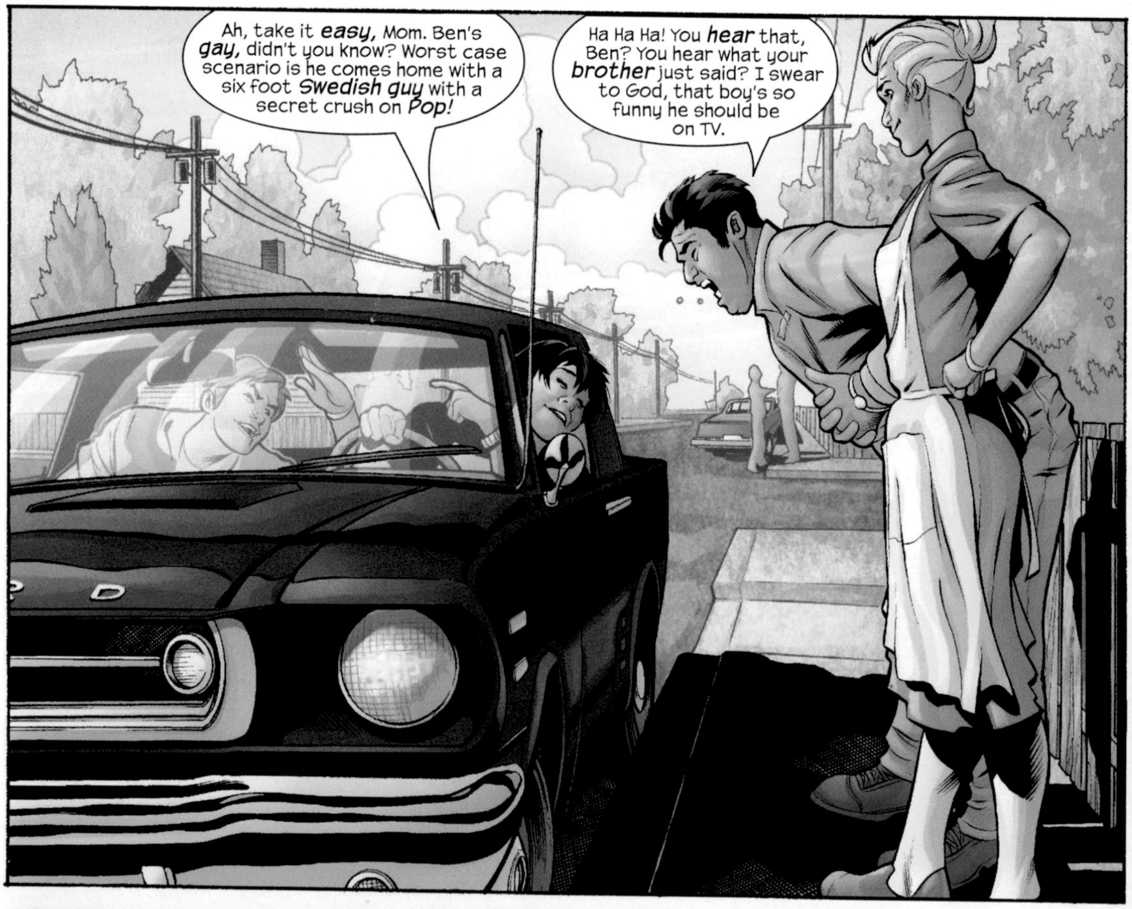
Ah, take it easy, Mom. Ben's gay, didn't you know? Worst case scenario is he comes home with a six foot Swedish guy with a secret crush on Pop!
Ha Ha Ha! You hear that, Ben? You hear what your brother just said? I swear to God, that boy's so funny he should be on TV.

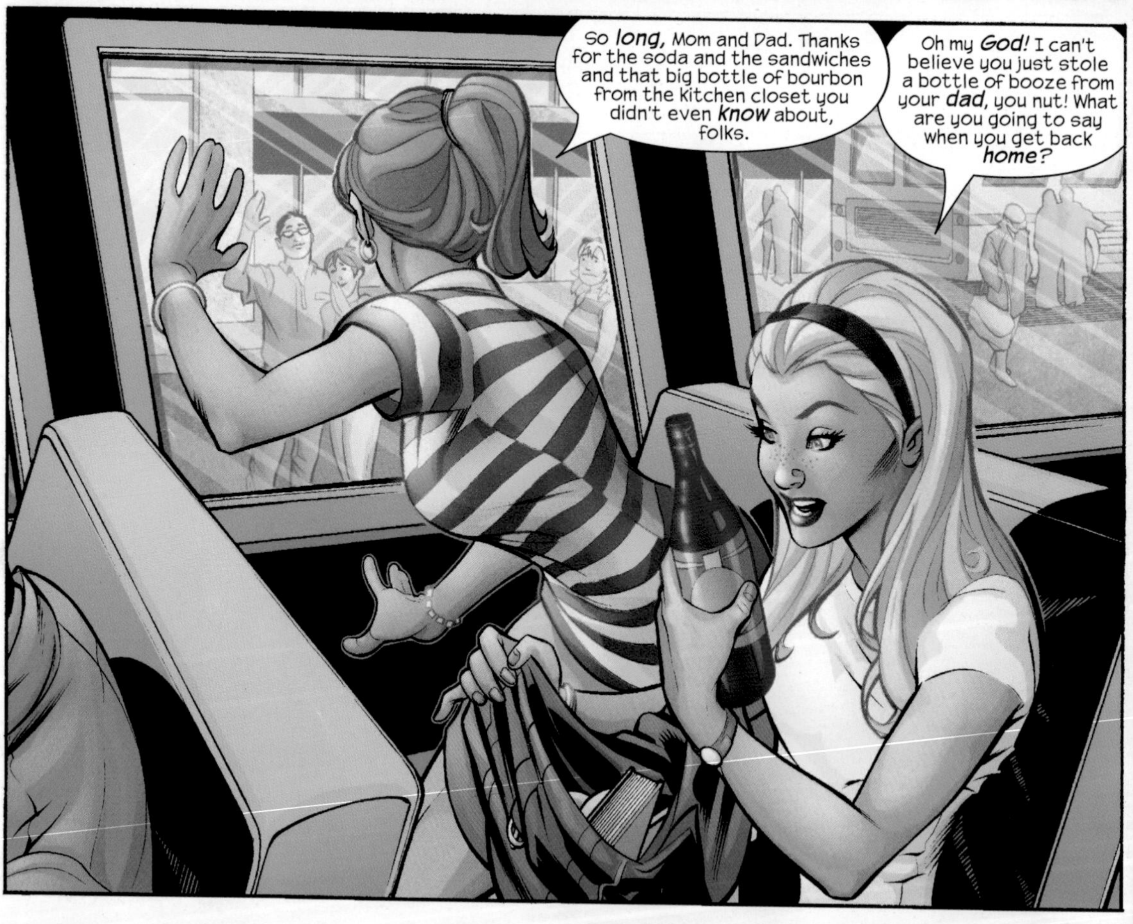
So long, Mom and Dad. Thanks for the soda and the sandwiches and that big bottle of bourbon from the kitchen closet you didn't even know about, folks.
Oh my God! I can't believe you just stole a bottle of booze from your dad, you nut! What are you going to say when you get back home?

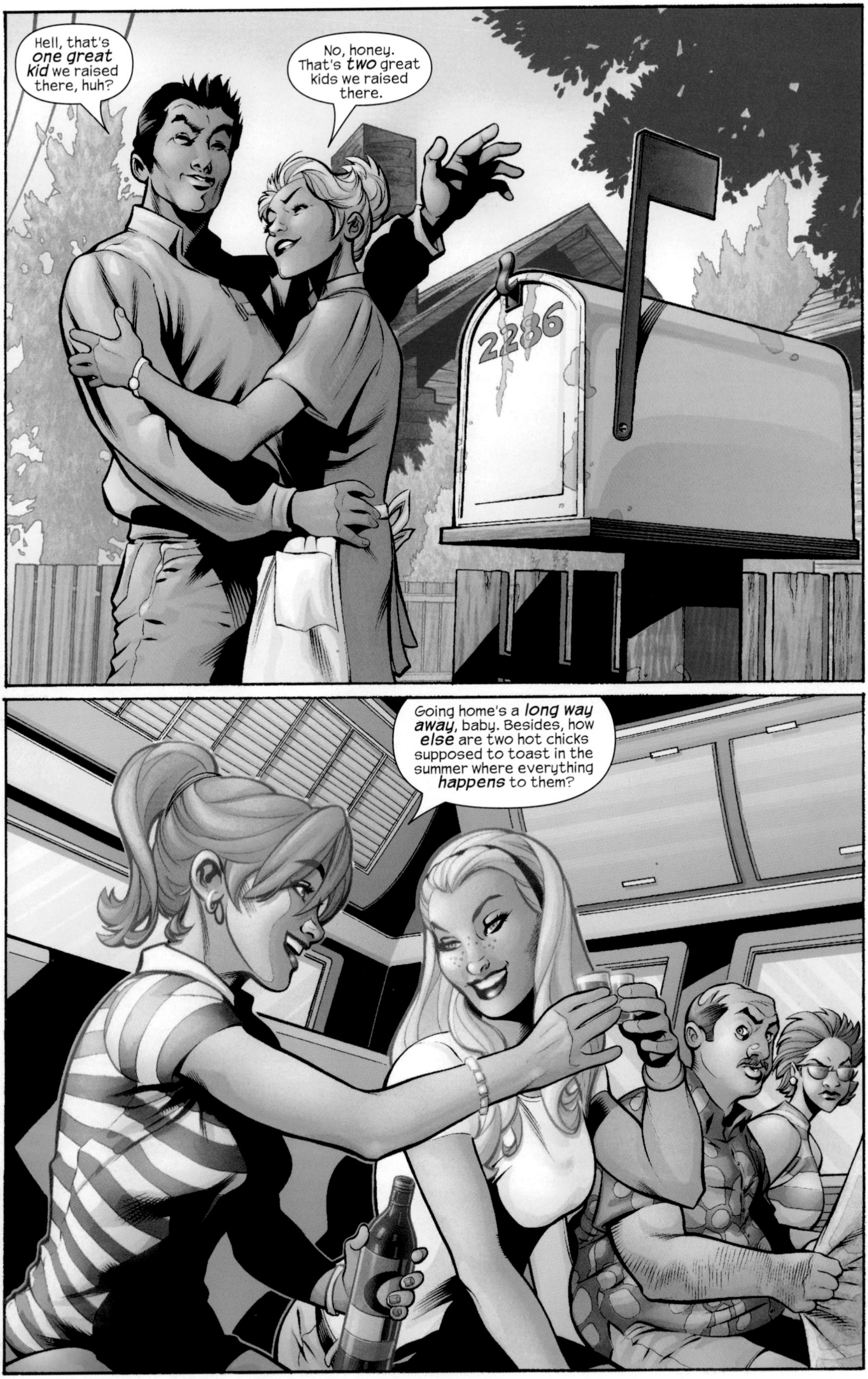

Hell, that's *one great kid* we raised there, huh?
No, honey. That's *two* great kids we raised there.
2286
Going home's a *long way away*, baby. Besides, how *else* are two hot chicks supposed to toast in the summer where everything *happens* to them?

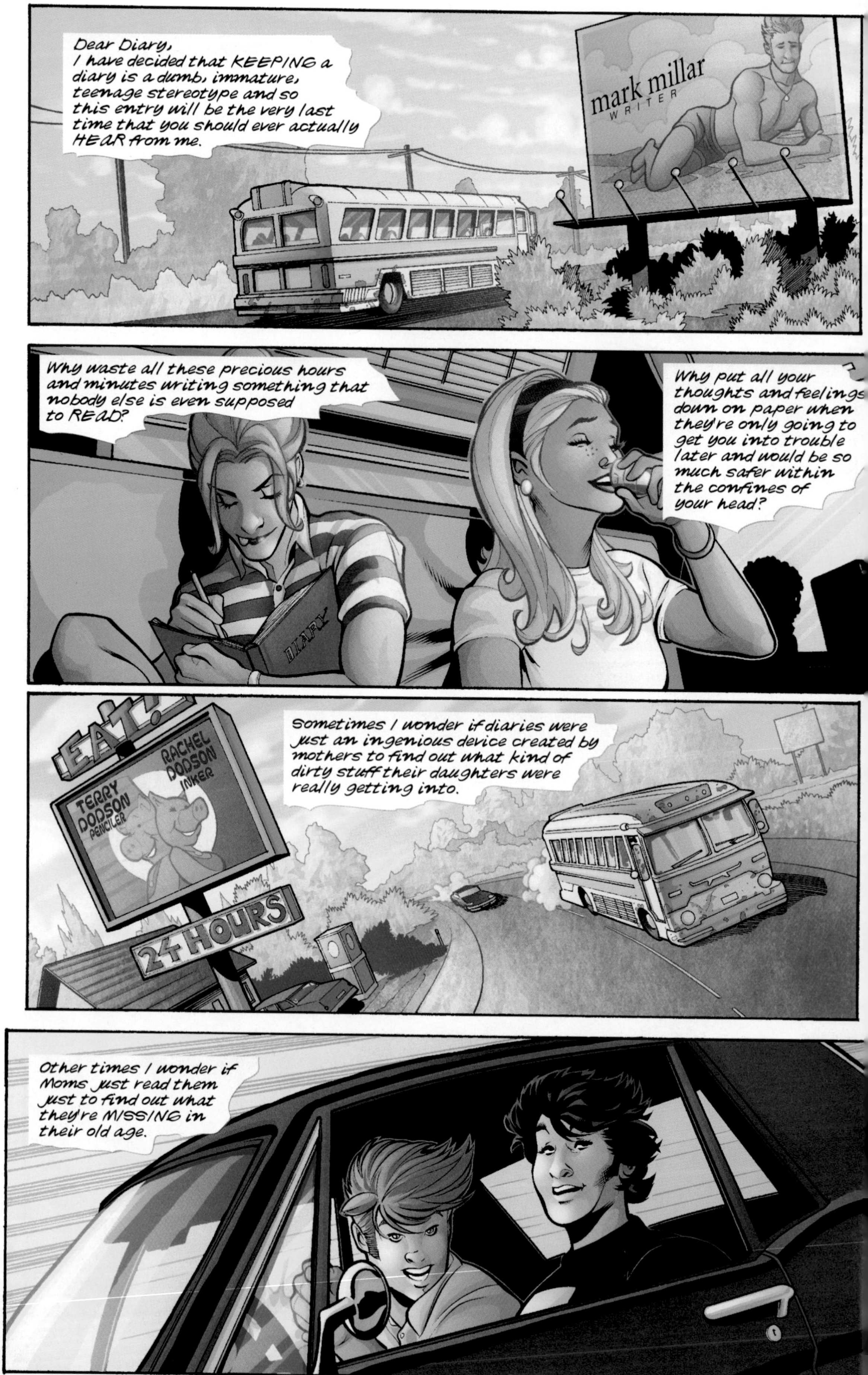

Dear Diary,
I have decided that KEEPING a diary is a dumb, immature, teenage stereotype and so this entry will be the very last time that you should ever actually HEAR from me.
mark millar
WRITER
Why waste all these precious hours and minutes writing something that nobody else is even supposed to READ?
Why put all your thoughts and feelings down on paper when they're only going to get you into trouble later and would be so much safer within the confines of your head?
DIARY
EAT
RACHEL DODSON INKER
TERRY DODSON PENCILER
24 HOURS
Sometimes I wonder if diaries were just an ingenious device created by mothers to find out what kind of dirty stuff their daughters were really getting into.
Other times I wonder if Moms just read them just to find out what they're MISSING in their old age.

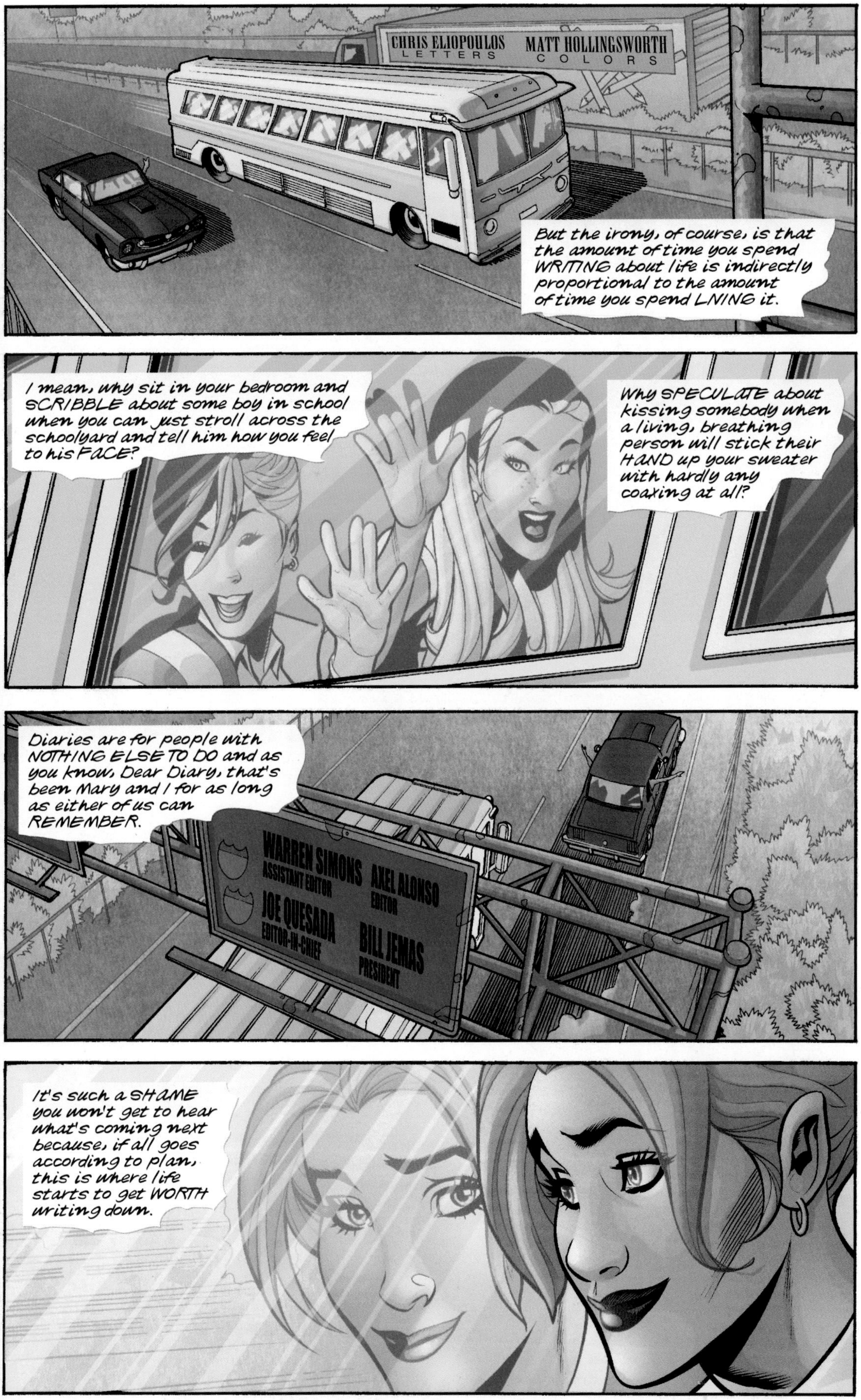
CHRIS ELIOPOULOS LETTERS
MATT HOLLINGSWORTH COLORS
But the irony, of course, is that the amount of time you spend WRITING about life is indirectly proportional to the amount of time you spend LIVING it.
I mean, why sit in your bedroom and SCRIBBLE about some boy in school when you can just stroll across the schoolyard and tell him how you feel to his FACE?
Why SPECULATE about kissing somebody when a living, breathing person will stick their HAND up your sweater with hardly any coaxing at all?
Diaries are for people with NOTHING ELSE TO DO and as you know, Dear Diary, that's been Mary and I for as long as either of us can REMEMBER.
WARREN SIMONS ASSISTANT EDITOR
AXEL ALONSO EDITOR
JOE QUESADA EDITOR-IN-CHIEF
BILL JEMAS PRESIDENT
It's such a SHAME you won't get to hear what's coming next because, if all goes according to plan, this is where life starts to get WORTH writing down.

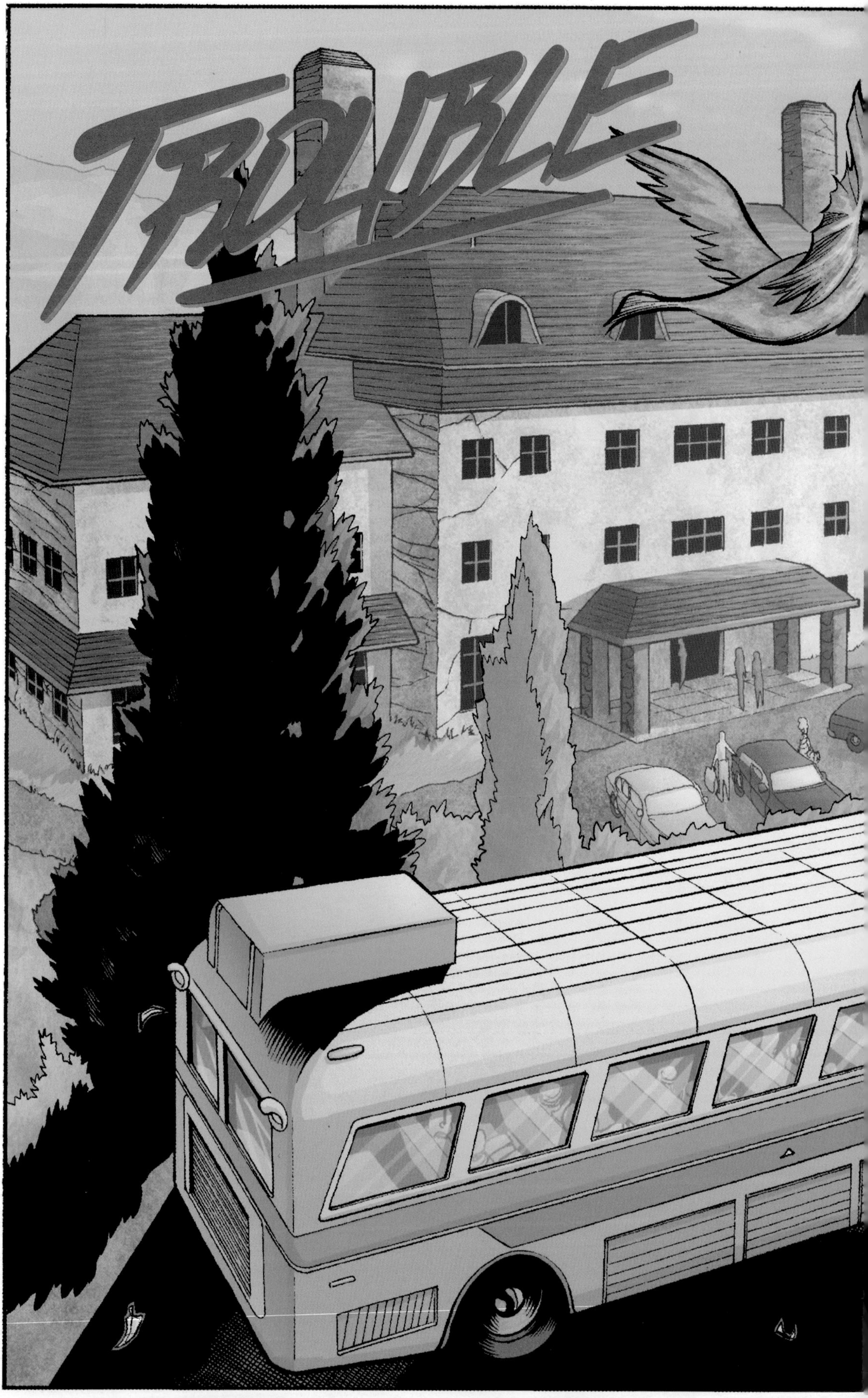
TROUBLE

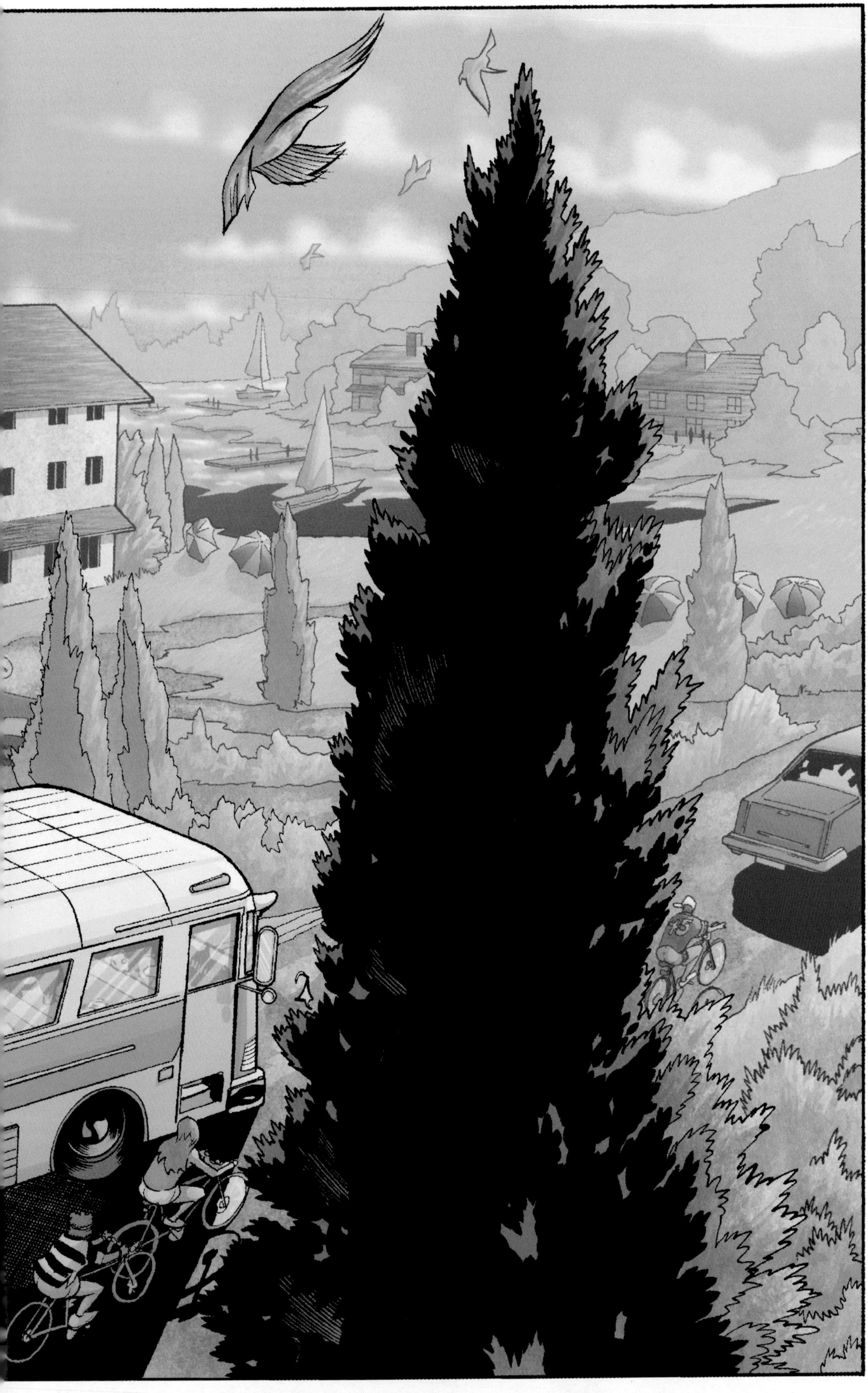

Good evening, ladies and gentlemen. My name is *Peter Howard Shelby* and it's my great pleasure to welcome you to the staff of *The East Hamptons Resort.*

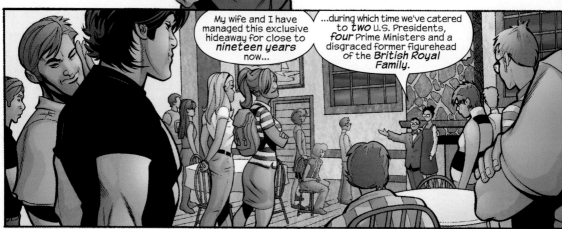

My wife and I have managed this exclusive hideaway for close to *nineteen years* now...

...during which time we've catered to *two* U.S. Presidents, *four* Prime Ministers and a disgraced former figurehead of the *British Royal Family.*

As we show you around, you will all understand why *East Hampton* is one of the three most *prestigious locales* in an already *prestigious area.*

You will also hear about the strict rules under which we work, the first of which is: no *intimate relations* between unmarried members of the *service staff.*

In my thirty years experience in these various forms of *hotel management,* I've learned that *intimacy* breeds *distraction* and *distraction* breeds *incompetence.*

In other words: please keep your *John Thomases* safely in your *trousers.* Do I make myself clear?

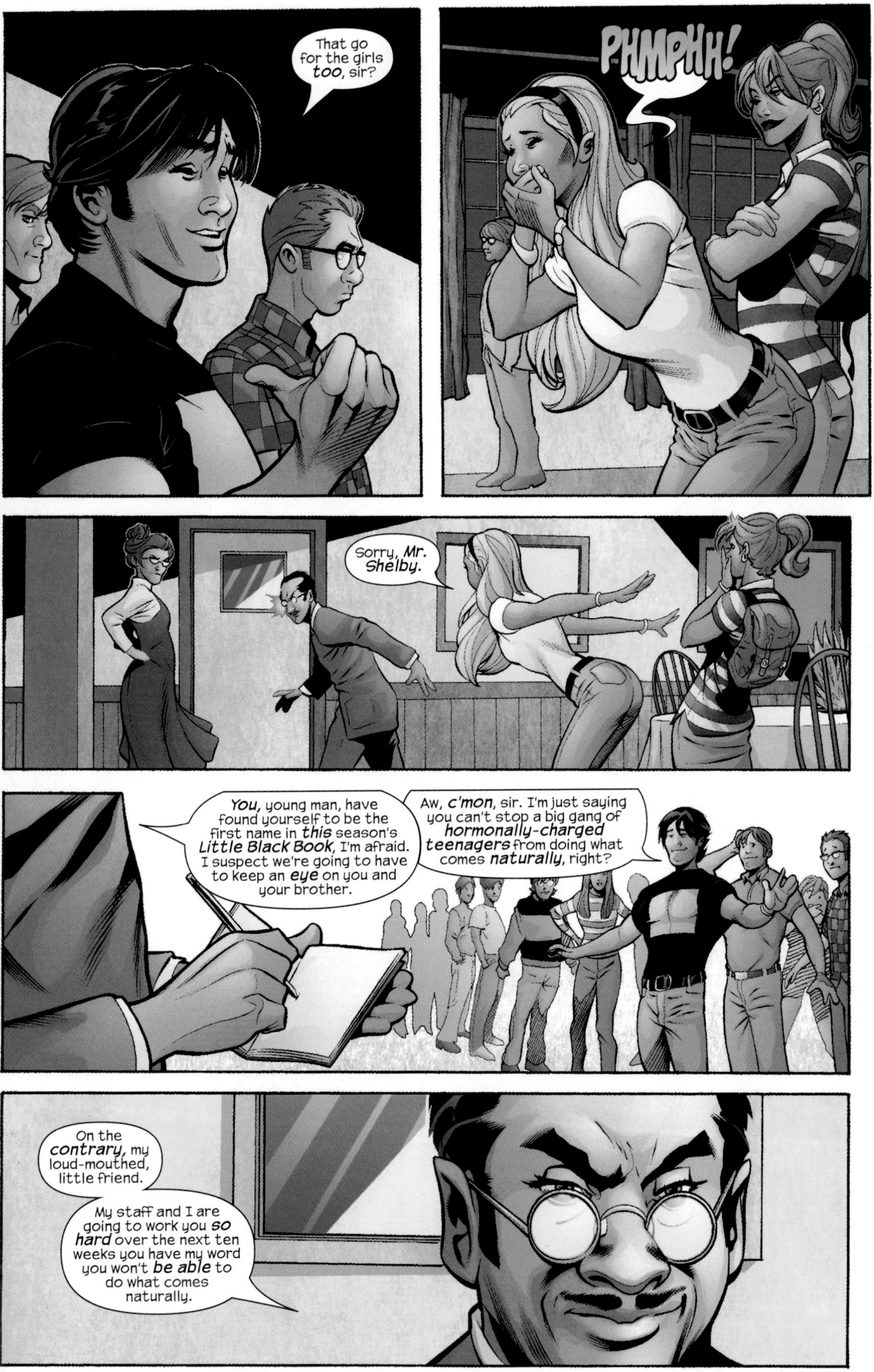
That go for the girls too, sir?
PHMPHH!
Sorry, Mr. Shelby.
You, young man, have found yourself to be the first name in this season's Little Black Book, I'm afraid. I suspect we're going to have to keep an eye on you and your brother.
Aw, c'mon, sir. I'm just saying you can't stop a big gang of hormonally-charged teenagers from doing what comes naturally, right?
On the contrary, my loud-mouthed, little friend.
My staff and I are going to work you so hard over the next ten weeks you have my word you won't be able to do what comes naturally.

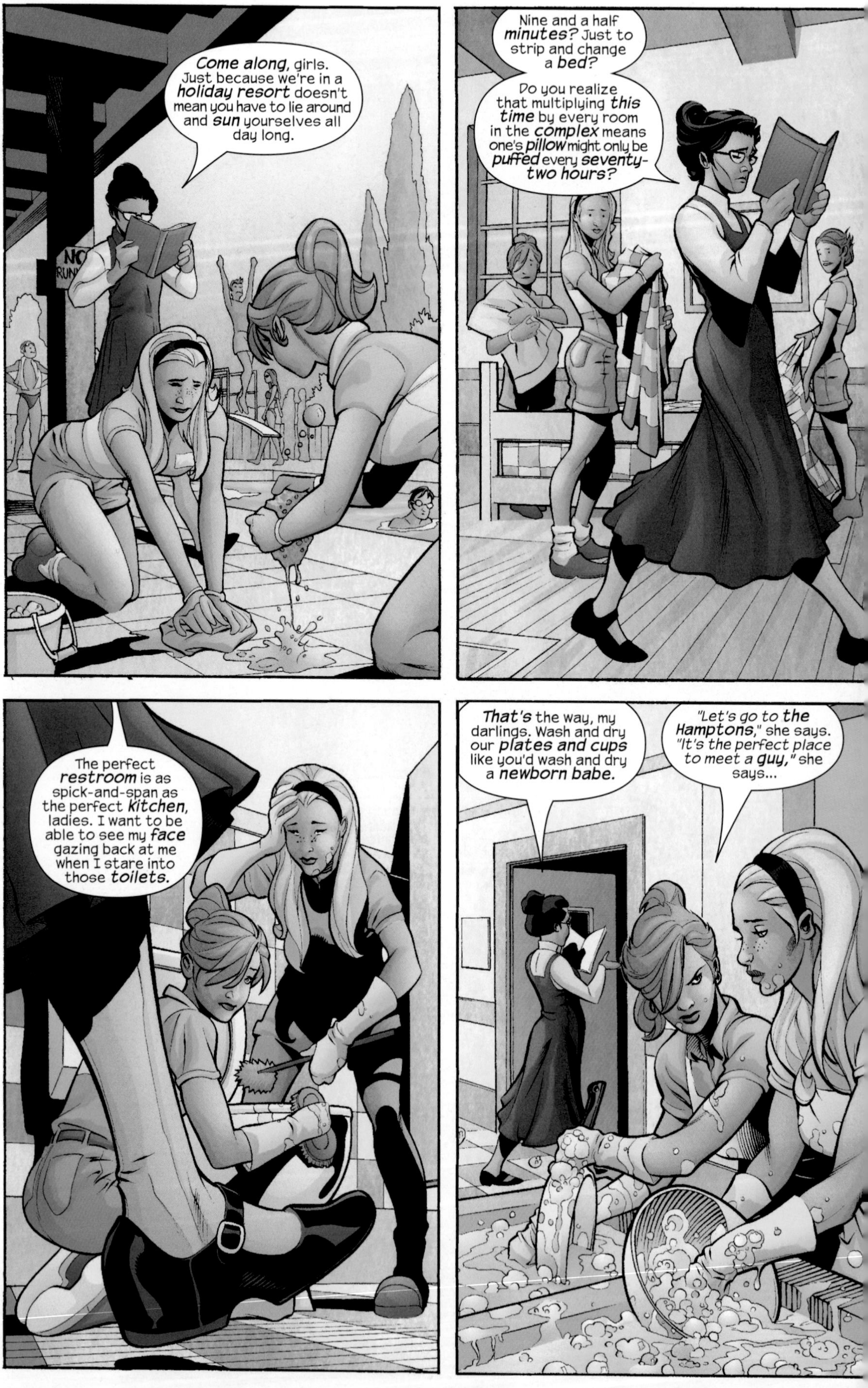
Come along, girls. Just because we're in a holiday resort doesn't mean you have to lie around and sun yourselves all day long.
Nine and a half minutes? Just to strip and change a bed?
Do you realize that multiplying this time by every room in the complex means one's pillow might only be puffed every seventy-two hours?
The perfect restroom is as spick-and-span as the perfect kitchen, ladies. I want to be able to see my face gazing back at me when I stare into those toilets.
That's the way, my darlings. Wash and dry our plates and cups like you'd wash and dry a newborn babe.
"Let's go to the Hamptons," she says. "It's the perfect place to meet a guy," she says...

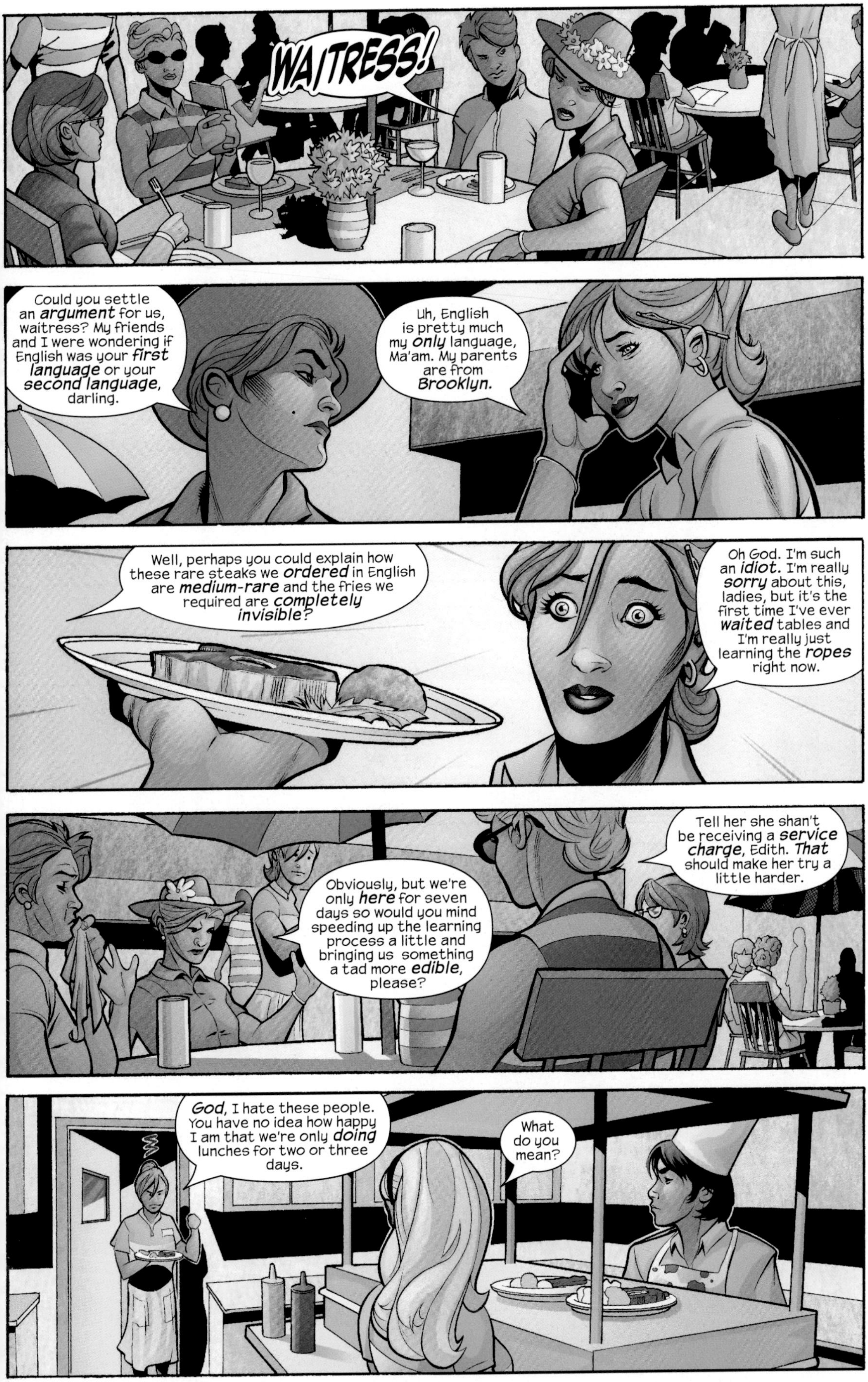
WAITRESS!
Could you settle an argument for us, waitress? My friends and I were wondering if English was your first language or your second language, darling.
Uh, English is pretty much my only language, Ma'am. My parents are from Brooklyn.
Well, perhaps you could explain how these rare steaks we ordered in English are medium-rare and the fries we required are completely invisible?
Oh God. I'm such an idiot. I'm really sorry about this, ladies, but it's the first time I've ever waited tables and I'm really just learning the ropes right now.
Obviously, but we're only here for seven days so would you mind speeding up the learning process a little and bringing us something a tad more edible, please?
Tell her she shan't be receiving a service charge, Edith. That should make her try a little harder.
God, I hate these people. You have no idea how happy I am that we're only doing lunches for two or three days.
What do you mean?

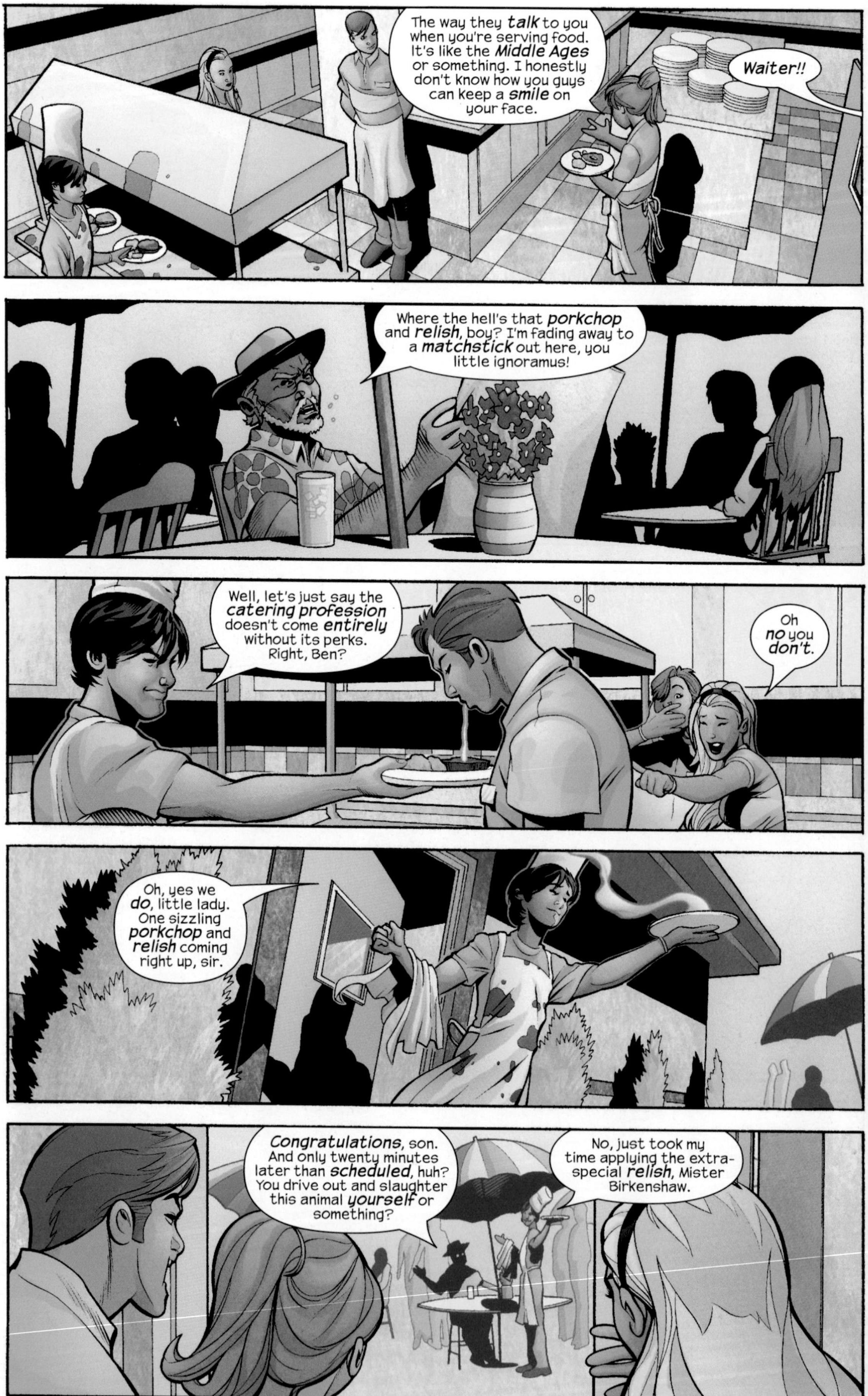
The way they talk to you when you're serving food. It's like the Middle Ages or something. I honestly don't know how you guys can keep a smile on your face.
Waiter!!
Where the hell's that porkchop and relish, boy? I'm fading away to a matchstick out here, you little ignoramus!
Well, let's just say the catering profession doesn't come entirely without its perks. Right, Ben?
Oh no you don't.
Oh, yes we do, little lady. One sizzling porkchop and relish coming right up, sir.
Congratulations, son. And only twenty minutes later than scheduled, huh? You drive out and slaughter this animal yourself or something?
No, just took my time applying the extra-special relish, Mister Birkenshaw.

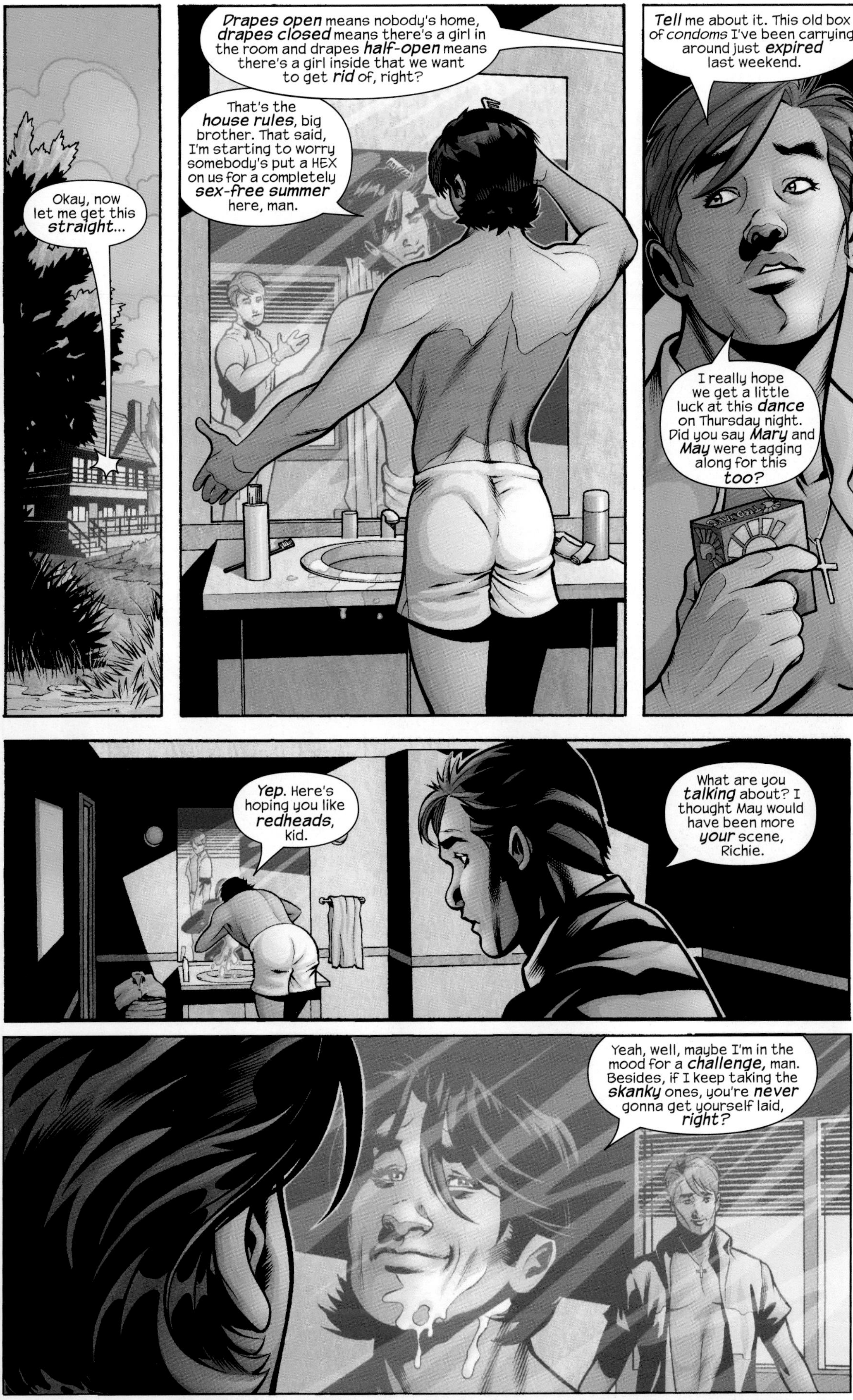
Okay, now let me get this straight...
Drapes open means nobody's home, drapes closed means there's a girl in the room and drapes half-open means there's a girl inside that we want to get rid of, right?
That's the house rules, big brother. That said, I'm starting to worry somebody's put a HEX on us for a completely sex-free summer here, man.
Tell me about it. This old box of condoms I've been carrying around just expired last weekend.
I really hope we get a little luck at this dance on Thursday night. Did you say Mary and May were tagging along for this too?
Yep. Here's hoping you like redheads, kid.
What are you talking about? I thought May would have been more your scene, Richie.
Yeah, well, maybe I'm in the mood for a challenge, man. Besides, if I keep taking the skanky ones, you're never gonna get yourself laid, right?

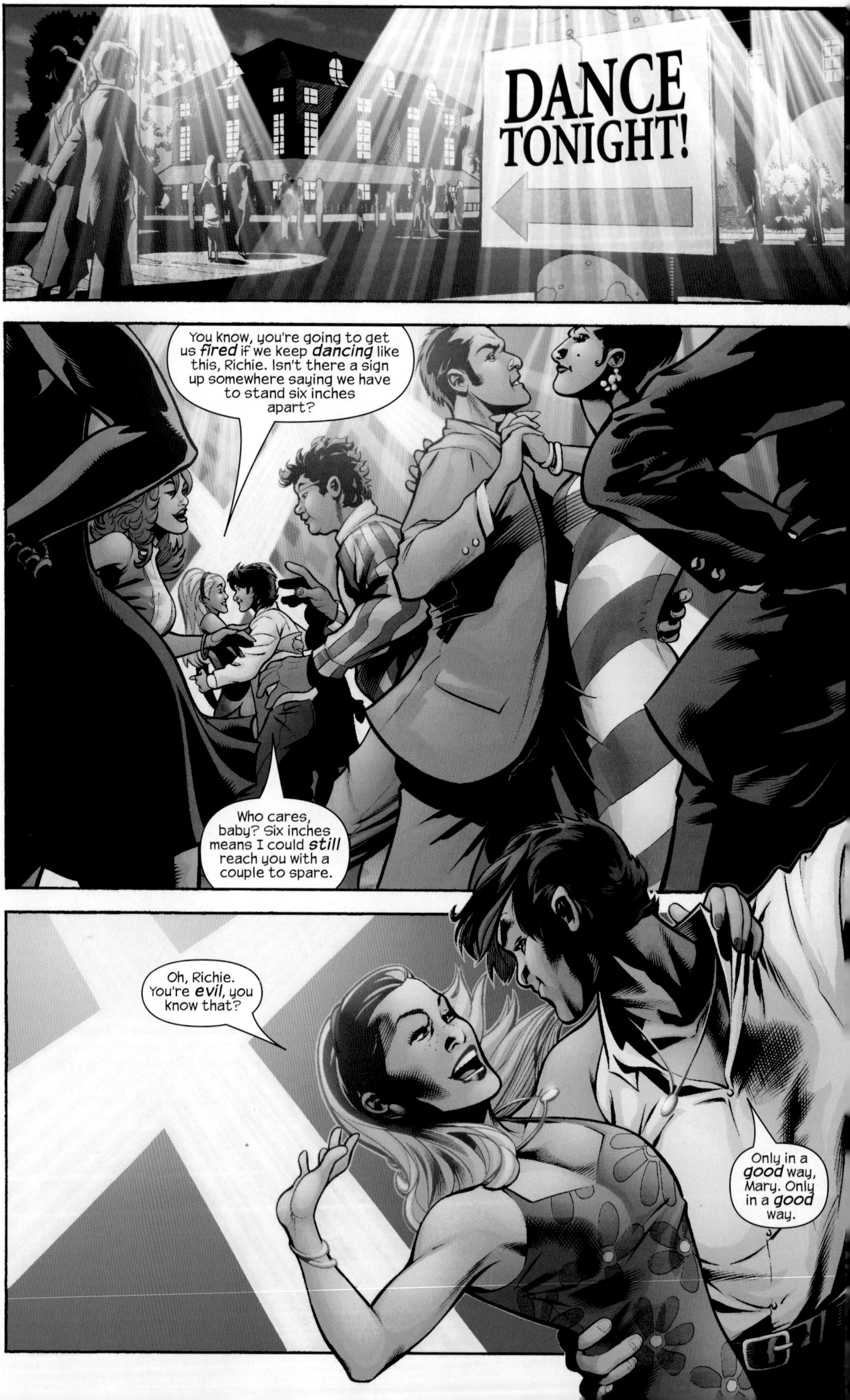
DANCE TONIGHT!
You know, you're going to get us fired if we keep dancing like this, Richie. Isn't there a sign up somewhere saying we have to stand six inches apart?
Who cares, baby? Six inches means I could still reach you with a couple to spare.
Oh, Richie. You're evil, you know that?
Only in a good way, Mary. Only in a good way.

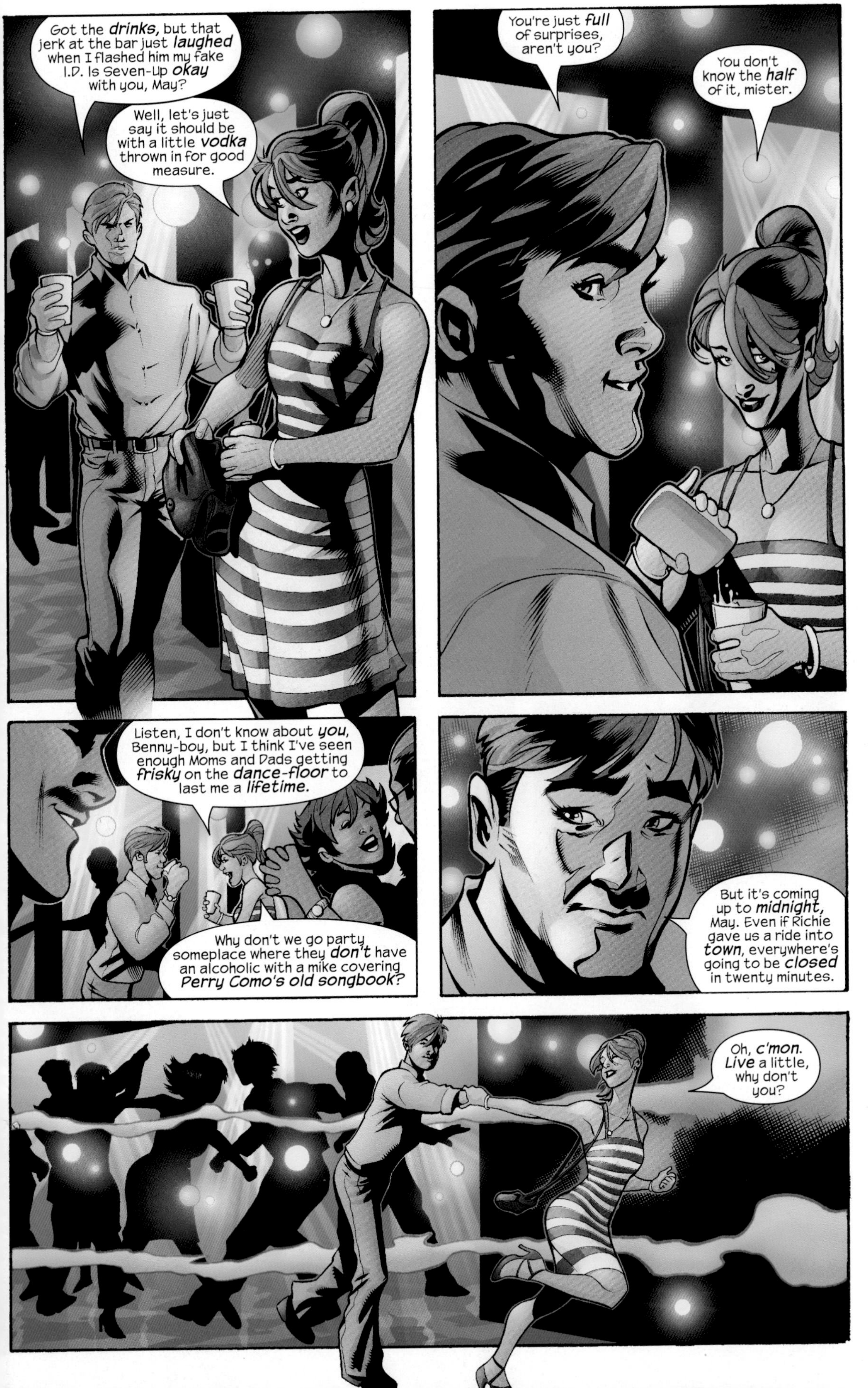
Got the drinks, but that jerk at the bar just laughed when I flashed him my fake I.D. Is Seven-Up okay with you, May?
Well, let's just say it should be with a little vodka thrown in for good measure.
You're just full of surprises, aren't you?
You don't know the half of it, mister.
Listen, I don't know about you, Benny-boy, but I think I've seen enough Moms and Dads getting frisky on the dance-floor to last me a lifetime.
Why don't we go party someplace where they don't have an alcoholic with a mike covering Perry Como's old songbook?
But it's coming up to midnight, May. Even if Richie gave us a ride into town, everywhere's going to be closed in twenty minutes.
Oh, c'mon. Live a little, why don't you?

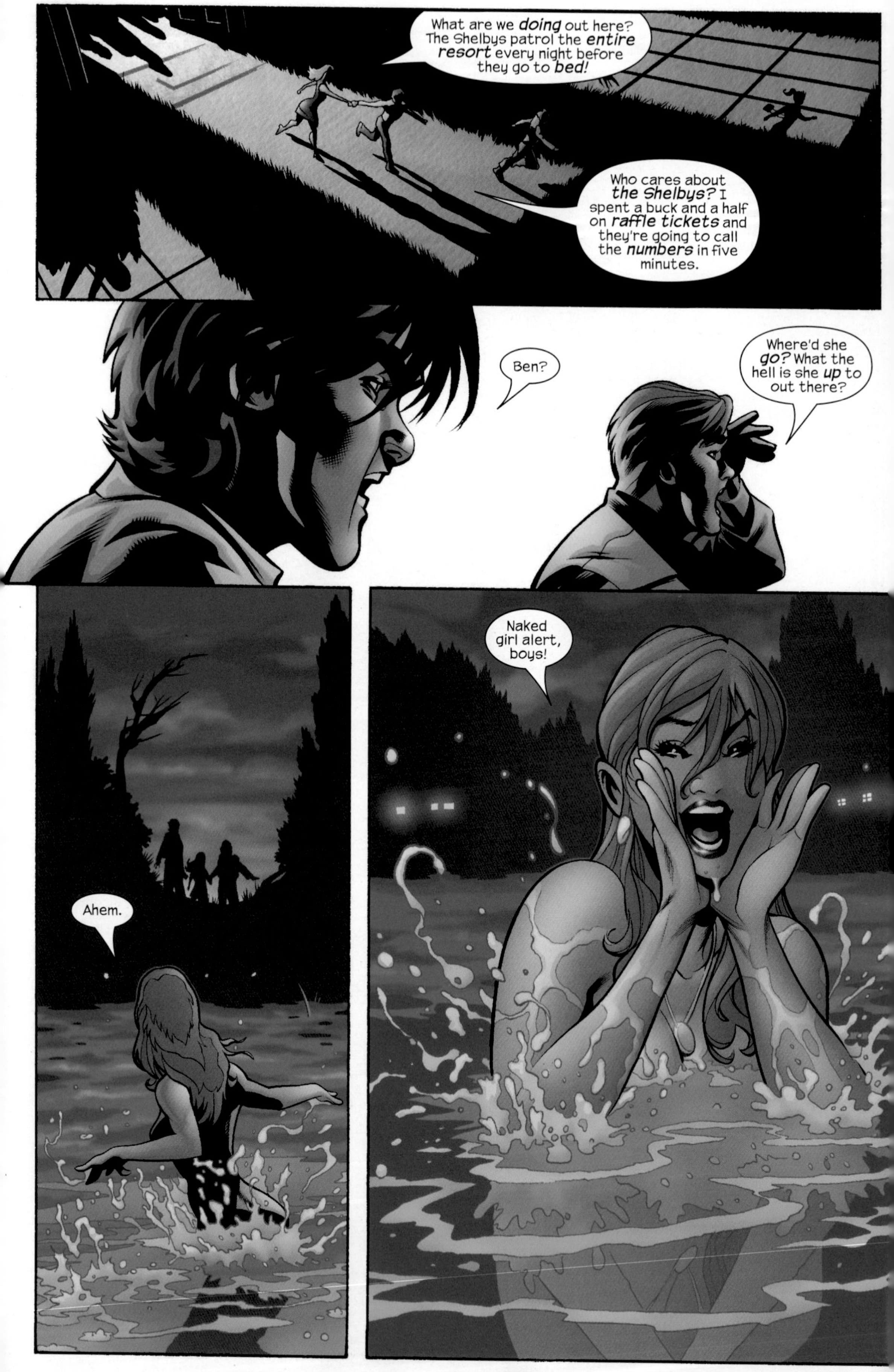
What are we doing out here? The Shelbys patrol the entire resort every night before they go to bed!
Who cares about the Shelbys? I spent a buck and a half on raffle tickets and they're going to call the numbers in five minutes.
Ben?
Where'd she go? What the hell is she up to out there?
Ahem.
Naked girl alert, boys!

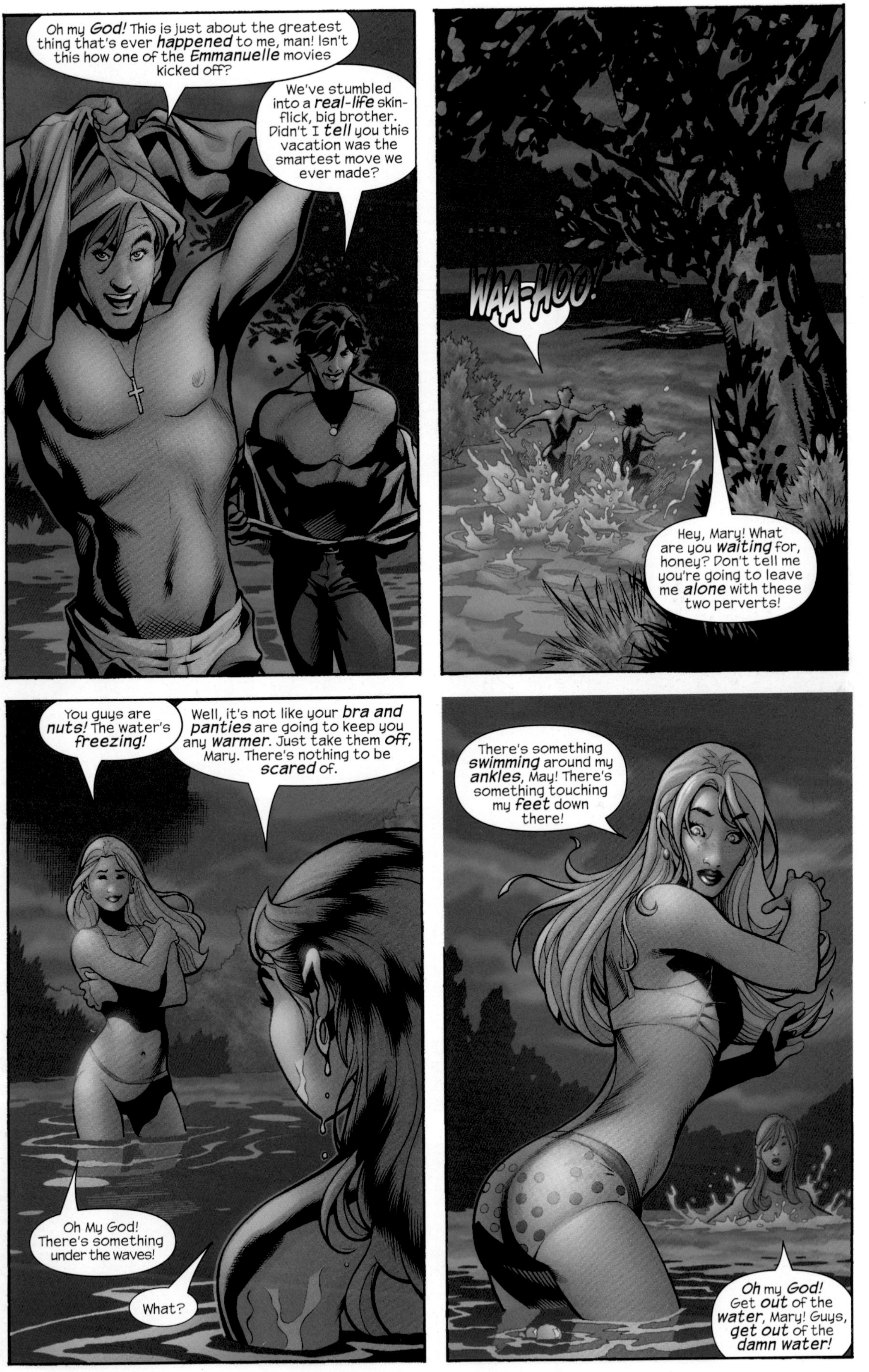
Oh my God! This is just about the greatest thing that's ever happened to me, man! Isn't this how one of the Emmanuelle movies kicked off?
We've stumbled into a real-life skin-flick, big brother. Didn't I tell you this vacation was the smartest move we ever made?
WAA-HOO!
Hey, Mary! What are you waiting for, honey? Don't tell me you're going to leave me alone with these two perverts!
You guys are nuts! The water's freezing!
Well, it's not like your bra and panties are going to keep you any warmer. Just take them off, Mary. There's nothing to be scared of.
Oh My God! There's something under the waves!
What?
There's something swimming around my ankles, May! There's something touching my feet down there!
Oh my God! Get out of the water, Mary! Guys, get out of the damn water!

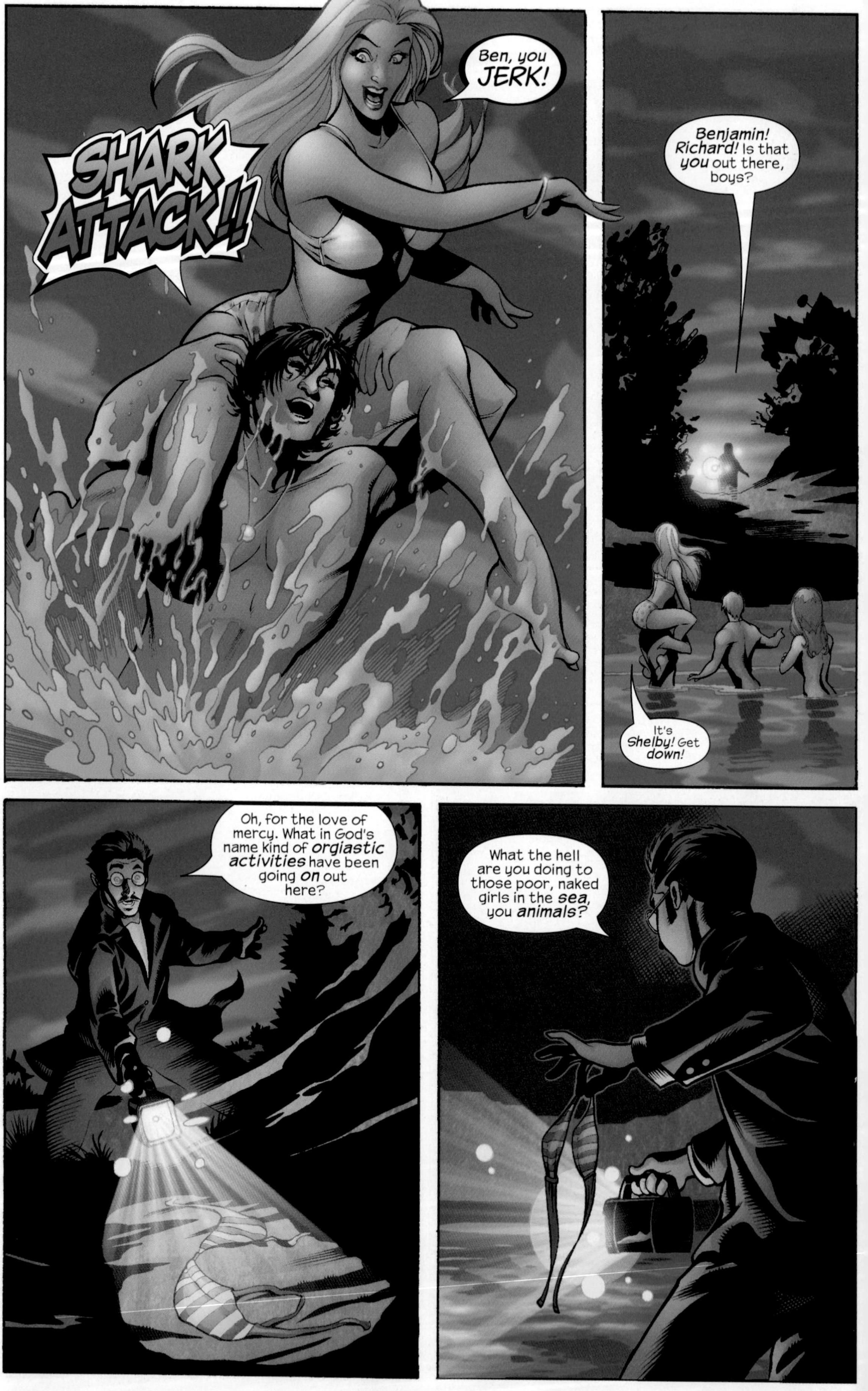

SHARK ATTACK!!
Ben, you JERK!
Benjamin! Richard! Is that you out there, boys?
It's Shelby! Get down!
Oh, for the love of mercy. What in God's name kind of orgiastic activities have been going on out here?
What the hell are you doing to those poor, naked girls in the sea, you animals?

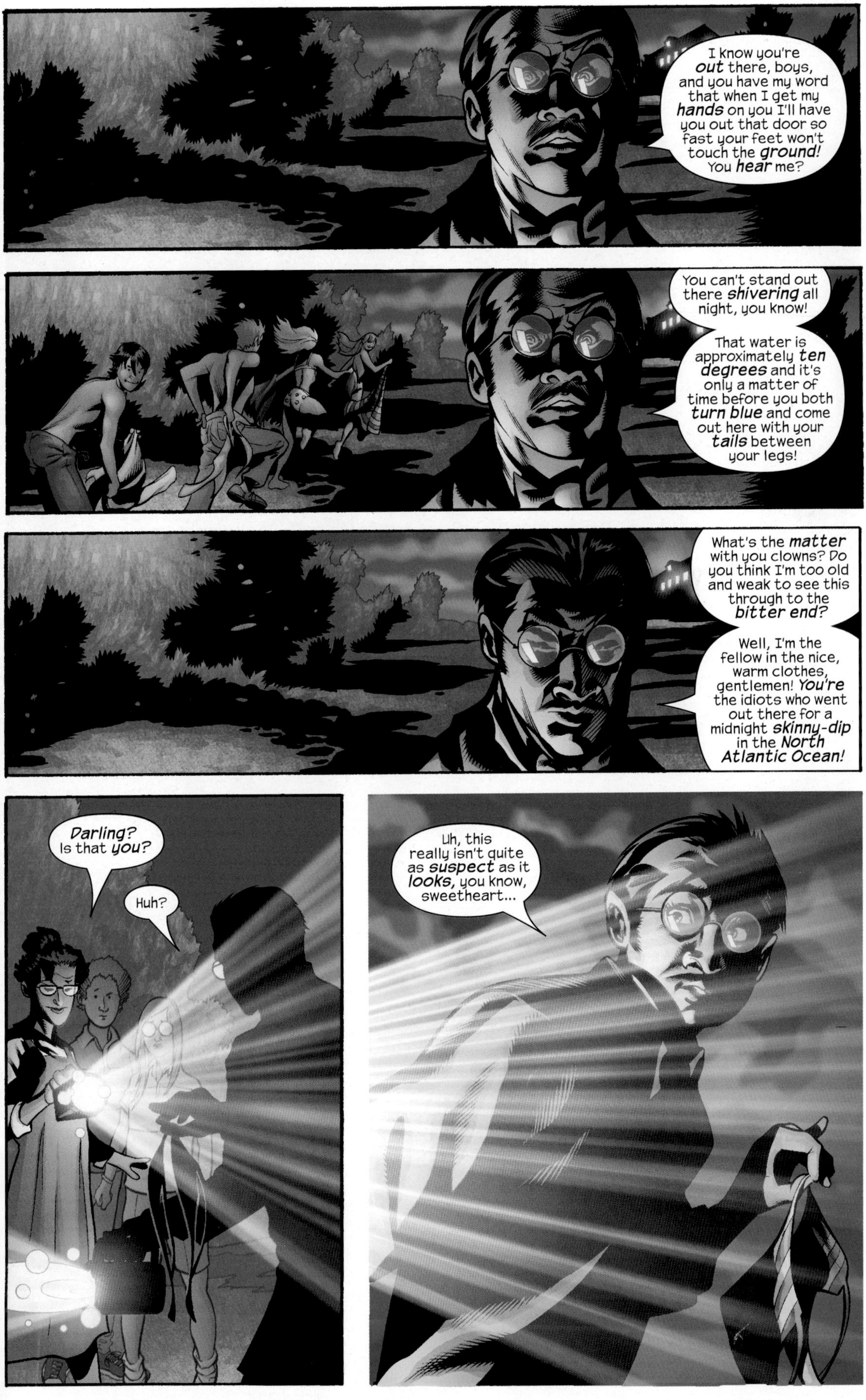
I know you're *out* there, boys, and you have my word that when I get my *hands* on you I'll have you out that door so fast your feet won't touch the *ground!* You *hear* me?
You can't stand out there *shivering* all night, you know!
That water is approximately *ten degrees* and it's only a matter of time before you both *turn blue* and come out here with your *tails* between your legs!
What's the *matter* with you clowns? Do you think I'm too old and weak to see this through to the *bitter end?*
Well, I'm the fellow in the nice, warm clothes, gentlemen! *You're* the idiots who went out there for a midnight *skinny-dip* in the *North Atlantic Ocean!*
Darling? Is that *you?*
Huh?
Uh, this really isn't quite as *suspect* as it *looks,* you know, sweetheart...

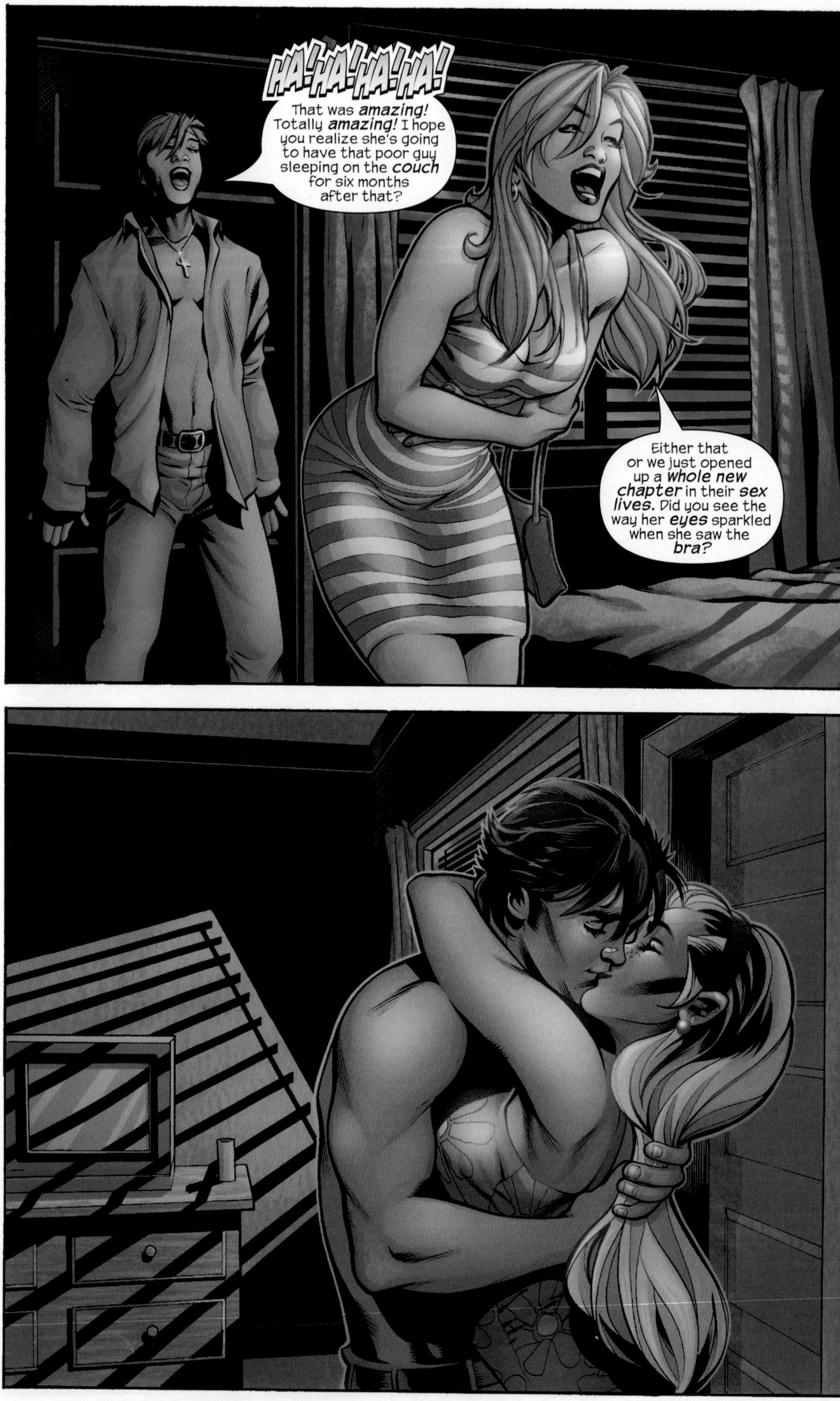
HA!HA!HA!HA!
That was amazing! Totally amazing! I hope you realize she's going to have that poor guy sleeping on the couch for six months after that?
Either that or we just opened up a whole new chapter in their sex lives. Did you see the way her eyes sparkled when she saw the bra?

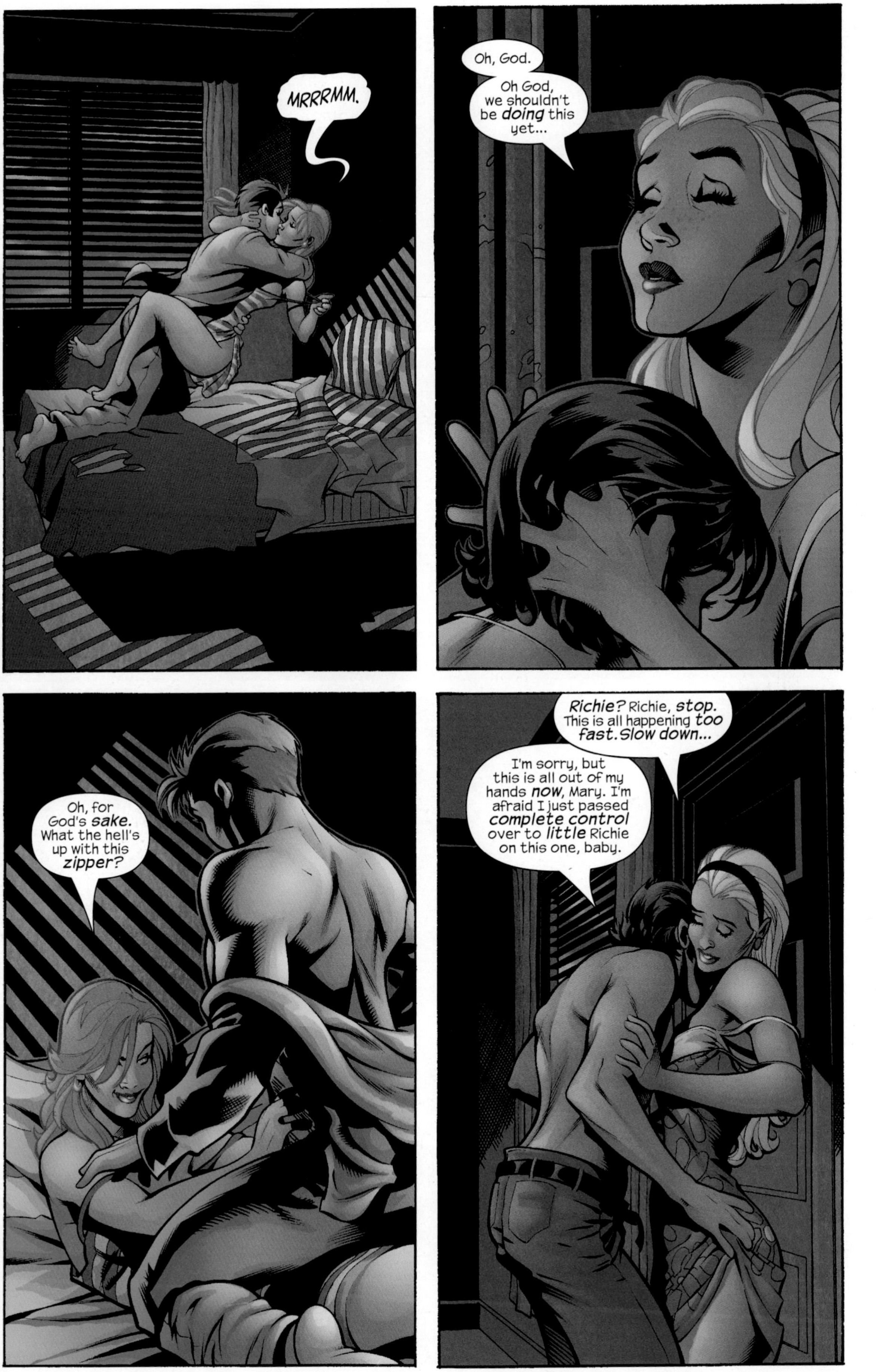
MRRRMM.
Oh, God.
Oh God, we shouldn't be doing this yet...
Oh, for God's sake. What the hell's up with this zipper?
Richie? Richie, stop. This is all happening too fast. Slow down...
I'm sorry, but this is all out of my hands now, Mary. I'm afraid I just passed complete control over to little Richie on this one, baby.

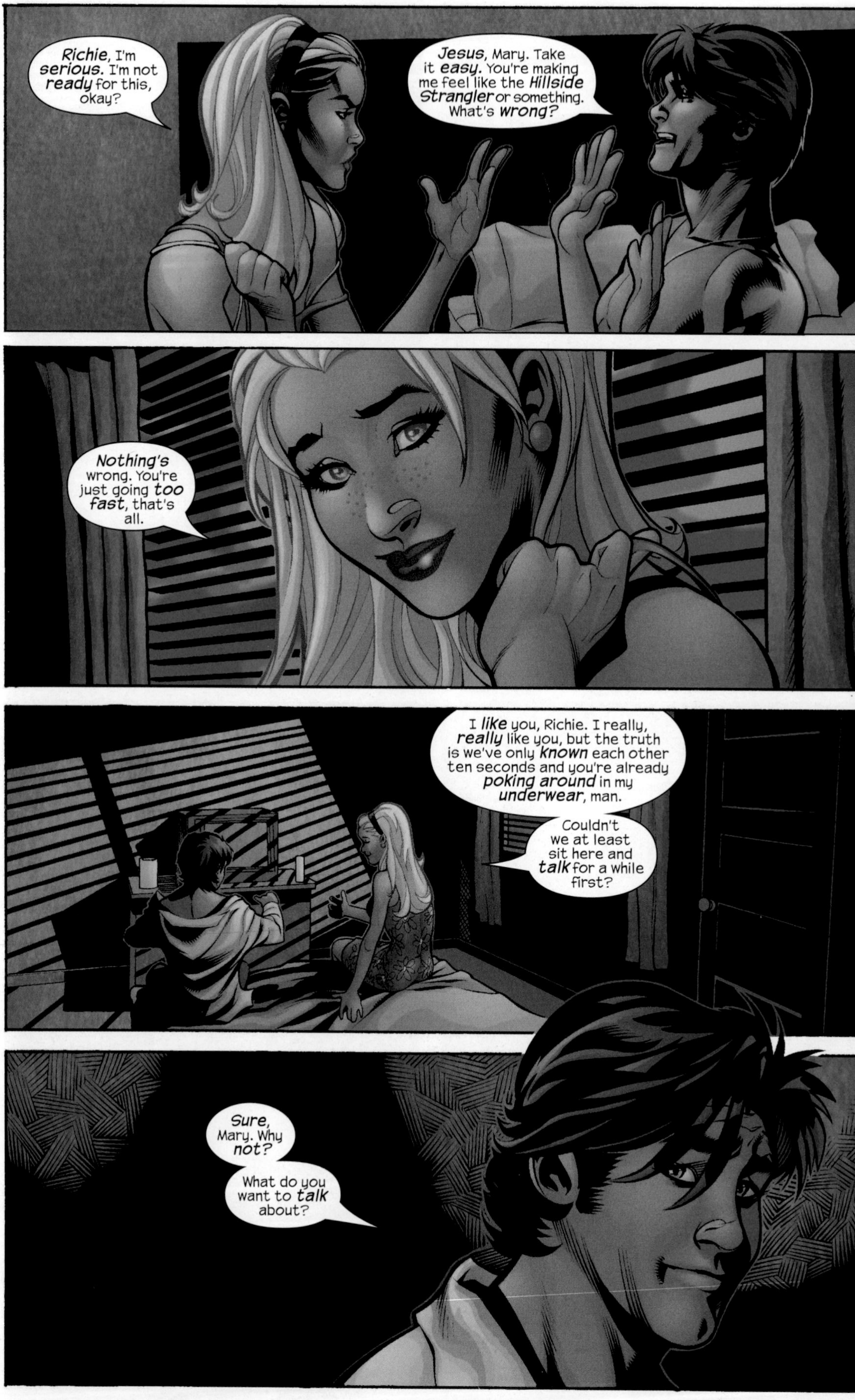
Richie, I'm serious. I'm not ready for this, okay?
Jesus, Mary. Take it easy. You're making me feel like the Hillside Strangler or something. What's wrong?
Nothing's wrong. You're just going too fast, that's all.
I like you, Richie. I really, really like you, but the truth is we've only known each other ten seconds and you're already poking around in my underwear, man.
Couldn't we at least sit here and talk for a while first?
Sure, Mary. Why not?
What do you want to talk about?

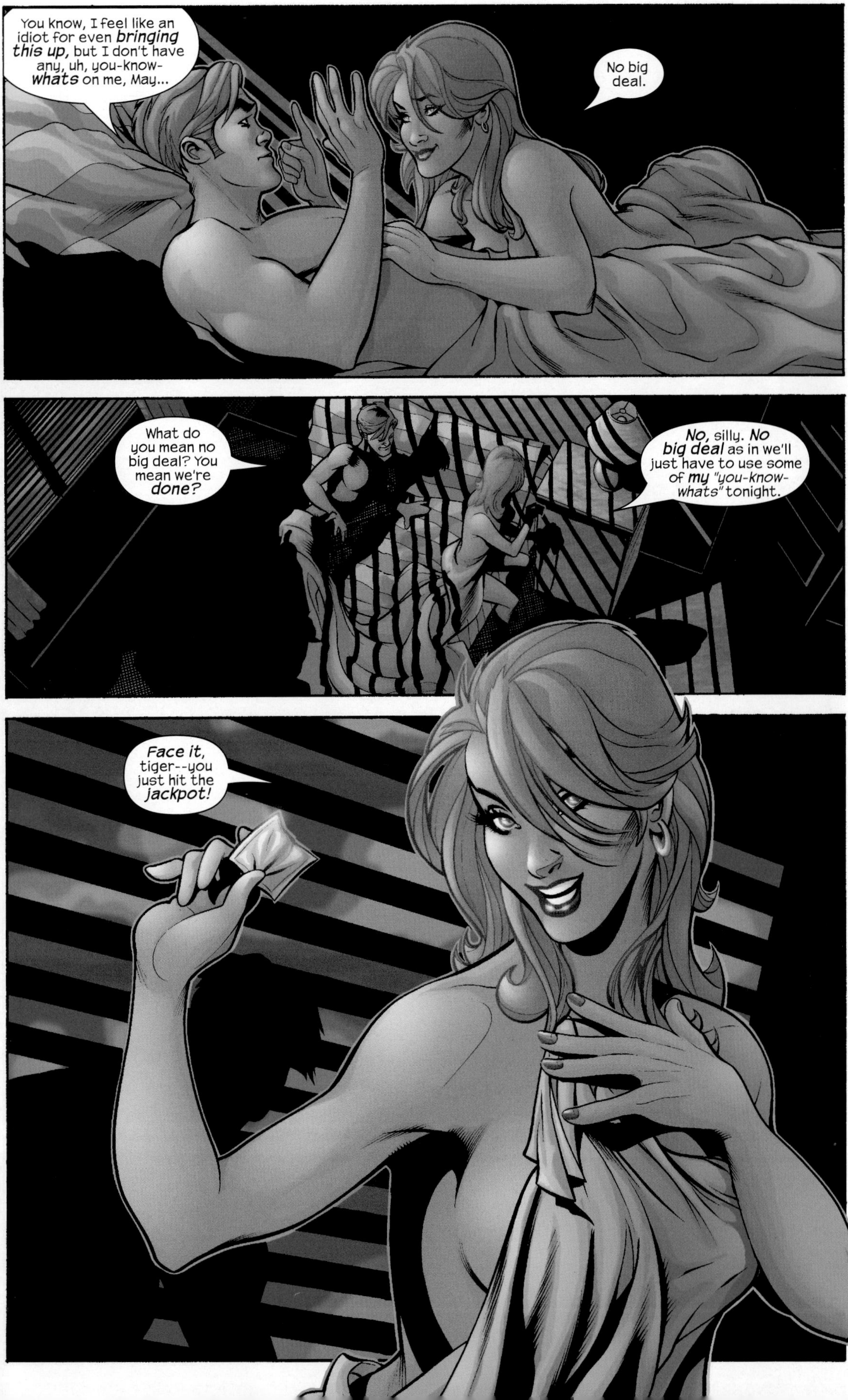
You know, I feel like an idiot for even *bringing this up*, but I don't have any, uh, you-know-*whats* on me, May...
No big deal.
What do you mean no big deal? You mean we're *done*?
No, silly. *No big deal* as in we'll just have to use some of *my* "you-know-whats" tonight.
Face it, tiger--you just hit the *jackpot*!

Trouble

part two of five

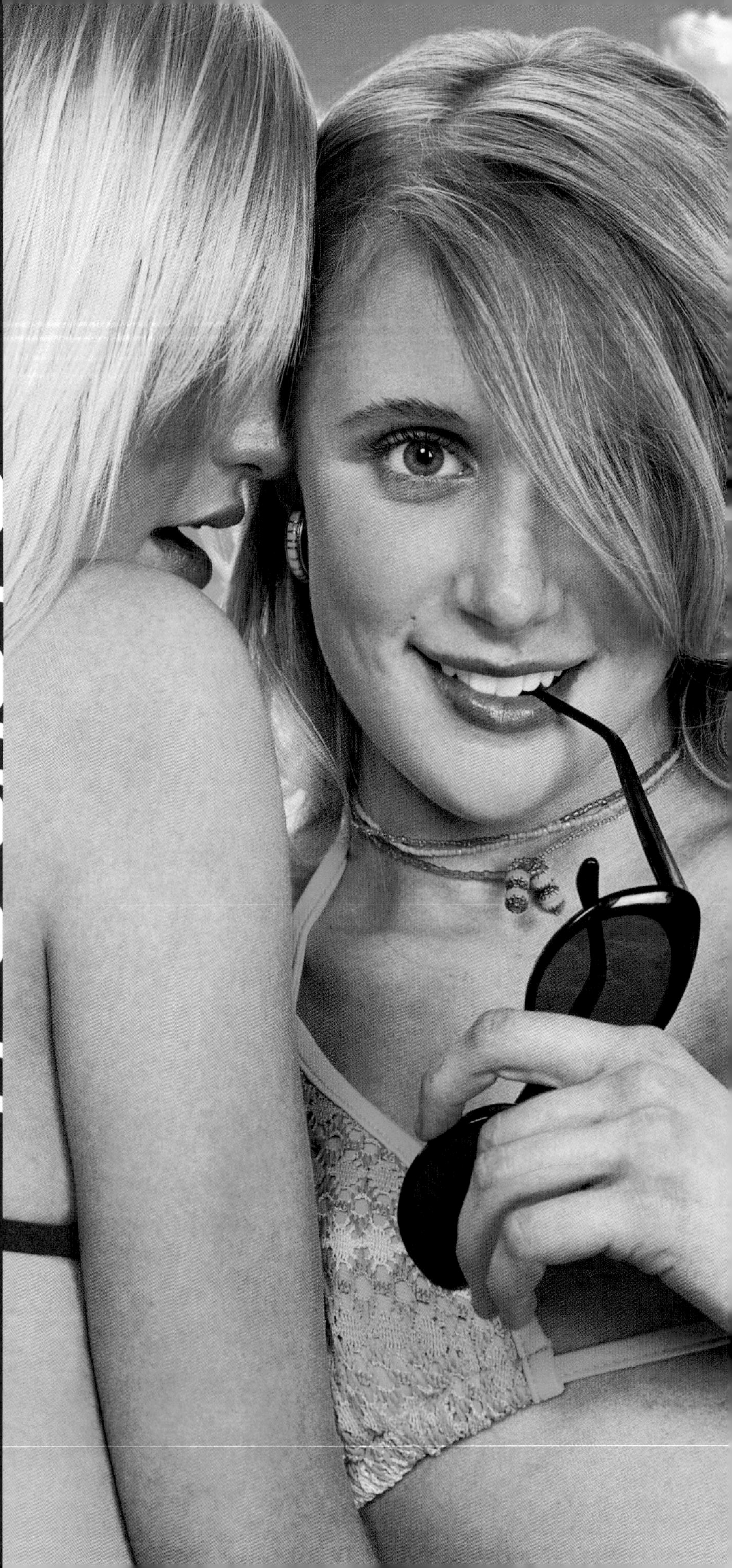

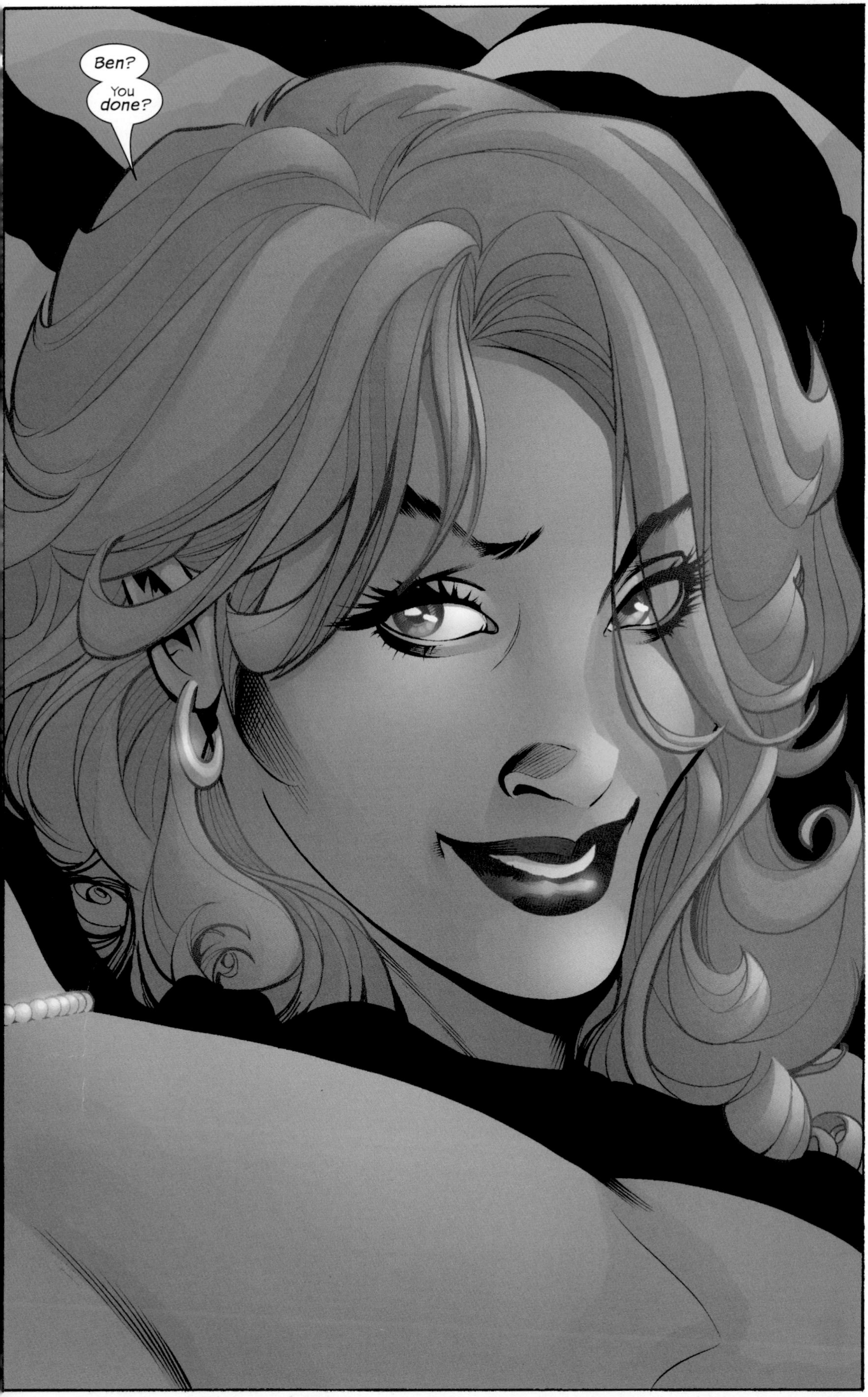
Ben?
You done?

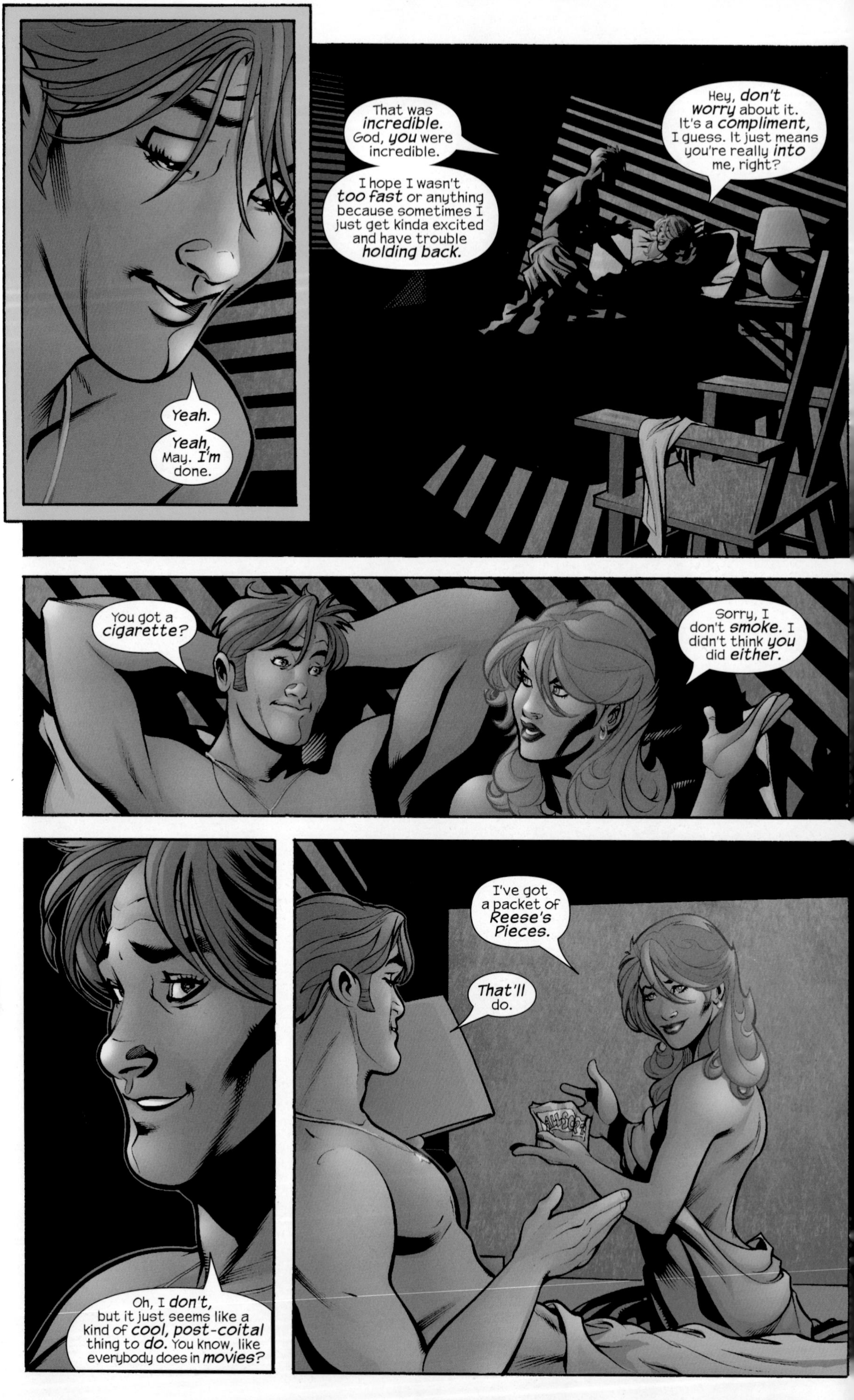

Yeah.
Yeah, May. I'm done.
That was incredible. God, you were incredible.
I hope I wasn't too fast or anything because sometimes I just get kinda excited and have trouble holding back.
Hey, don't worry about it. It's a compliment, I guess. It just means you're really into me, right?
You got a cigarette?
Sorry, I don't smoke. I didn't think you did either.
Oh, I don't, but it just seems like a kind of cool, post-coital thing to do. You know, like everybody does in movies?
I've got a packet of Reese's Pieces.
That'll do.

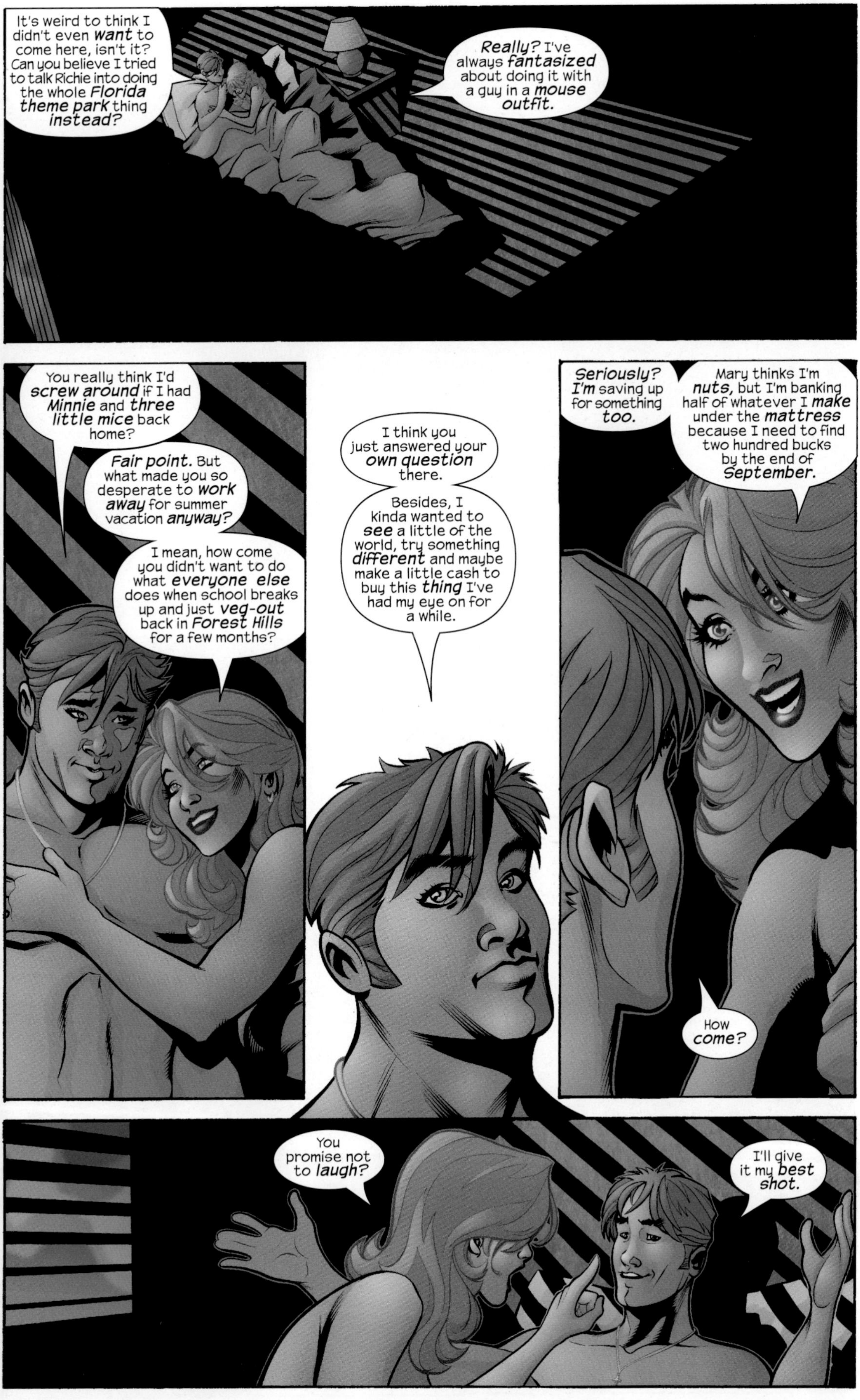
It's weird to think I didn't even want to come here, isn't it? Can you believe I tried to talk Richie into doing the whole Florida theme park thing instead?
Really? I've always fantasized about doing it with a guy in a mouse outfit.
You really think I'd screw around if I had Minnie and three little mice back home?
Fair point. But what made you so desperate to work away for summer vacation anyway?
I mean, how come you didn't want to do what everyone else does when school breaks up and just veg-out back in Forest Hills for a few months?
I think you just answered your own question there.
Besides, I kinda wanted to see a little of the world, try something different and maybe make a little cash to buy this thing I've had my eye on for a while.
Seriously? I'm saving up for something too.
Mary thinks I'm nuts, but I'm banking half of whatever I make under the mattress because I need to find two hundred bucks by the end of September.
How come?
You promise not to laugh?
I'll give it my best shot.

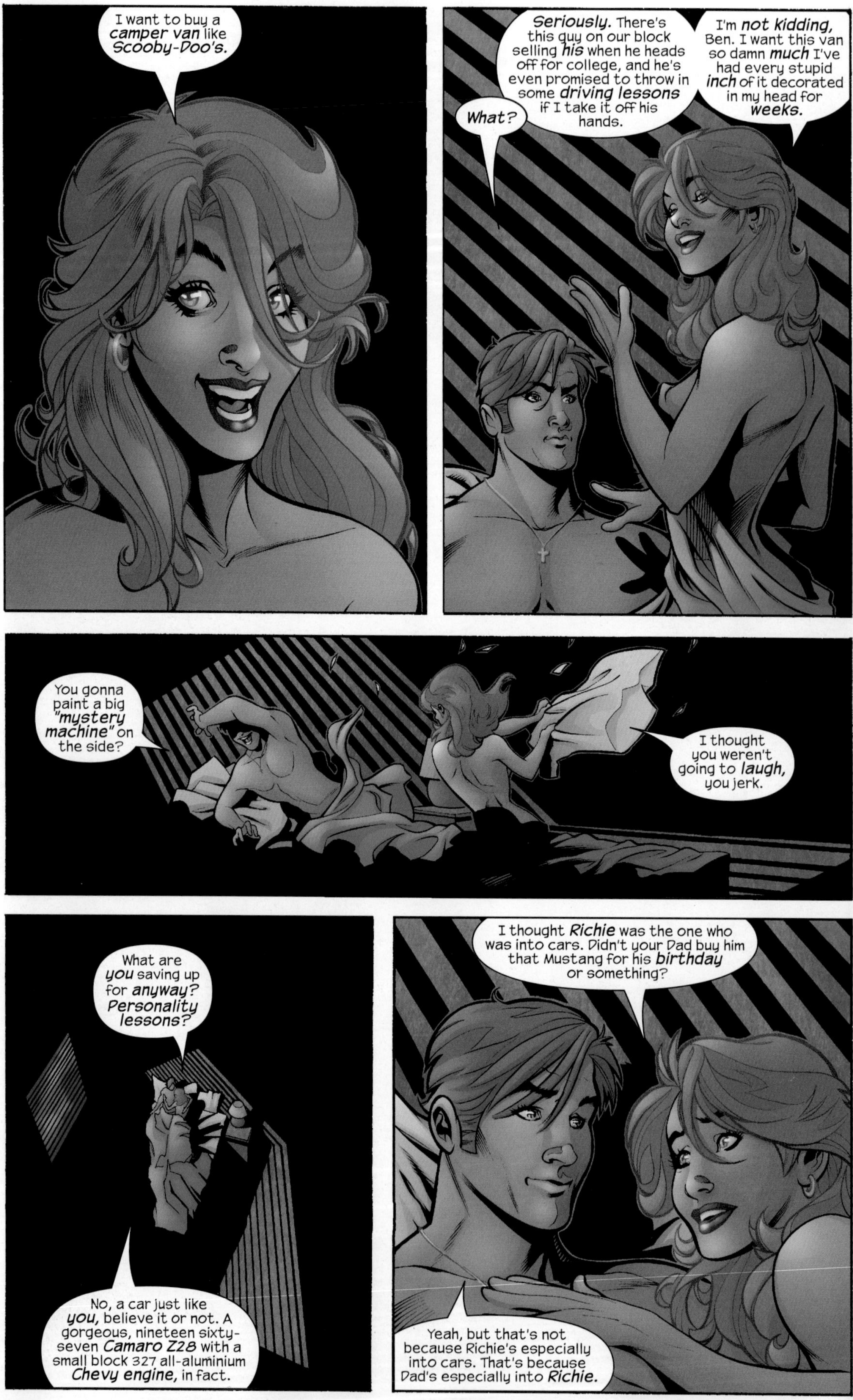
I want to buy a camper van like Scooby-Doo's.
What?
Seriously. There's this guy on our block selling his when he heads off for college, and he's even promised to throw in some driving lessons if I take it off his hands.
I'm not kidding, Ben. I want this van so damn much I've had every stupid inch of it decorated in my head for weeks.
You gonna paint a big "mystery machine" on the side?
I thought you weren't going to laugh, you jerk.
What are you saving up for anyway? Personality lessons?
No, a car just like you, believe it or not. A gorgeous, nineteen sixty-seven Camaro Z28 with a small block 327 all-aluminium Chevy engine, in fact.
I thought Richie was the one who was into cars. Didn't your Dad buy him that Mustang for his birthday or something?
Yeah, but that's not because Richie's especially into cars. That's because Dad's especially into Richie.

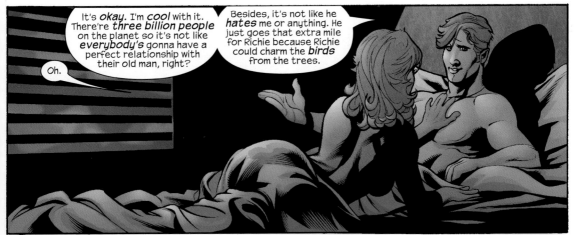

It's *okay.* I'm *cool* with it. There're *three billion people* on the planet so it's not like *everybody's* gonna have a perfect relationship with their old man, right?

Oh.

Besides, it's not like he *hates* me or anything. He just goes that extra mile for Richie because Richie could charm the *birds* from the trees.

I was always in and out of the *hospital* as a kid, whereas Richie was the *super-fit, super-funny* guy. Growing up, I just got used to *everybody* liking him better.

Which brings to me a question I've really got to *ask:*

Based on the fact you could have had *either one* of us, how come a cool chick like you settled for Little Richie's unspectacular *big brother?*

Why?

Because that's a question Little Richie would never have *asked* me, baby.

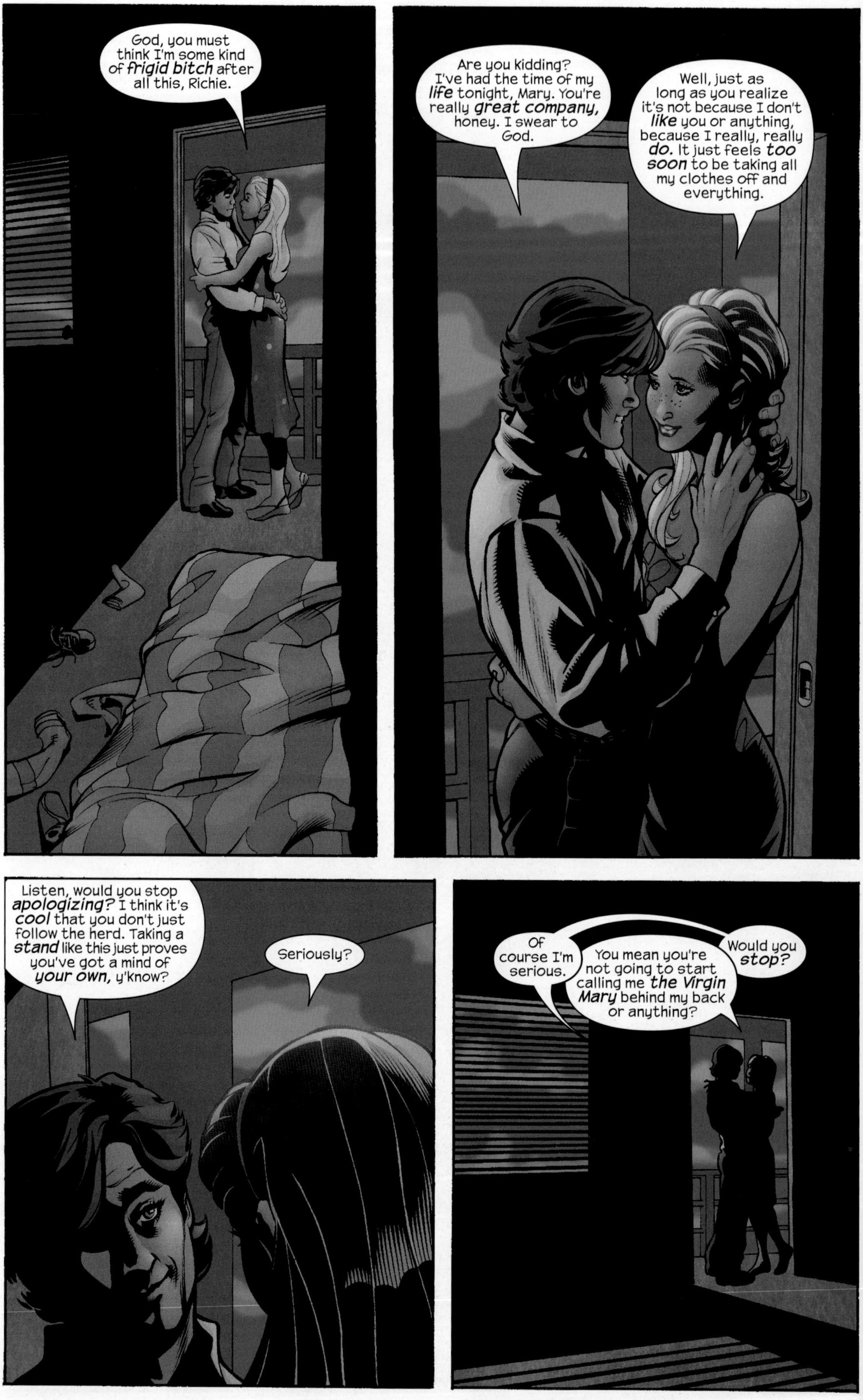
God, you must think I'm some kind of frigid bitch after all this, Richie.
Are you kidding? I've had the time of my life tonight, Mary. You're really great company, honey. I swear to God.
Well, just as long as you realize it's not because I don't like you or anything, because I really, really do. It just feels too soon to be taking all my clothes off and everything.
Listen, would you stop apologizing? I think it's cool that you don't just follow the herd. Taking a stand like this just proves you've got a mind of your own, y'know?
Seriously?
Of course I'm serious.
You mean you're not going to start calling me the Virgin Mary behind my back or anything?
Would you stop?

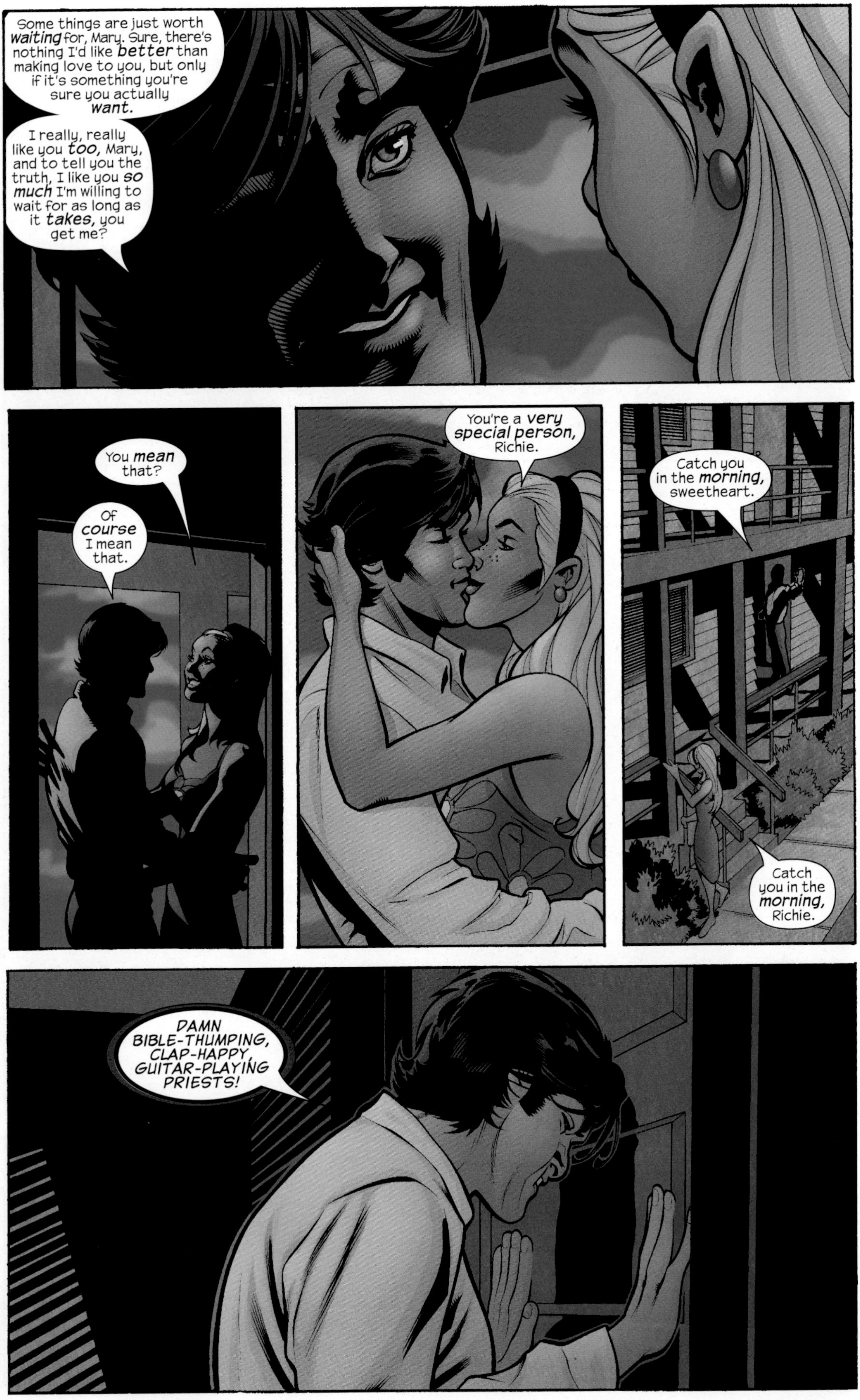
Some things are just worth waiting for, Mary. Sure, there's nothing I'd like better than making love to you, but only if it's something you're sure you actually want.
I really, really like you too, Mary, and to tell you the truth, I like you so much I'm willing to wait for as long as it takes, you get me?
You mean that?
Of course I mean that.
You're a very special person, Richie.
Catch you in the morning, sweetheart.
Catch you in the morning, Richie.
DAMN BIBLE-THUMPING, CLAP-HAPPY, GUITAR-PLAYING PRIESTS!

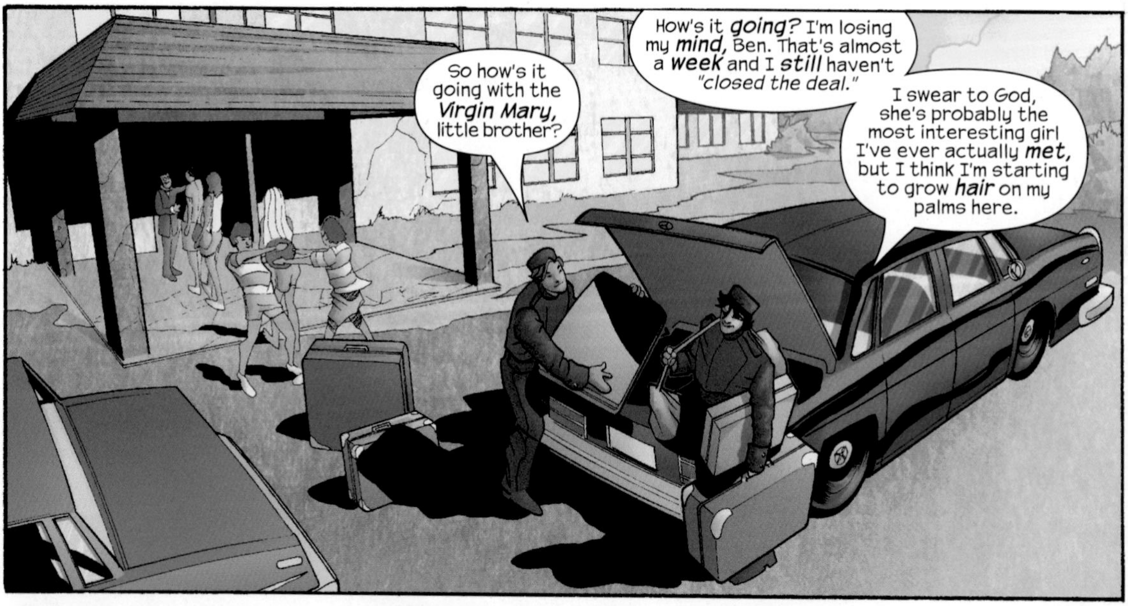
So how's it going with the Virgin Mary, little brother?
How's it going? I'm losing my mind, Ben. That's almost a week and I still haven't "closed the deal."
I swear to God, she's probably the most interesting girl I've ever actually met, but I think I'm starting to grow hair on my palms here.

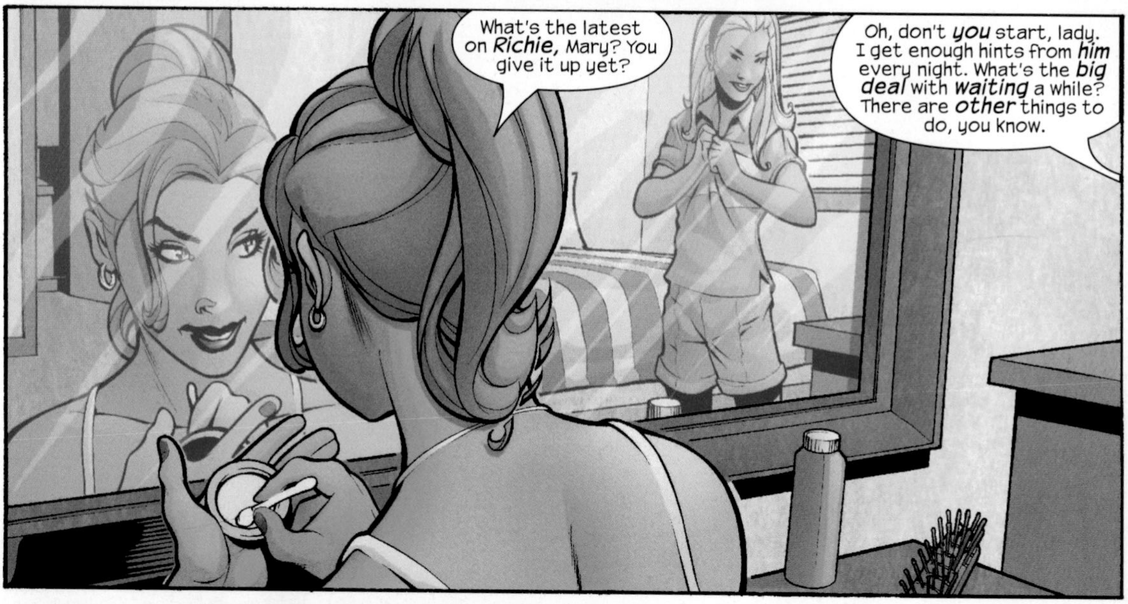
What's the latest on Richie, Mary? You give it up yet?
Oh, don't you start, lady. I get enough hints from him every night. What's the big deal with waiting a while? There are other things to do, you know.

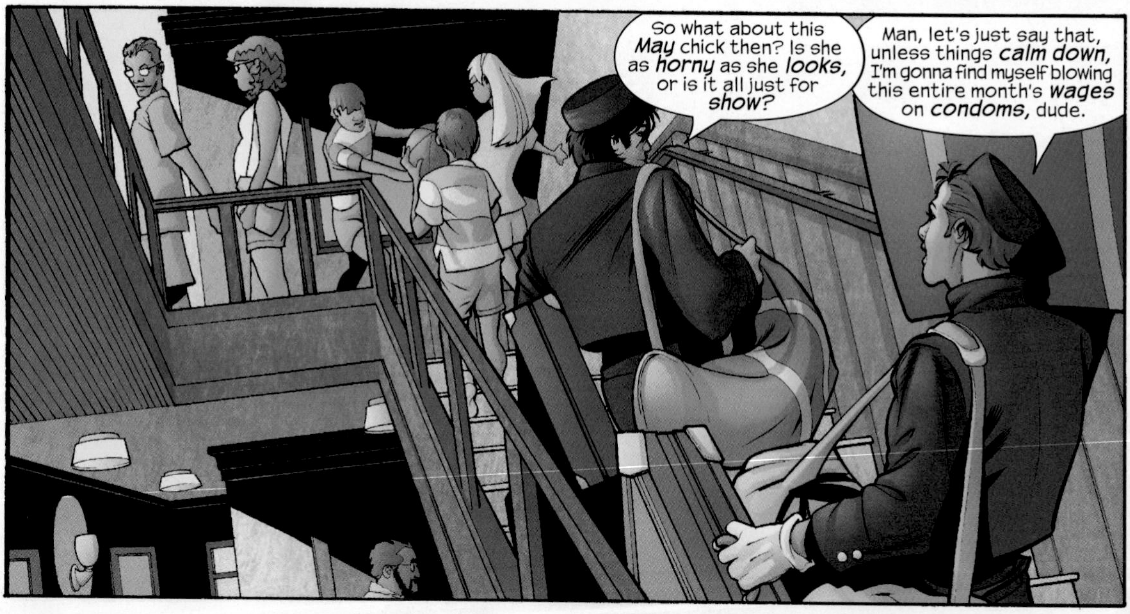
So what about this May chick then? Is she as horny as she looks, or is it all just for show?
Man, let's just say that, unless things calm down, I'm gonna find myself blowing this entire month's wages on condoms, dude.

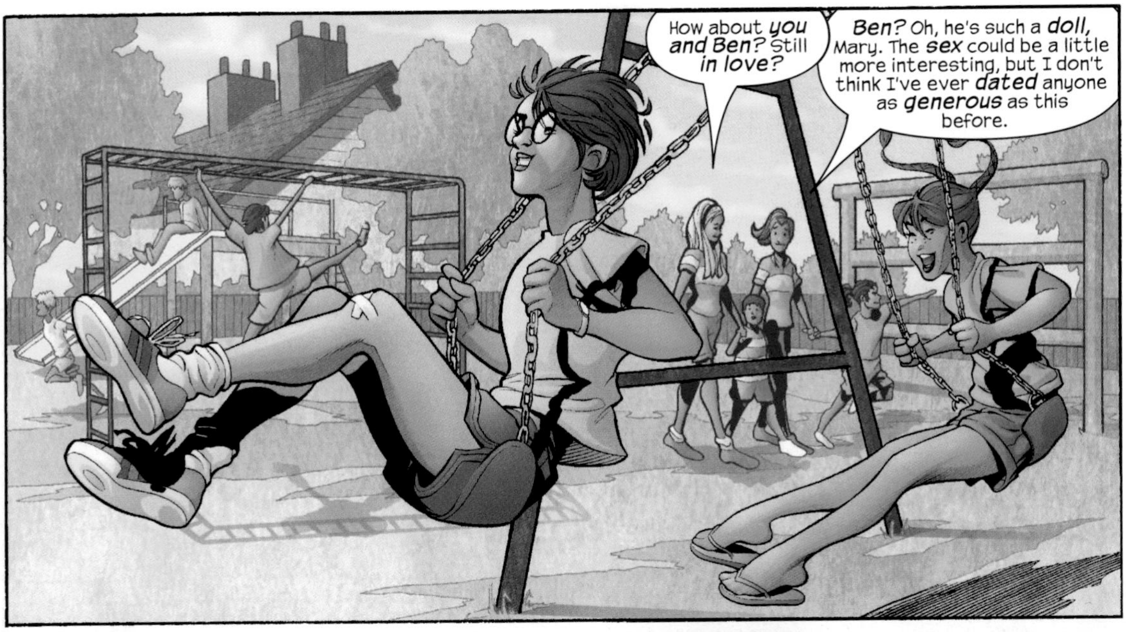
How about you and Ben? Still in love?
Ben? Oh, he's such a doll, Mary. The sex could be a little more interesting, but I don't think I've ever dated anyone as generous as this before.

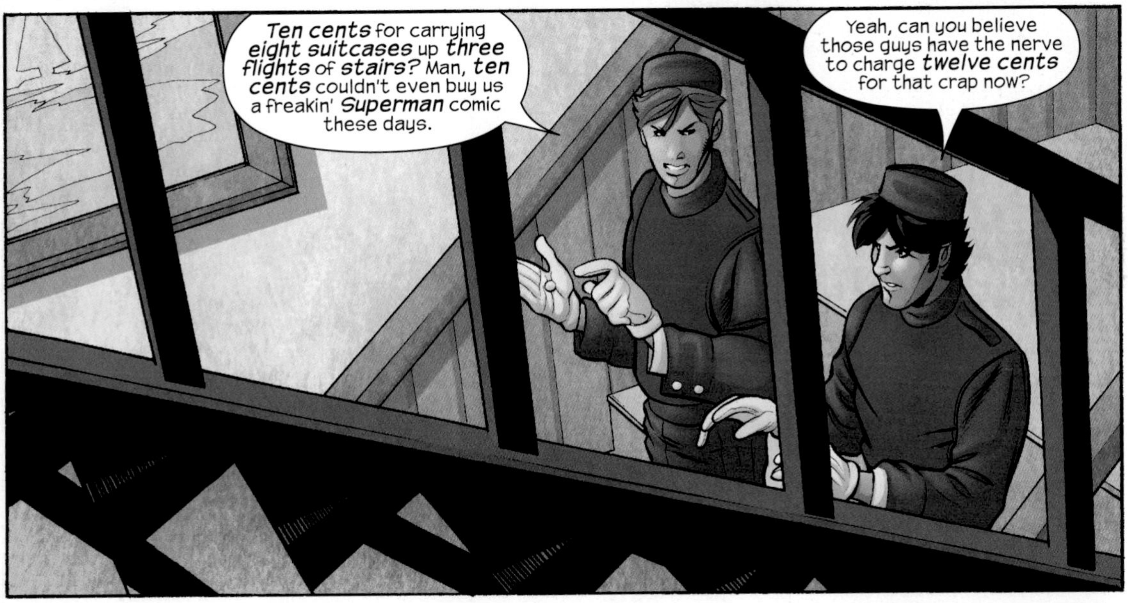
Ten cents for carrying eight suitcases up three flights of stairs? Man, ten cents couldn't even buy us a freakin' Superman comic these days.
Yeah, can you believe those guys have the nerve to charge twelve cents for that crap now?

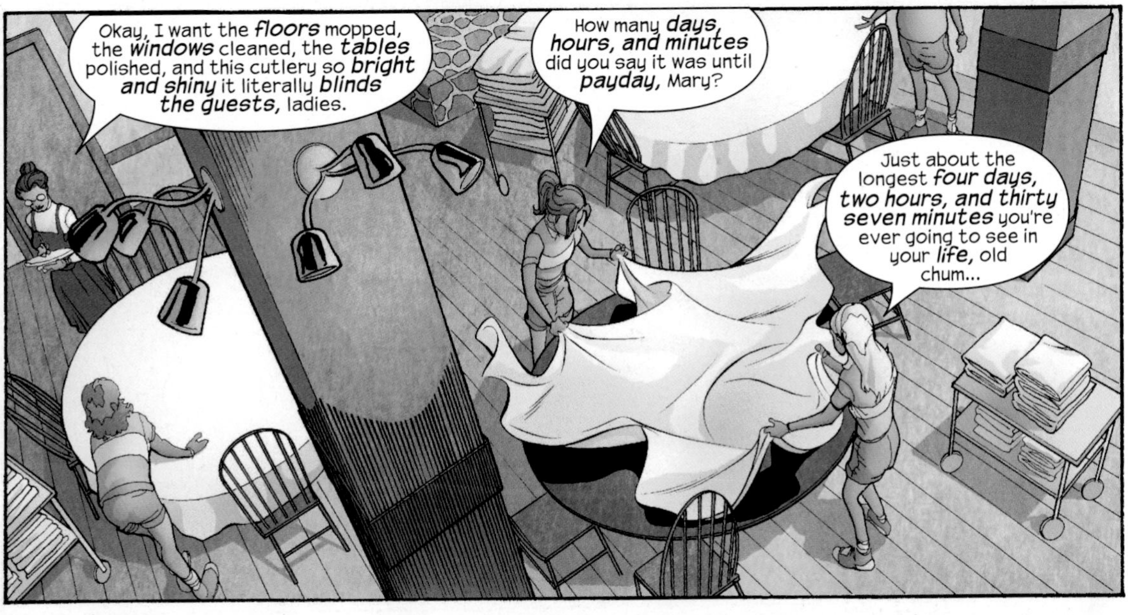
Okay, I want the floors mopped, the windows cleaned, the tables polished, and this cutlery so bright and shiny it literally blinds the guests, ladies.
How many days, hours, and minutes did you say it was until payday, Mary?
Just about the longest four days, two hours, and thirty seven minutes you're ever going to see in your life, old chum...

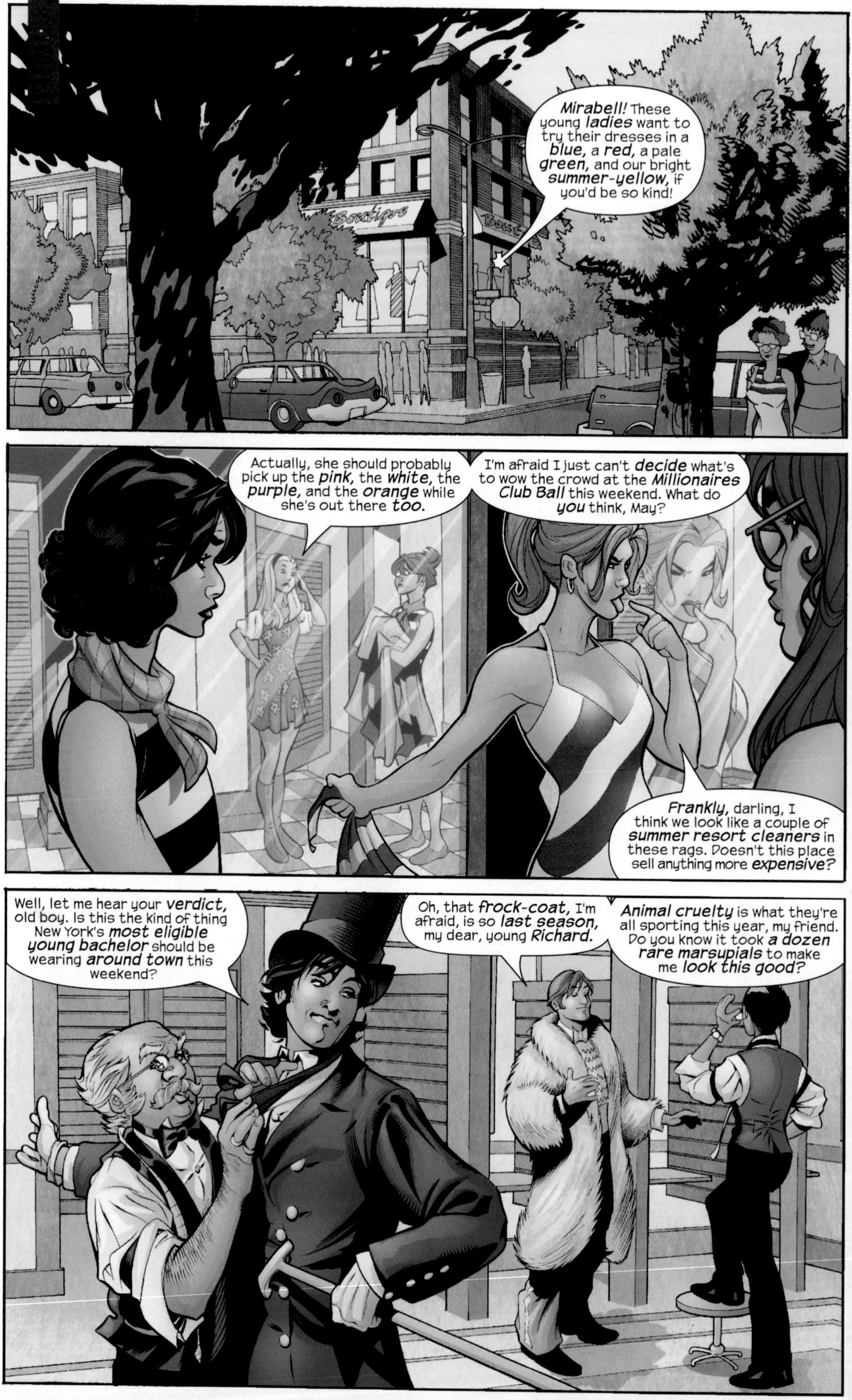
Mirabell! These young ladies want to try their dresses in a blue, a red, a pale green, and our bright summer-yellow, if you'd be so kind!
Boutique
Actually, she should probably pick up the pink, the white, the purple, and the orange while she's out there too.
I'm afraid I just can't decide what's to wow the crowd at the Millionaires Club Ball this weekend. What do you think, May?
Frankly, darling, I think we look like a couple of summer resort cleaners in these rags. Doesn't this place sell anything more expensive?
Well, let me hear your verdict, old boy. Is this the kind of thing New York's most eligible young bachelor should be wearing around town this weekend?
Oh, that frock-coat, I'm afraid, is so last season, my dear, young Richard.
Animal cruelty is what they're all sporting this year, my friend. Do you know it took a dozen rare marsupials to make me look this good?

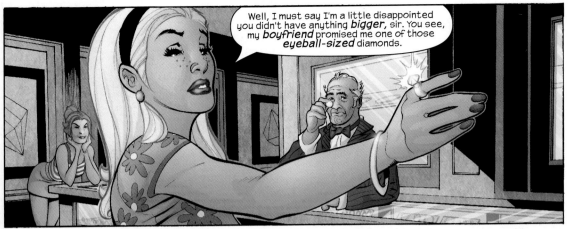

Well, I must say I'm a little disappointed you didn't have anything *bigger*, sir. You see, my *boyfriend* promised me one of those *eyeball-sized* diamonds.

Yes, yes, yes. I'm sure these *contemporary* artists all have *very promising futures*, my dear lady, but where are the *Rembrandts?* Where are the *Picassos?*

My God, you call yourselves *snobs*, and you don't even have a little *Degas* hanging on the walls?

Excuse me, darling, but you don't think an extra couple of diamond rings hanging on my *thumbs* would be verging on *tasteless*, do you?

Listen, between you and me--supposing we spent over a million dollars in *cash* in here today? Do you think we might be able to get one of these paperweights for *nothing?*

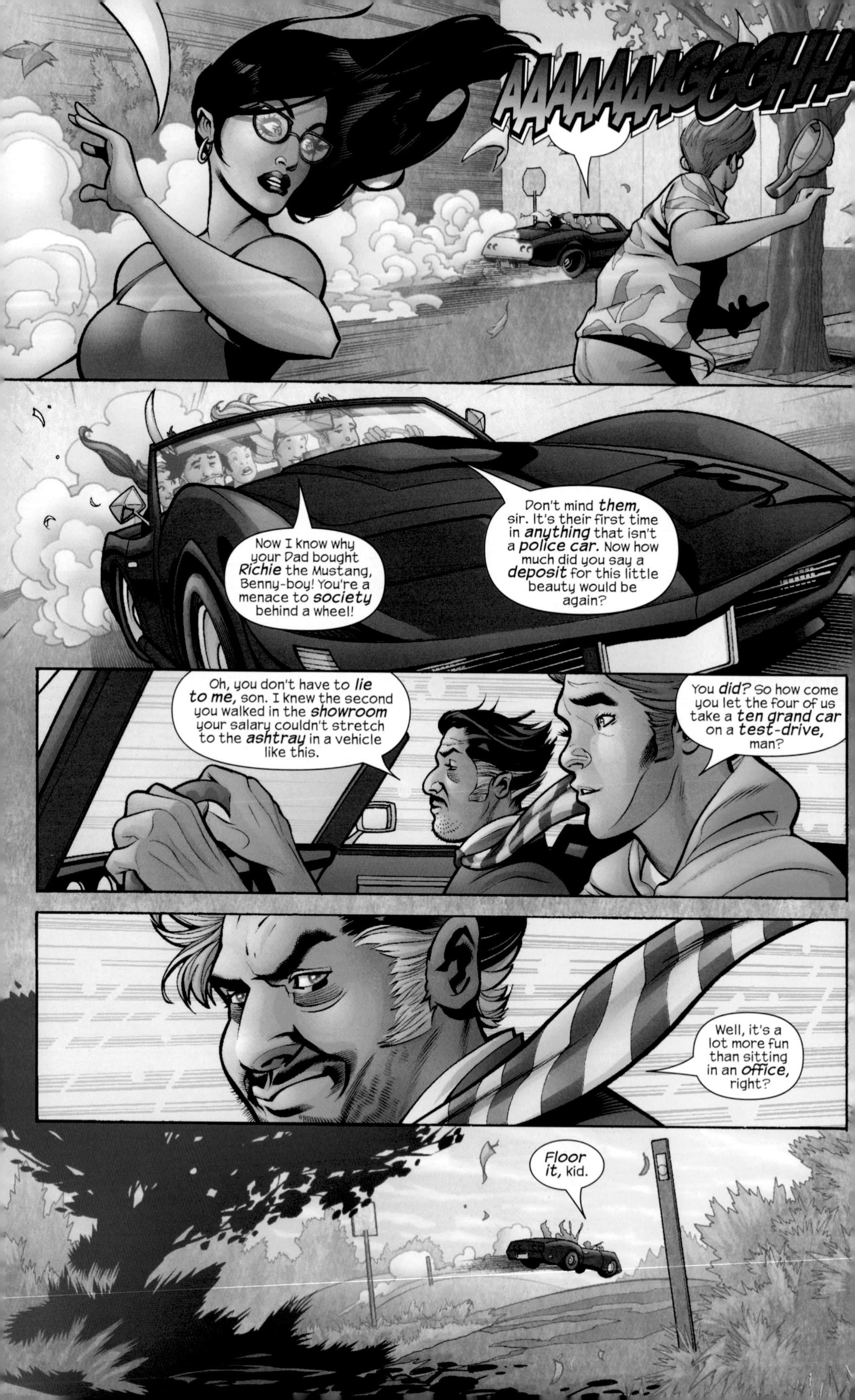
AAAAAAGGGHH!
Now I know why your Dad bought Richie the Mustang, Benny-boy! You're a menace to society behind a wheel!
Don't mind them, sir. It's their first time in anything that isn't a police car. Now how much did you say a deposit for this little beauty would be again?
Oh, you don't have to lie to me, son. I knew the second you walked in the showroom your salary couldn't stretch to the ashtray in a vehicle like this.
You did? So how come you let the four of us take a ten grand car on a test-drive, man?
Well, it's a lot more fun than sitting in an office, right?
Floor it, kid.

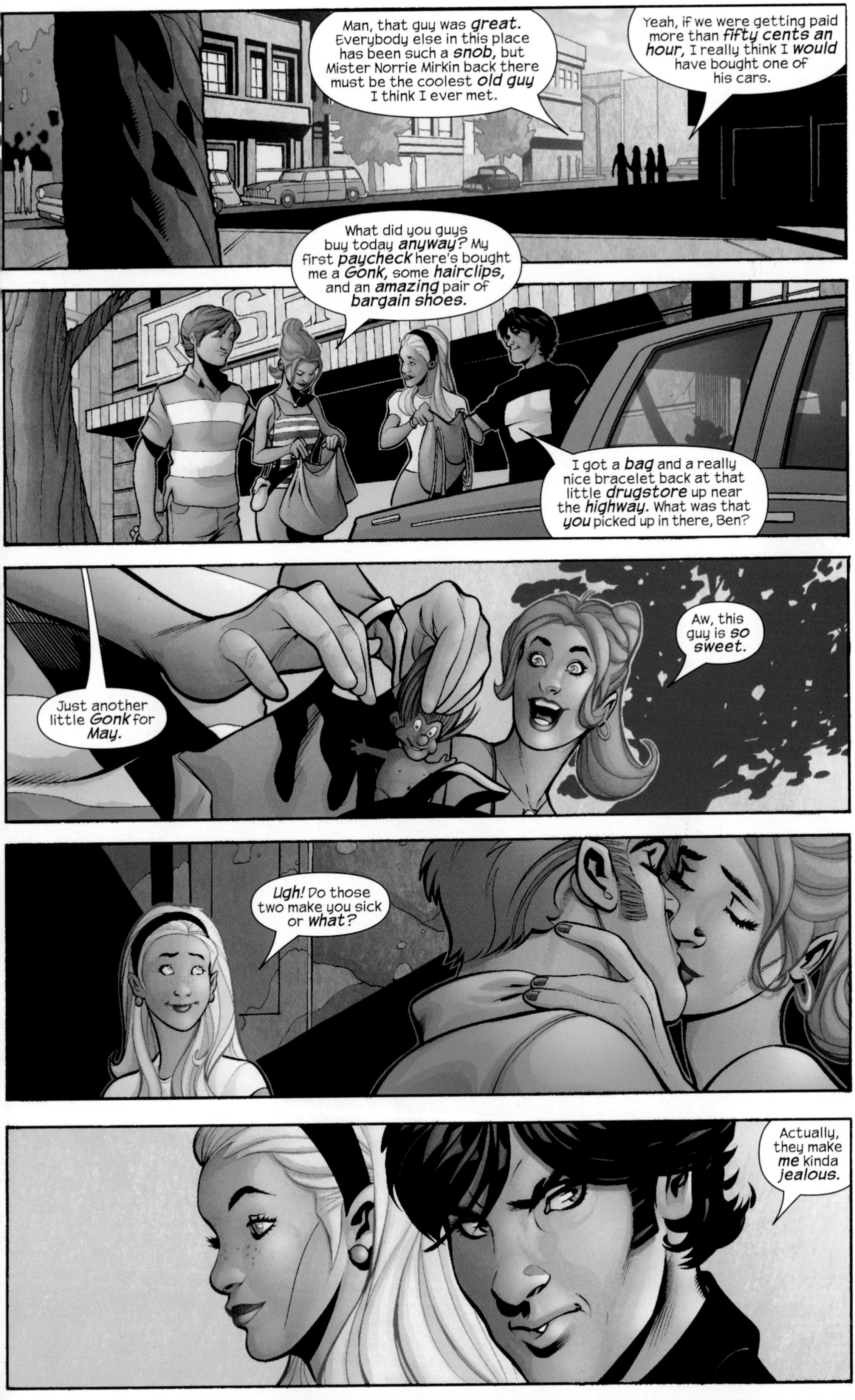
Man, that guy was great. Everybody else in this place has been such a snob, but Mister Norrie Mirkin back there must be the coolest old guy I think I ever met.
Yeah, if we were getting paid more than fifty cents an hour, I really think I would have bought one of his cars.
What did you guys buy today anyway? My first paycheck here's bought me a Gonk, some hairclips, and an amazing pair of bargain shoes.
I got a bag and a really nice bracelet back at that little drugstore up near the highway. What was that you picked up in there, Ben?
Just another little Gonk for May.
Aw, this guy is so sweet.
Ugh! Do those two make you sick or what?
Actually, they make me kinda jealous.

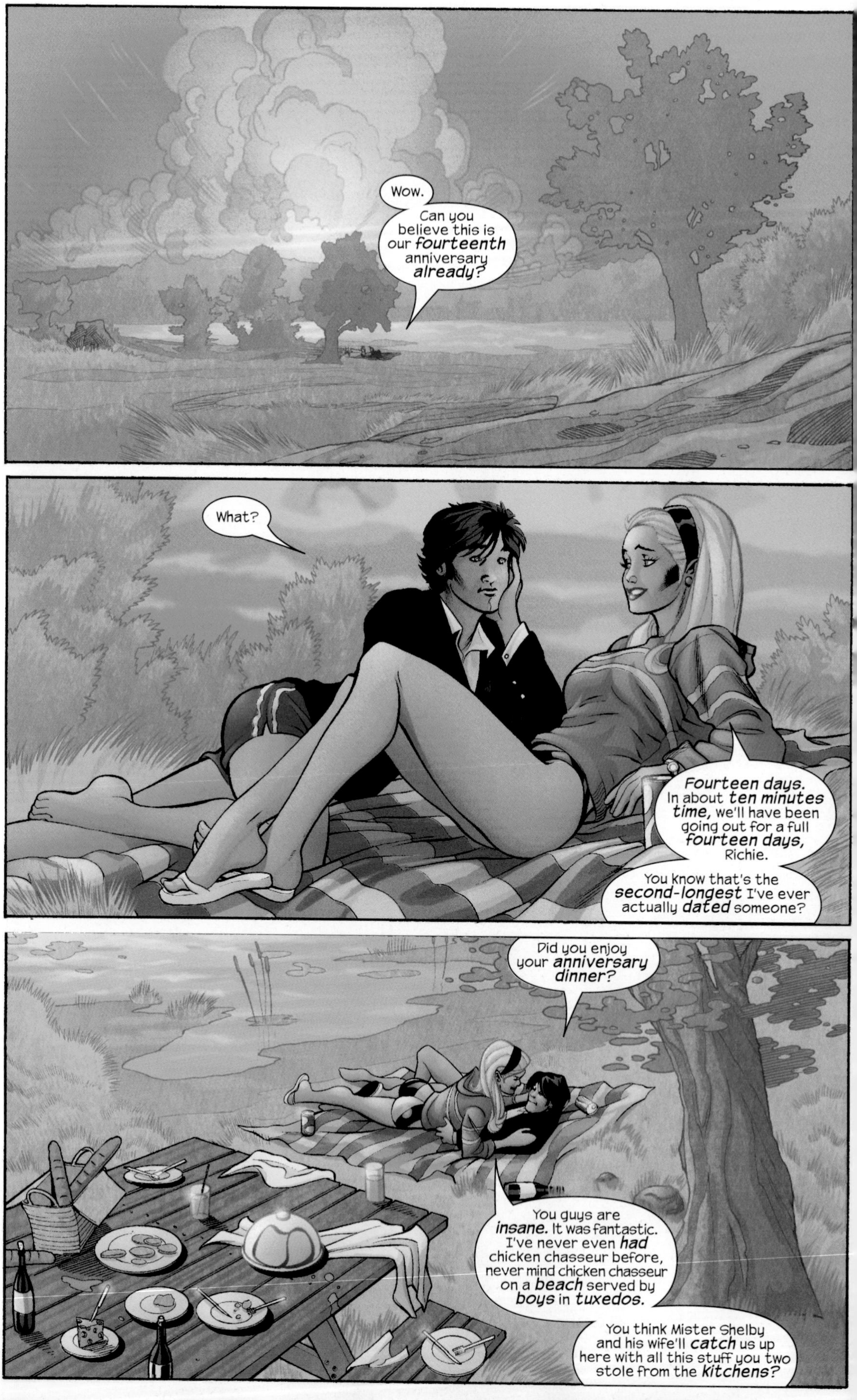
Wow.
Can you believe this is our fourteenth anniversary already?
What?
Fourteen days. In about ten minutes time, we'll have been going out for a full fourteen days, Richie.
You know that's the second-longest I've ever actually dated someone?
Did you enjoy your anniversary dinner?
You guys are insane. It was fantastic. I've never even had chicken chasseur before, never mind chicken chasseur on a beach served by boys in tuxedos.
You think Mister Shelby and his wife'll catch us up here with all this stuff you two stole from the kitchens?

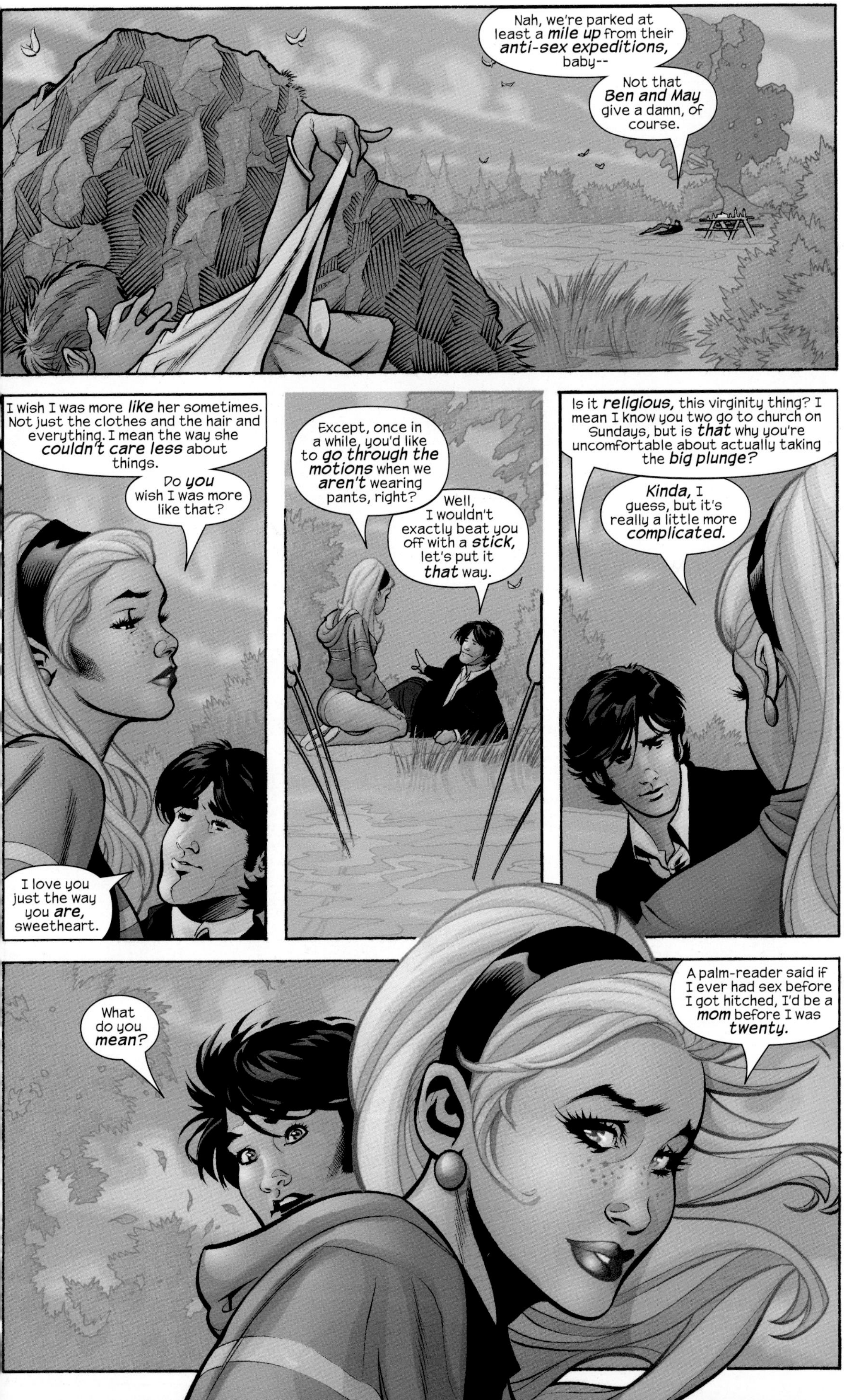

Nah, we're parked at least a mile up from their anti-sex expeditions, baby--
Not that Ben and May give a damn, of course.
I wish I was more like her sometimes. Not just the clothes and the hair and everything. I mean the way she couldn't care less about things.
Do you wish I was more like that?
I love you just the way you are, sweetheart.
Except, once in a while, you'd like to go through the motions when we aren't wearing pants, right?
Well, I wouldn't exactly beat you off with a stick, let's put it that way.
Is it religious, this virginity thing? I mean I know you two go to church on Sundays, but is that why you're uncomfortable about actually taking the big plunge?
Kinda, I guess, but it's really a little more complicated.
What do you mean?
A palm-reader said if I ever had sex before I got hitched, I'd be a mom before I was twenty.

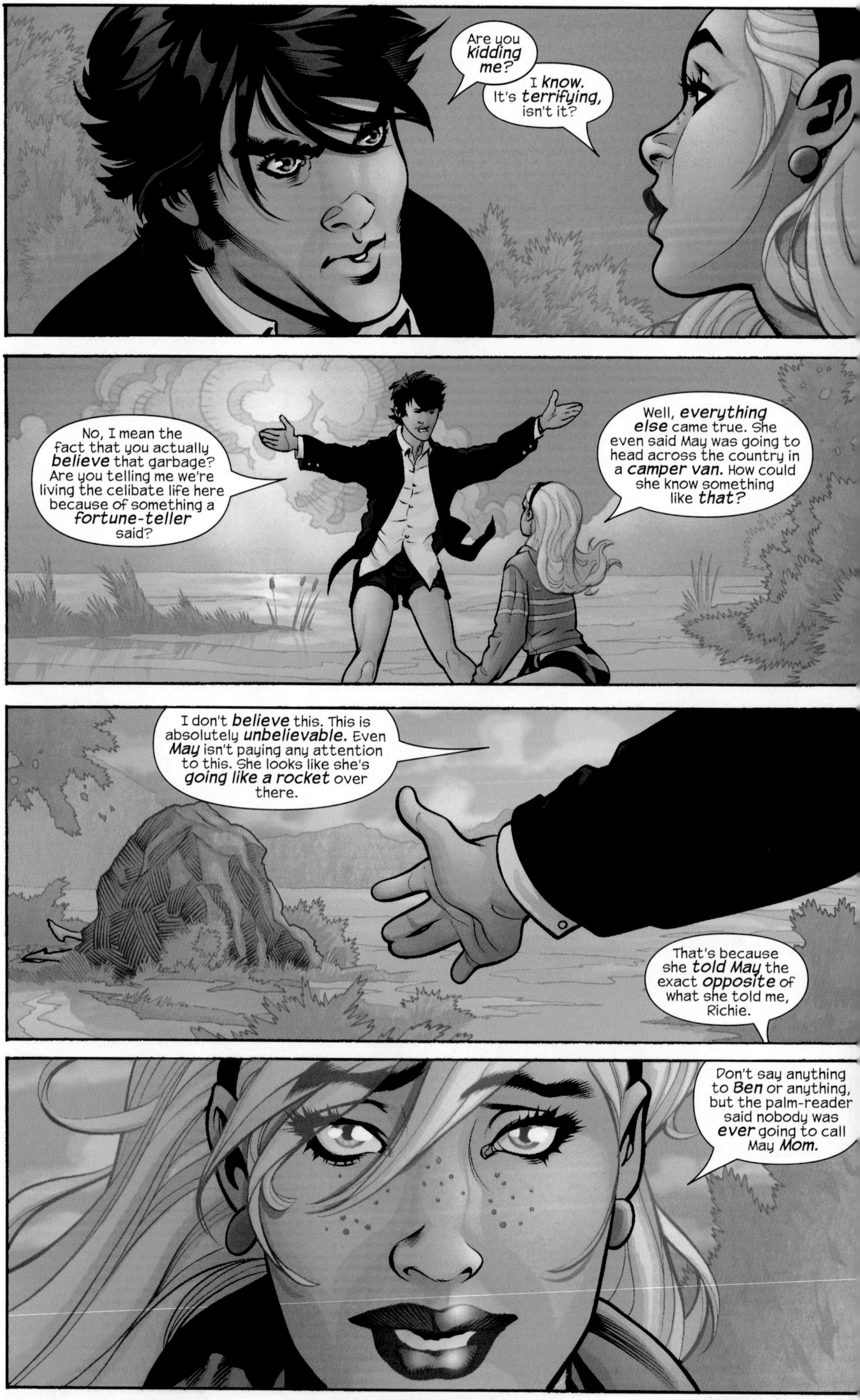

Are you kidding me?
I know. It's terrifying, isn't it?
No, I mean the fact that you actually believe that garbage? Are you telling me we're living the celibate life here because of something a fortune-teller said?
Well, everything else came true. She even said May was going to head across the country in a camper van. How could she know something like that?
I don't believe this. This is absolutely unbelievable. Even May isn't paying any attention to this. She looks like she's going like a rocket over there.
That's because she told May the exact opposite of what she told me, Richie.
Don't say anything to Ben or anything, but the palm-reader said nobody was ever going to call May Mom.

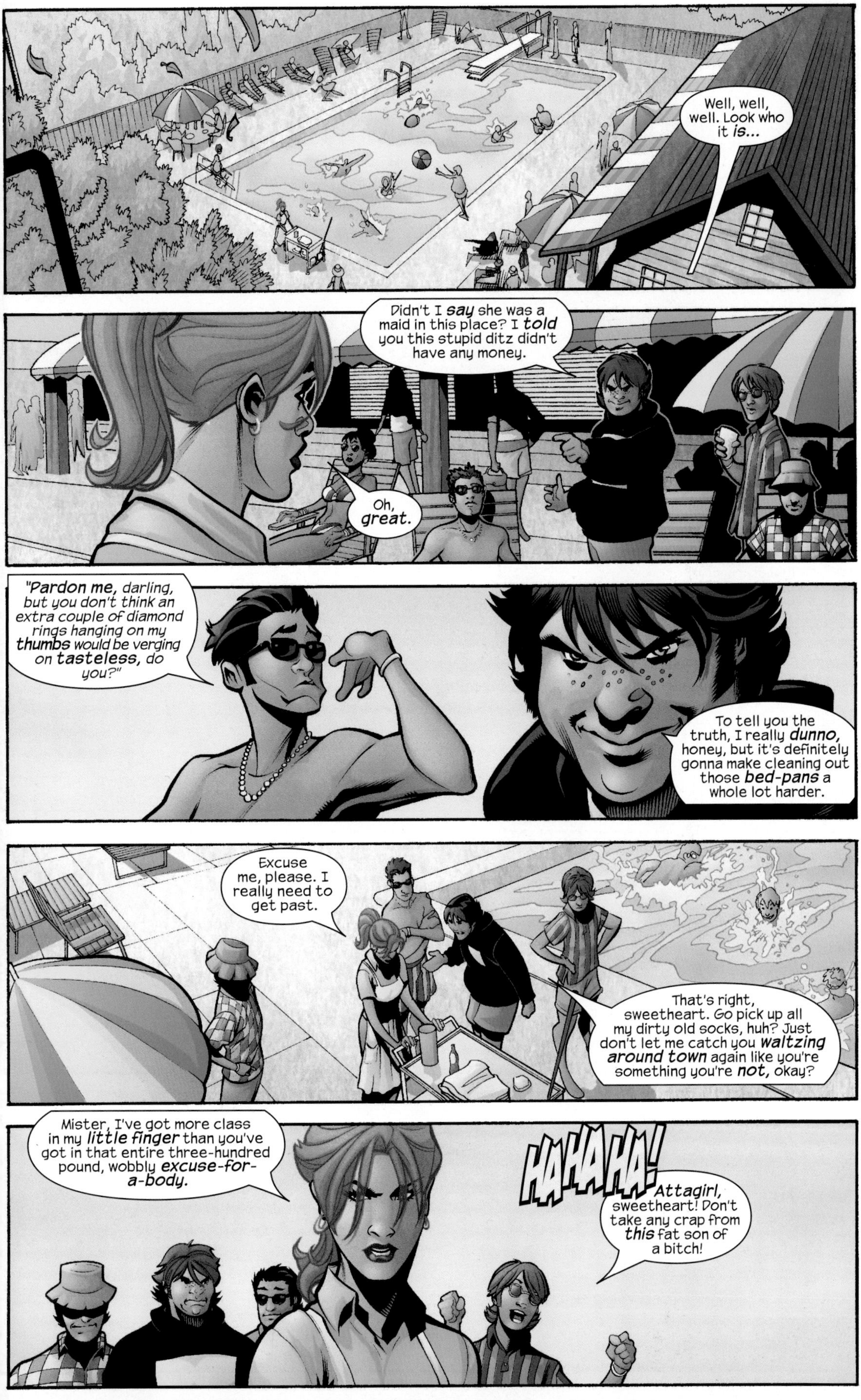
Well, well, well. Look who it is...
Didn't I say she was a maid in this place? I told you this stupid ditz didn't have any money.
Oh, great.
"Pardon me, darling, but you don't think an extra couple of diamond rings hanging on my thumbs would be verging on tasteless, do you?"
To tell you the truth, I really dunno, honey, but it's definitely gonna make cleaning out those bed-pans a whole lot harder.
Excuse me, please. I really need to get past.
That's right, sweetheart. Go pick up all my dirty old socks, huh? Just don't let me catch you waltzing around town again like you're something you're not, okay?
Mister, I've got more class in my little finger than you've got in that entire three-hundred pound, wobbly excuse-for-a-body.
HA HA HA!
Attagirl, sweetheart! Don't take any crap from this fat son of a bitch!

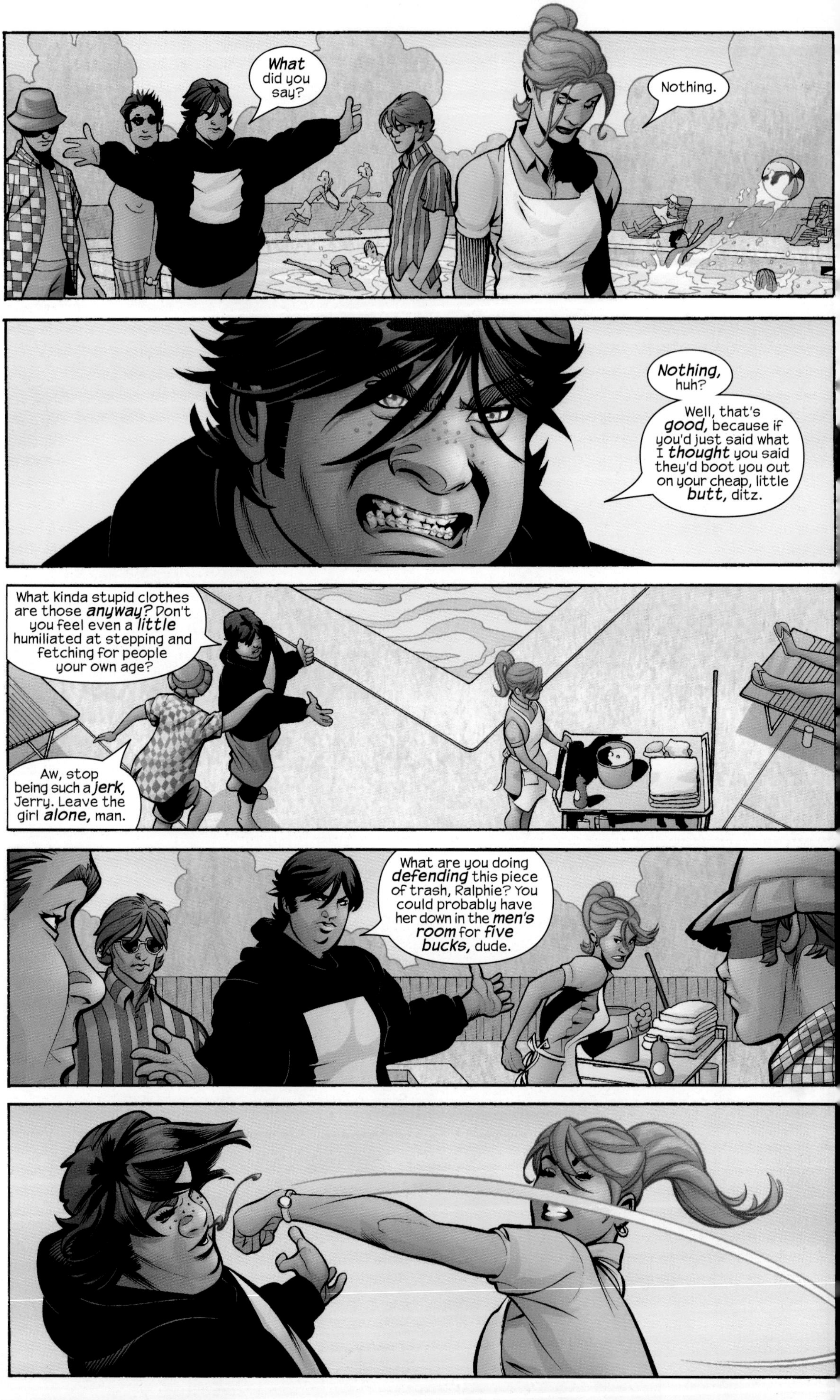
What did you say?
Nothing.
Nothing, huh?
Well, that's good, because if you'd just said what I thought you said they'd boot you out on your cheap, little butt, ditz.
What kinda stupid clothes are those anyway? Don't you feel even a little humiliated at stepping and fetching for people your own age?
Aw, stop being such a jerk, Jerry. Leave the girl alone, man.
What are you doing defending this piece of trash, Ralphie? You could probably have her down in the men's room for five bucks, dude.

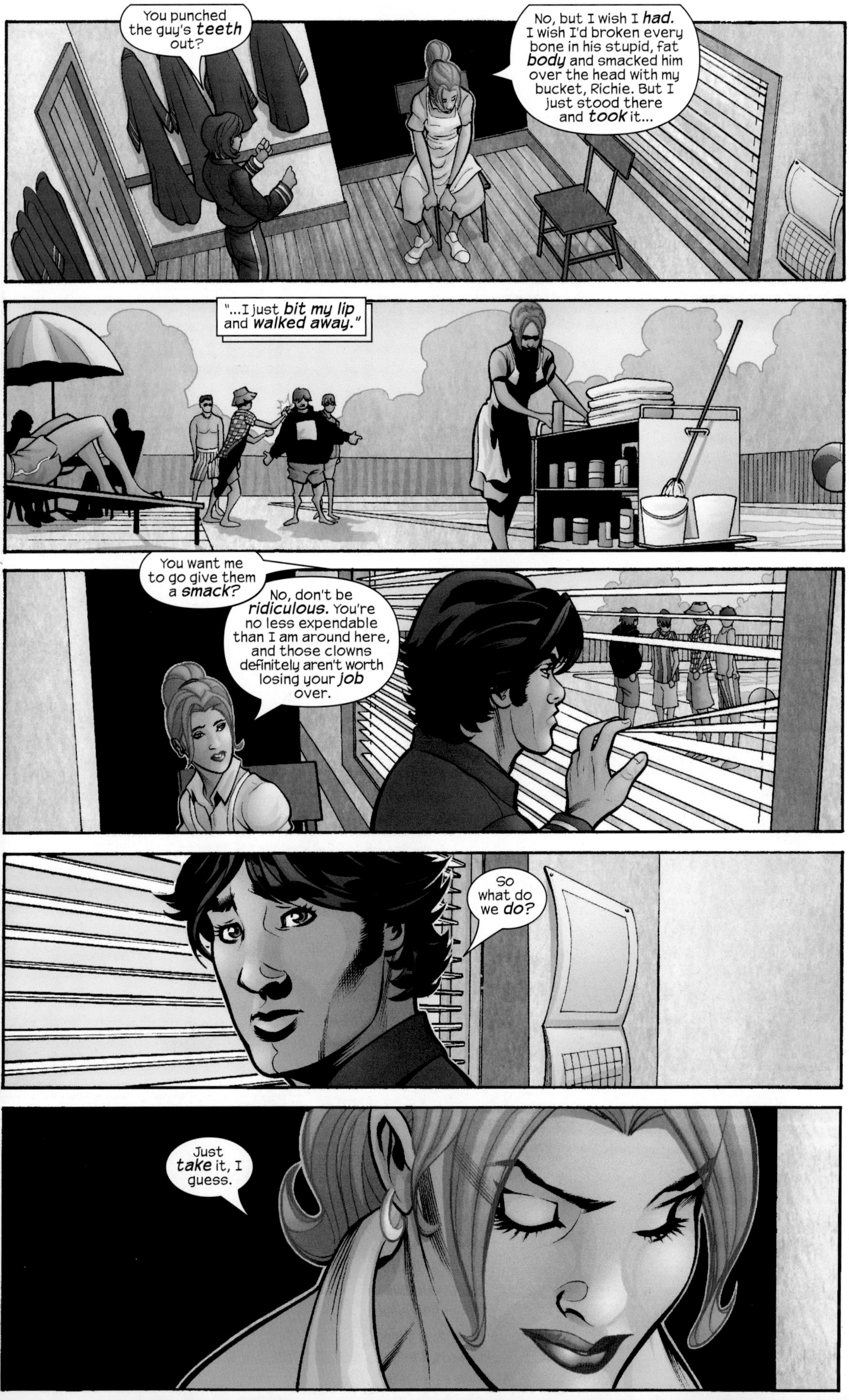
You punched the guy's *teeth* out?
No, but I wish I *had.* I wish I'd broken every bone in his stupid, fat *body* and smacked him over the head with my bucket, Richie. But I just stood there and *took* it...
"...I just *bit my lip* and *walked away.*"
You want me to go give them a *smack*?
No, don't be *ridiculous.* You're no less expendable than I am around here, and those clowns definitely aren't worth losing your *job* over.
So what do we *do*?
Just *take* it, I guess.

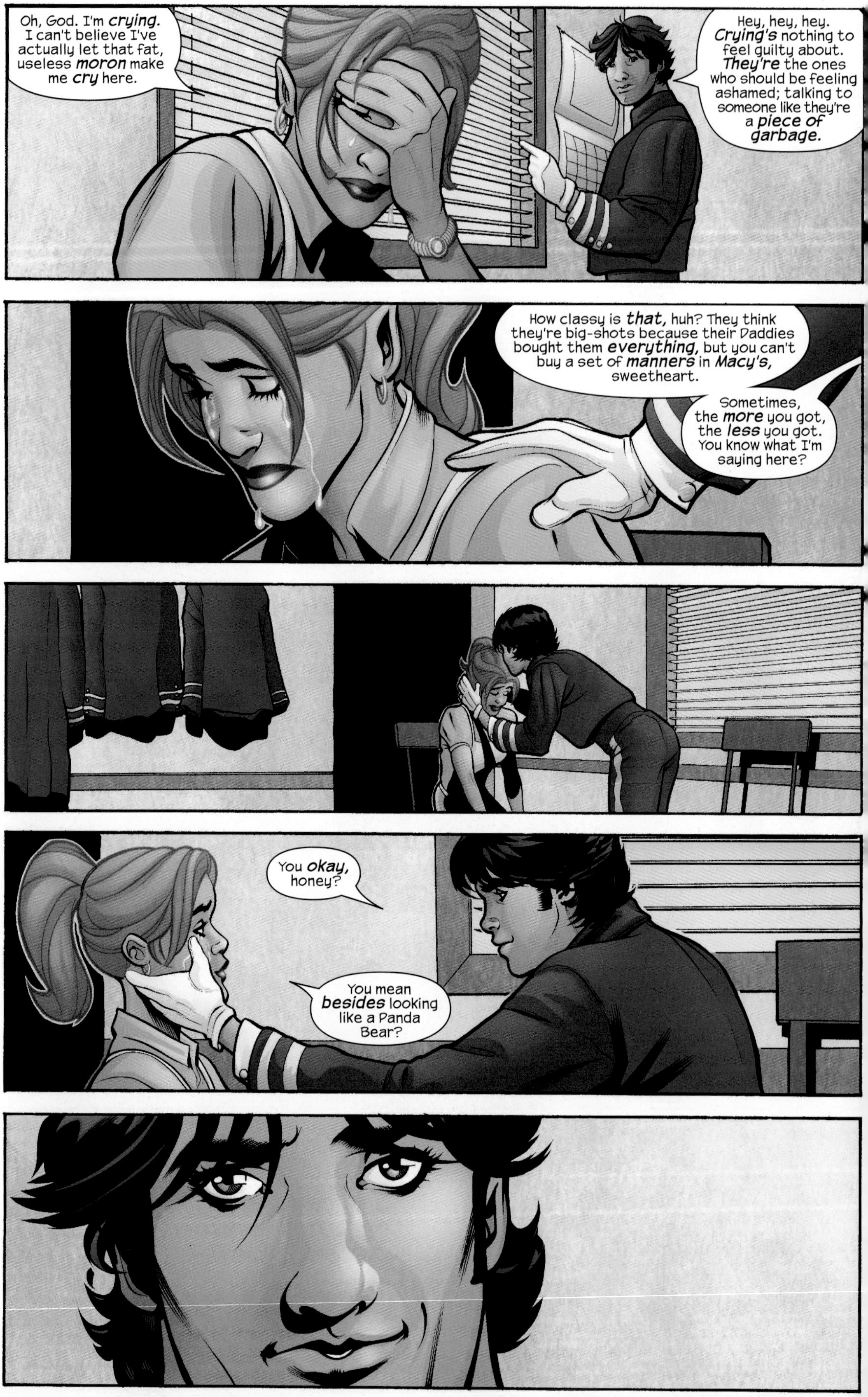
Oh, God. I'm crying. I can't believe I've actually let that fat, useless moron make me cry here.
Hey, hey, hey. Crying's nothing to feel guilty about. They're the ones who should be feeling ashamed; talking to someone like they're a piece of garbage.
How classy is that, huh? They think they're big-shots because their Daddies bought them everything, but you can't buy a set of manners in Macy's, sweetheart.
Sometimes, the more you got, the less you got. You know what I'm saying here?
You okay, honey?
You mean besides looking like a Panda Bear?

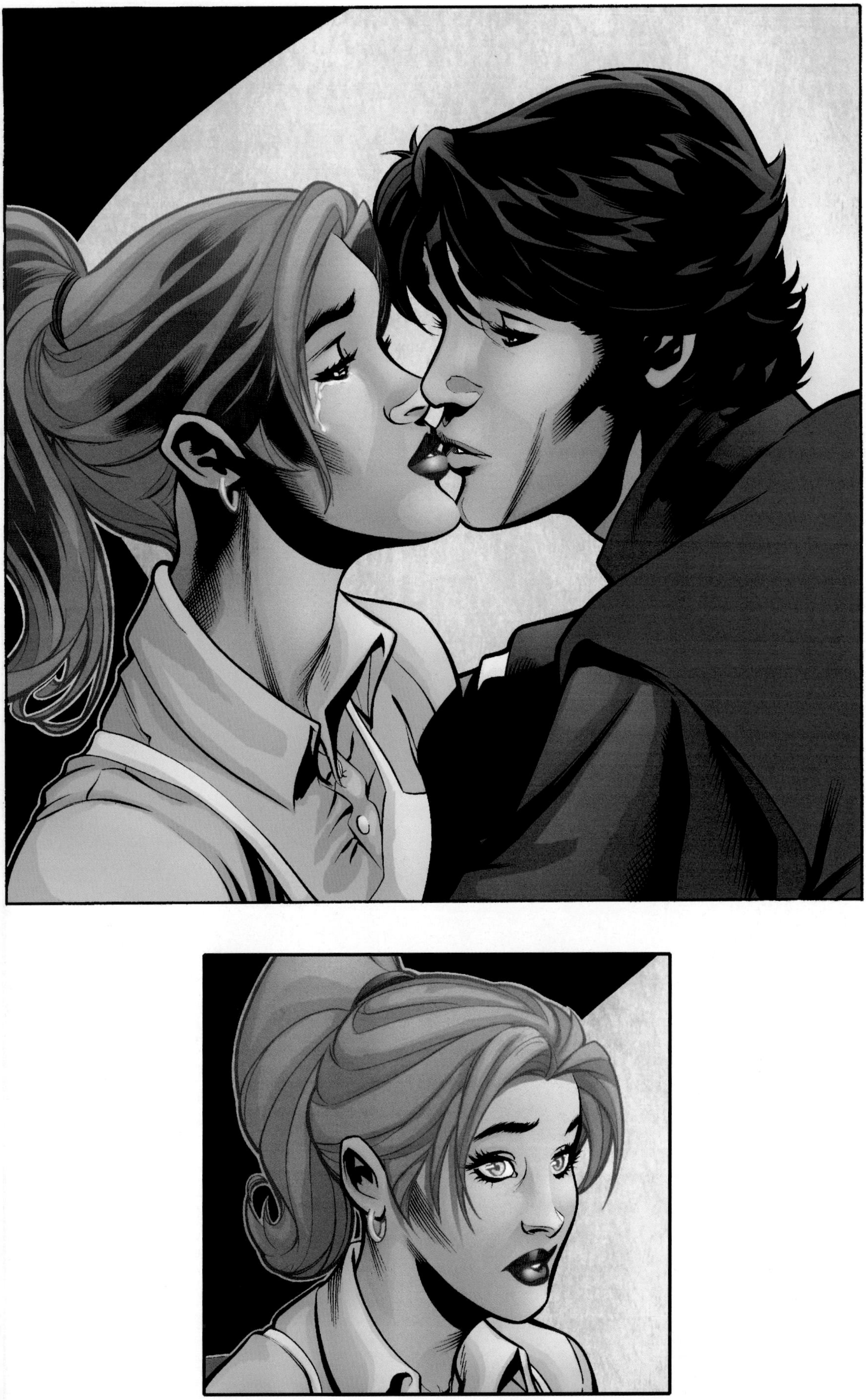

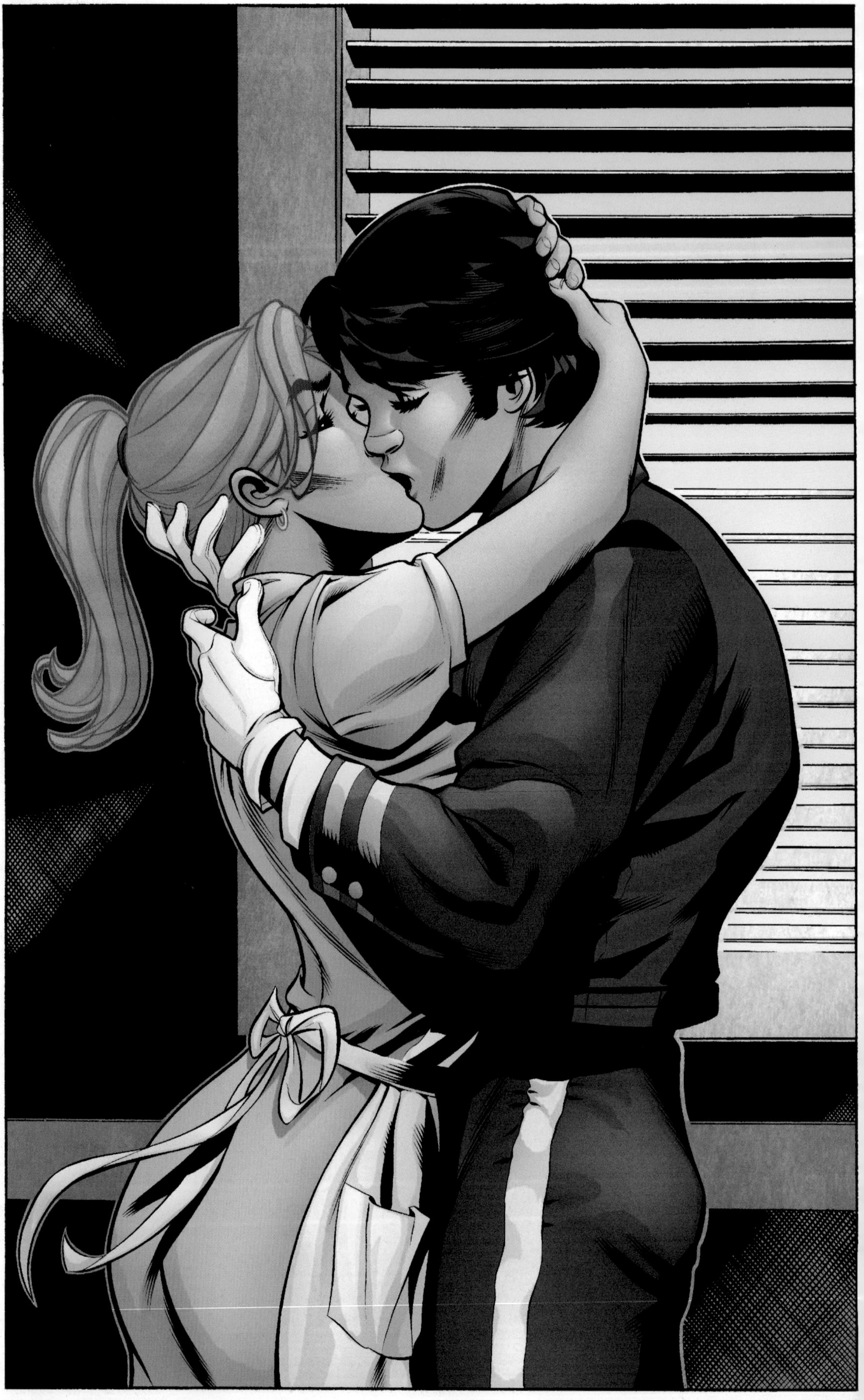

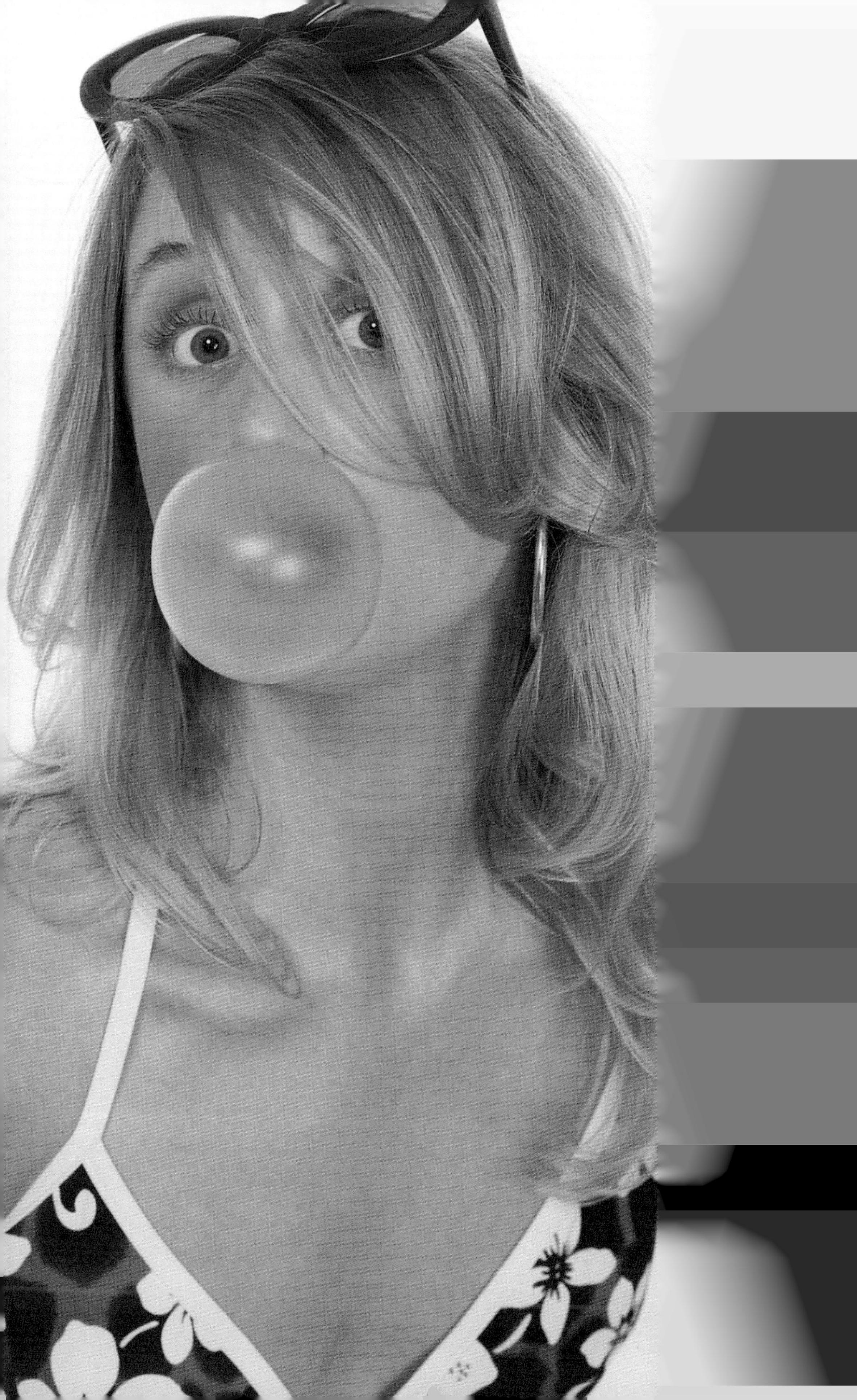

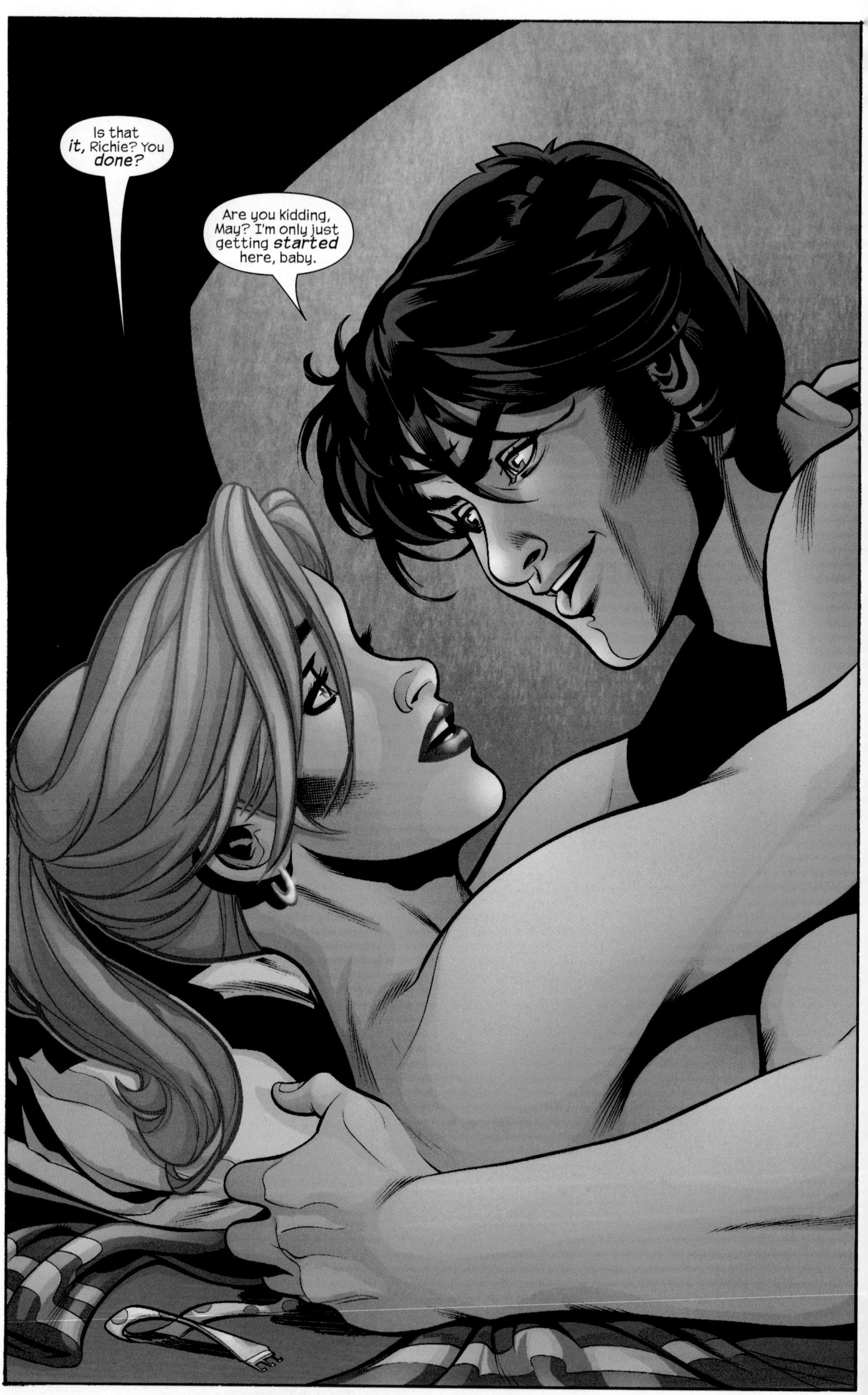
Is that *it,* Richie? You *done?*
Are you kidding, May? I'm only just getting *started* here, baby.

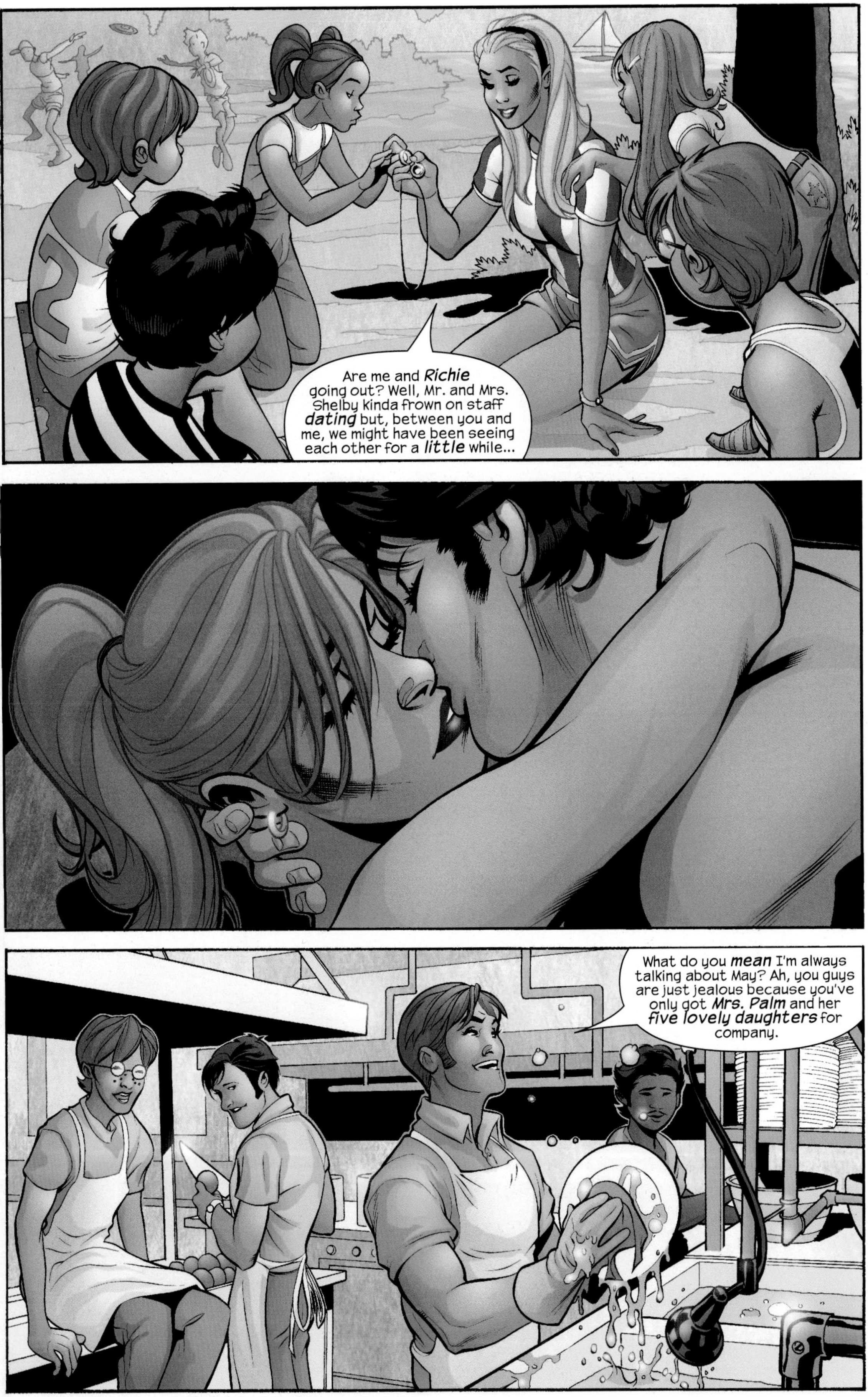
Are me and Richie going out? Well, Mr. and Mrs. Shelby kinda frown on staff dating but, between you and me, we might have been seeing each other for a little while...
What do you mean I'm always talking about May? Ah, you guys are just jealous because you've only got Mrs. Palm and her five lovely daughters for company.

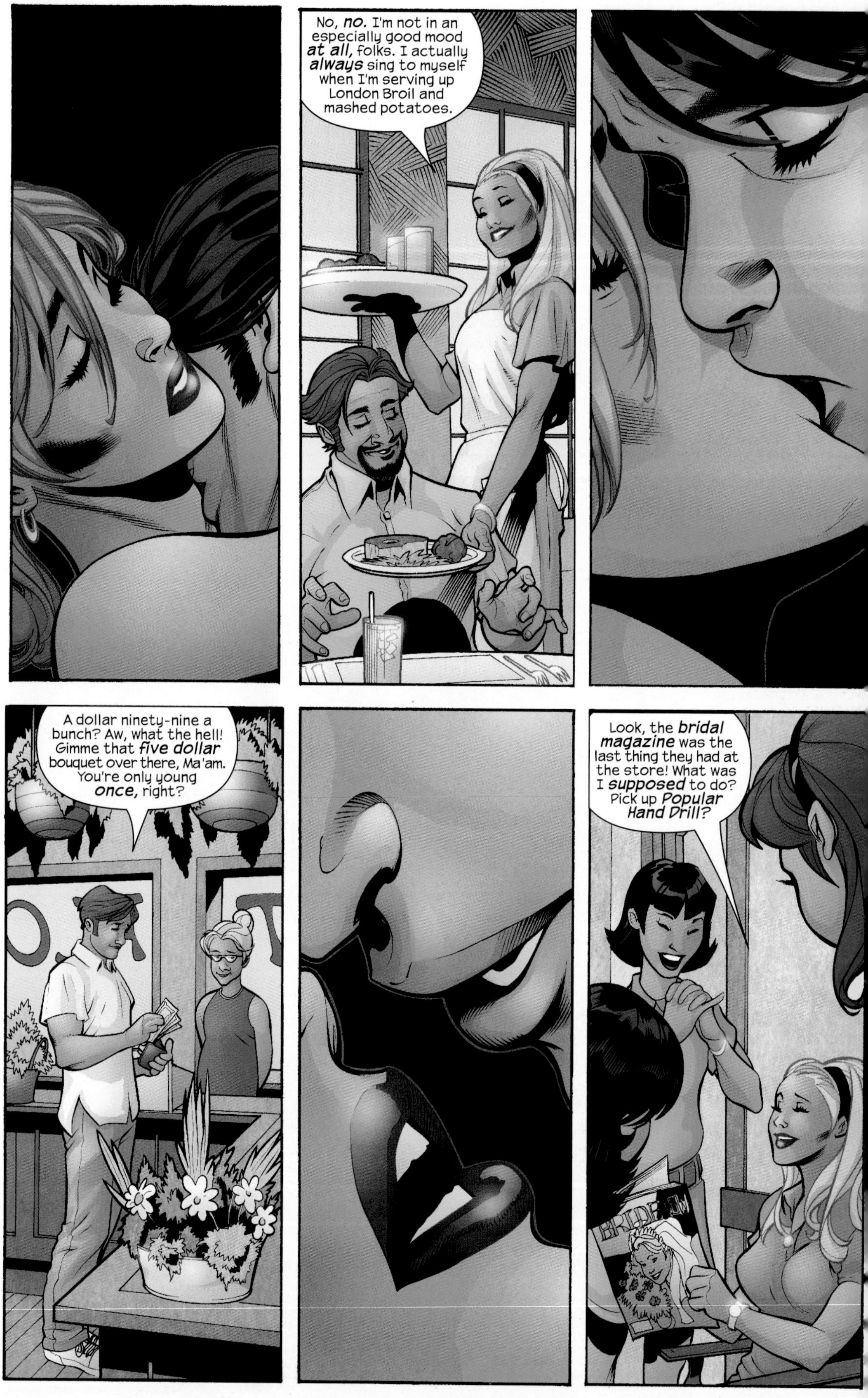
No, *no.* I'm not in an especially good mood *at all,* folks. I actually *always* sing to myself when I'm serving up London Broil and mashed potatoes.
A dollar ninety-nine a bunch? Aw, what the hell! Gimme that *five dollar* bouquet over there, Ma'am. You're only young *once,* right?
Look, the *bridal magazine* was the last thing they had at the store! What was I *supposed* to do? Pick up *Popular Hand Drill?*
BRIDE

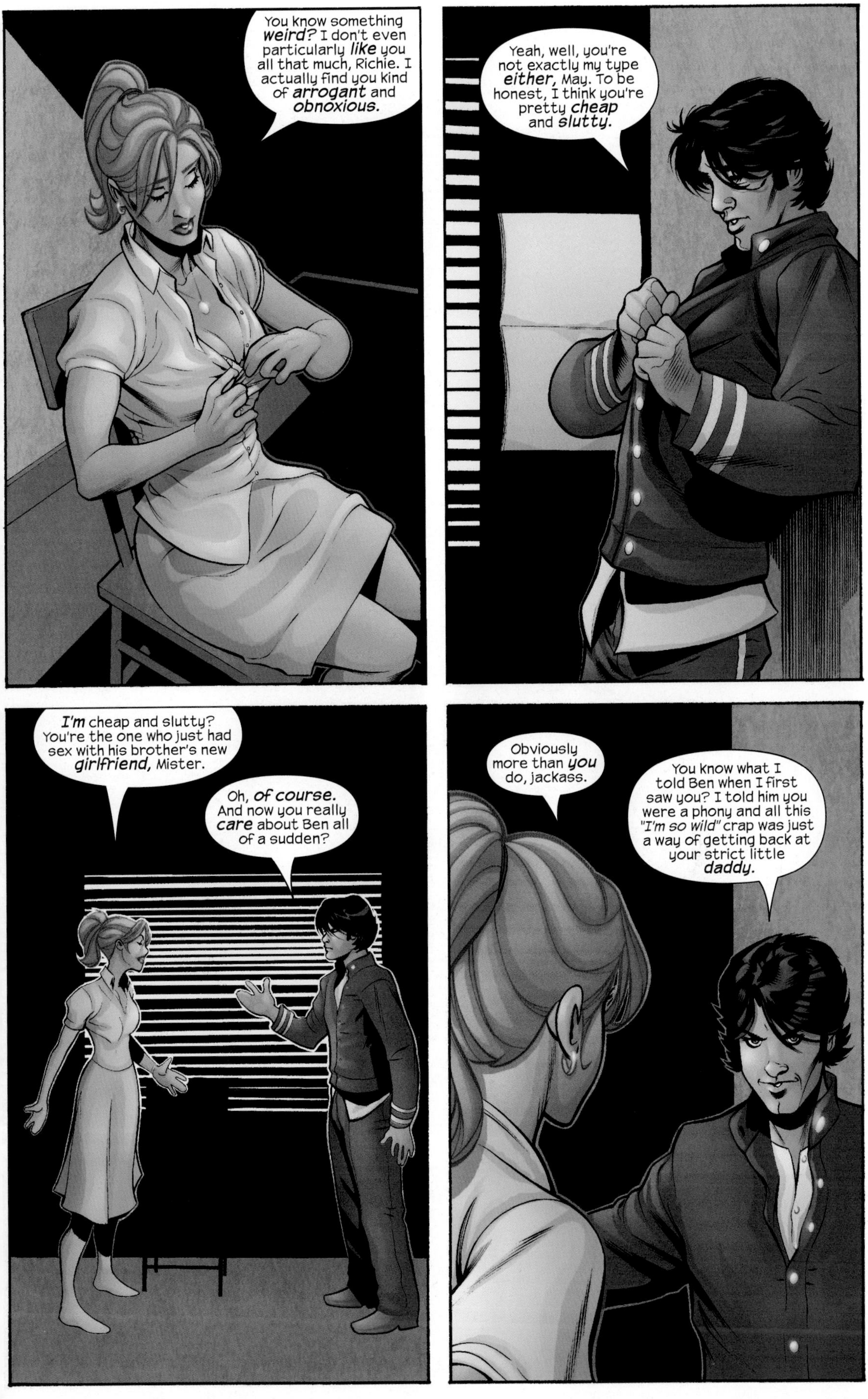
You know something weird? I don't even particularly like you all that much, Richie. I actually find you kind of arrogant and obnoxious.
Yeah, well, you're not exactly my type either, May. To be honest, I think you're pretty cheap and slutty.
I'm cheap and slutty? You're the one who just had sex with his brother's new girlfriend, Mister.
Oh, of course. And now you really care about Ben all of a sudden?
Obviously more than you do, jackass.
You know what I told Ben when I first saw you? I told him you were a phony and all this "I'm so wild" crap was just a way of getting back at your strict little daddy.

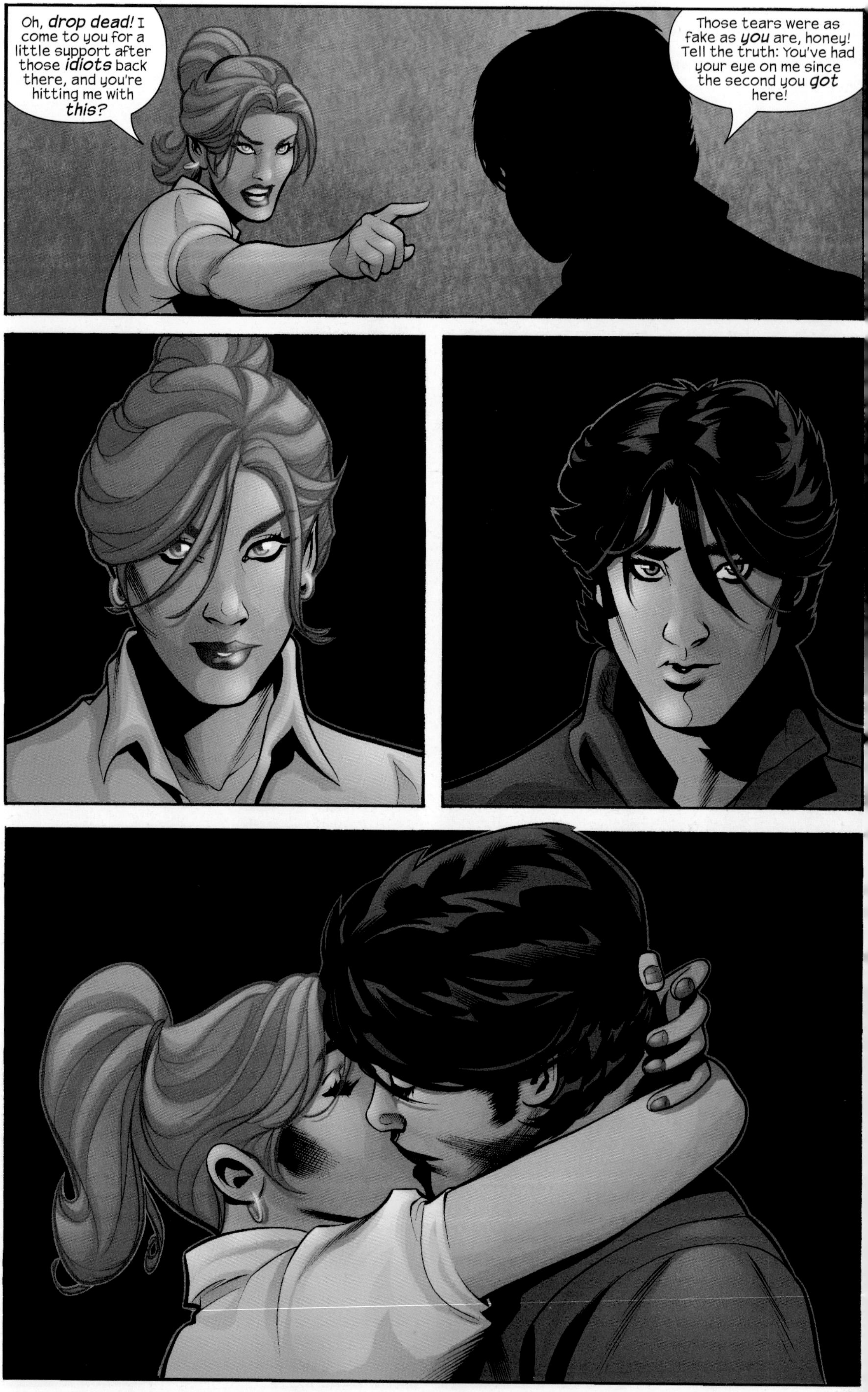
Oh, *drop dead!* I come to you for a little support after those *idiots* back there, and you're hitting me with *this?*
Those tears were as fake as *you* are, honey! Tell the truth: You've had your eye on me since the second you *got* here!

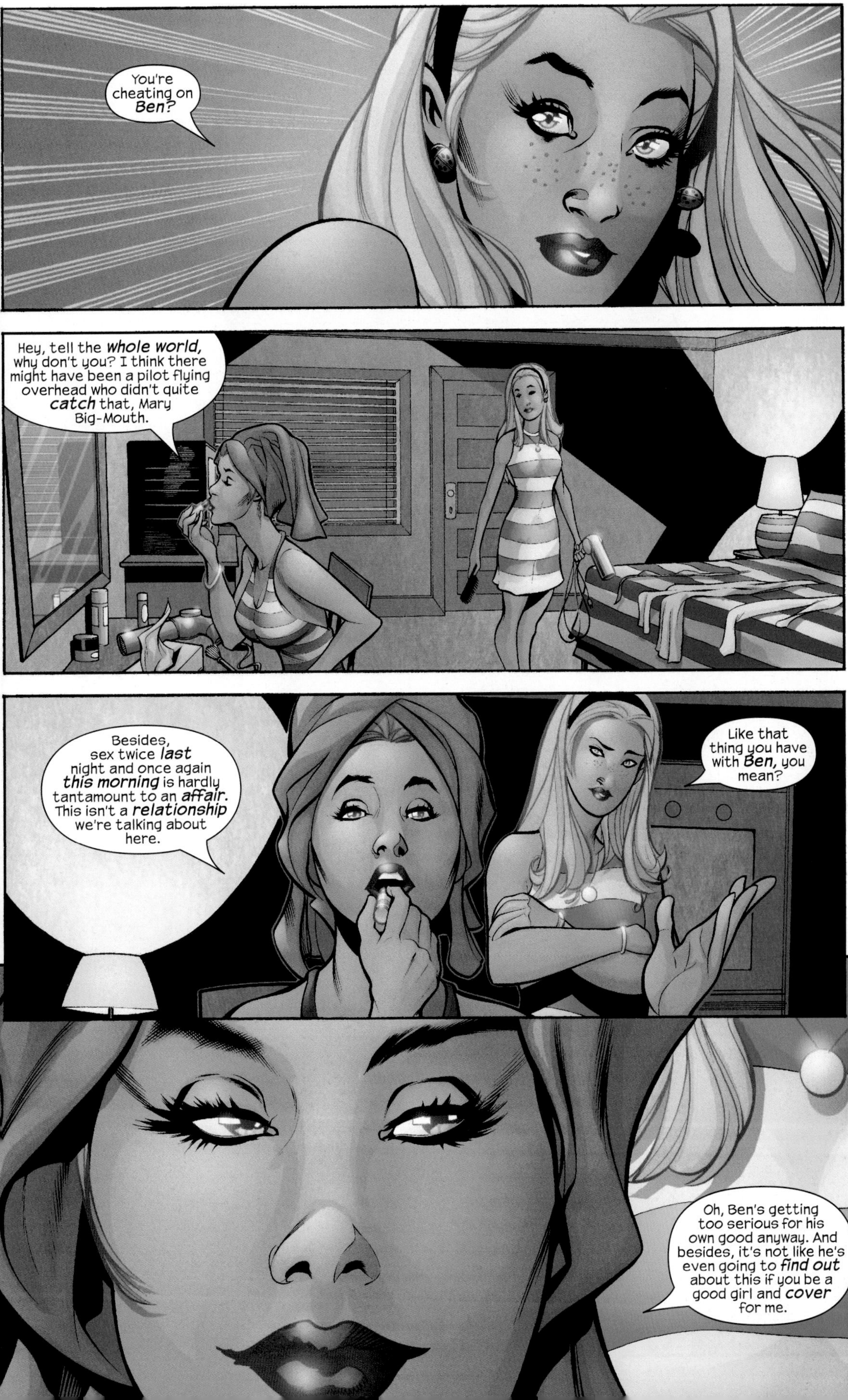

You're cheating on Ben?
Hey, tell the whole world, why don't you? I think there might have been a pilot flying overhead who didn't quite catch that, Mary Big-Mouth.
Besides, sex twice last night and once again this morning is hardly tantamount to an affair. This isn't a relationship we're talking about here.
Like that thing you have with Ben, you mean?
Oh, Ben's getting too serious for his own good anyway. And besides, it's not like he's even going to find out about this if you be a good girl and cover for me.

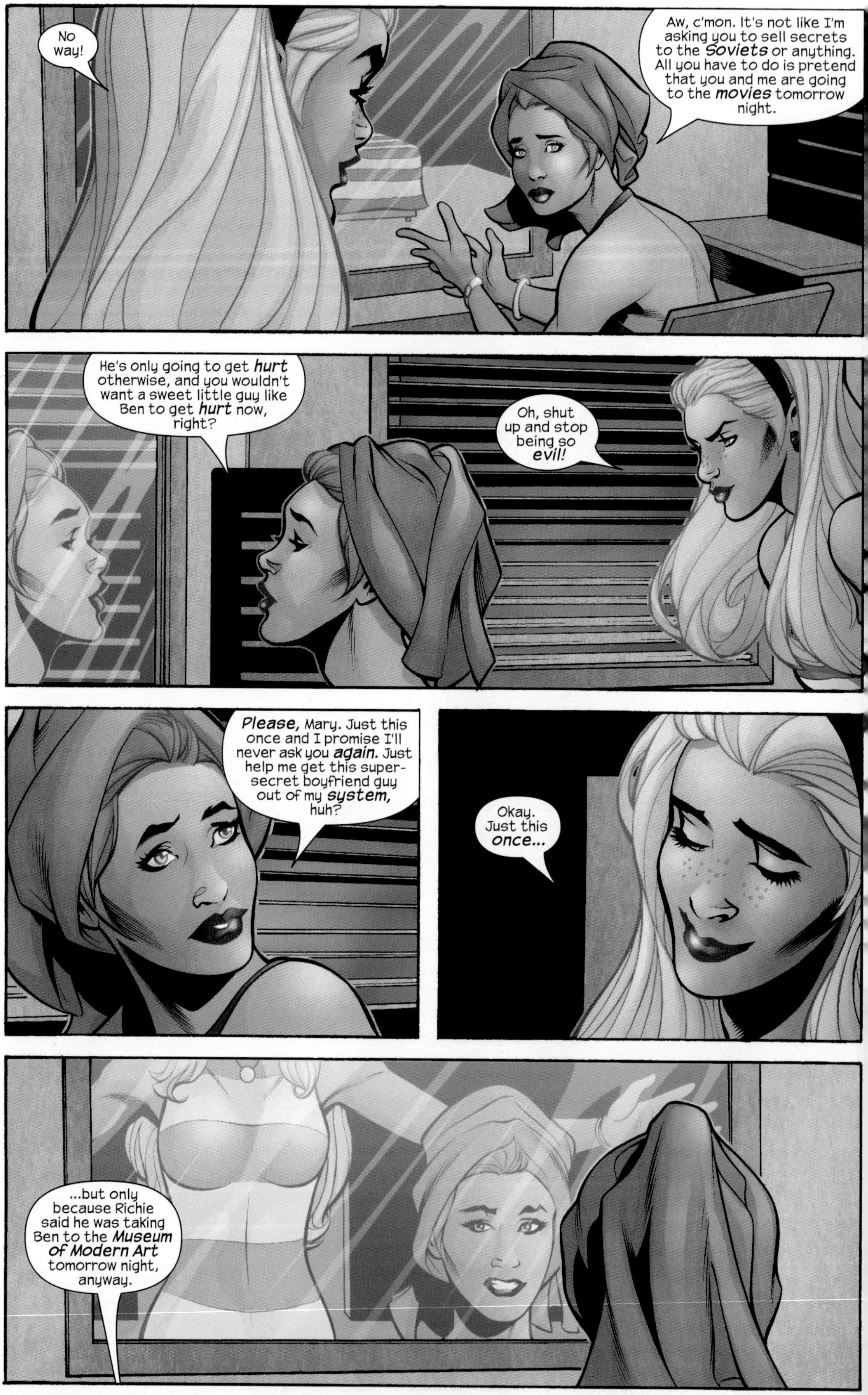
No way!
Aw, c'mon. It's not like I'm asking you to sell secrets to the Soviets or anything. All you have to do is pretend that you and me are going to the movies tomorrow night.
He's only going to get hurt otherwise, and you wouldn't want a sweet little guy like Ben to get hurt now, right?
Oh, shut up and stop being so evil!
Please, Mary. Just this once and I promise I'll never ask you again. Just help me get this super-secret boyfriend guy out of my system, huh?
Okay. Just this once...
...but only because Richie said he was taking Ben to the Museum of Modern Art tomorrow night, anyway.

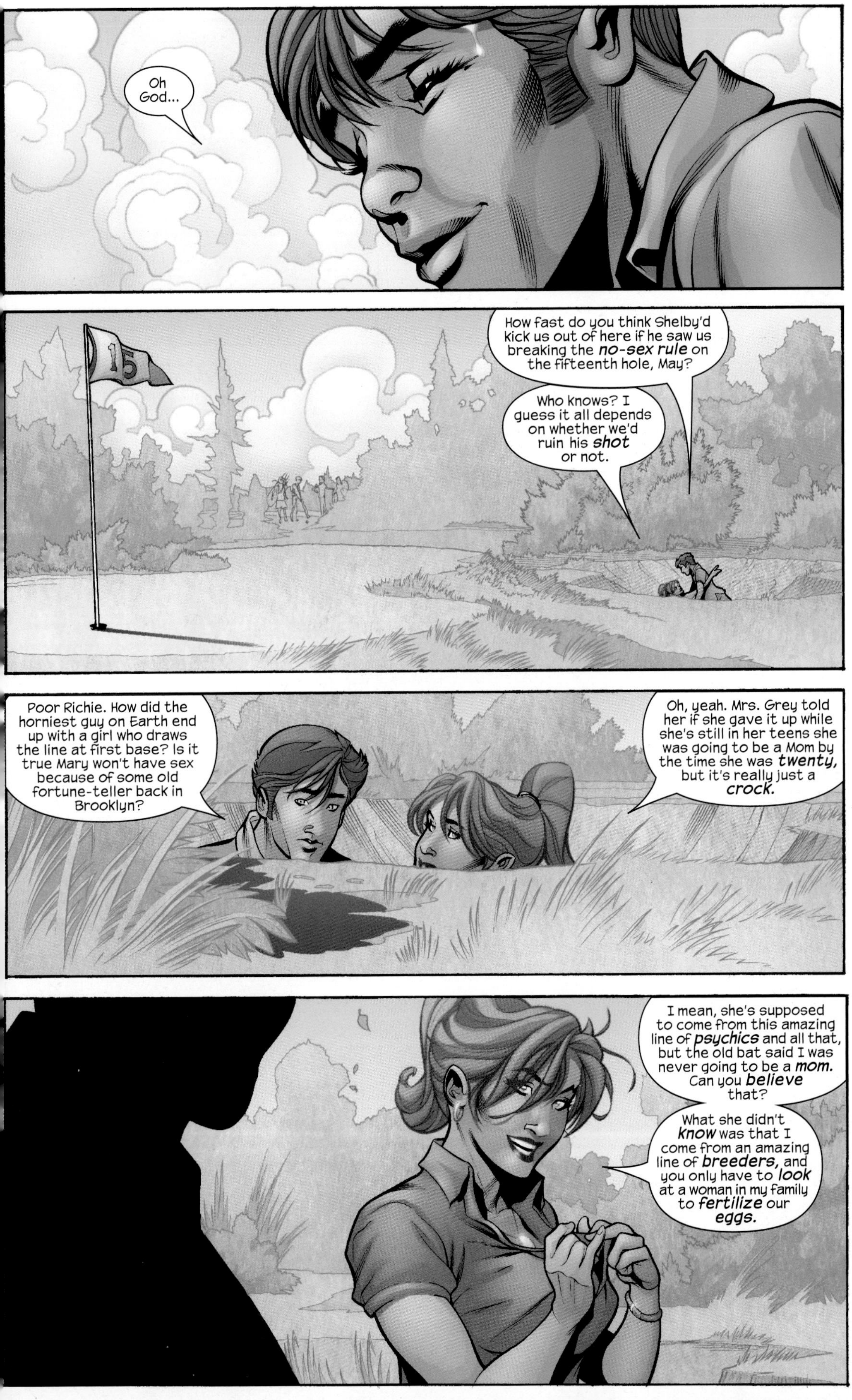
Oh God...
How fast do you think Shelby'd kick us out of here if he saw us breaking the no-sex rule on the fifteenth hole, May?
Who knows? I guess it all depends on whether we'd ruin his shot or not.
Poor Richie. How did the horniest guy on Earth end up with a girl who draws the line at first base? Is it true Mary won't have sex because of some old fortune-teller back in Brooklyn?
Oh, yeah. Mrs. Grey told her if she gave it up while she's still in her teens she was going to be a Mom by the time she was twenty, but it's really just a crock.
I mean, she's supposed to come from this amazing line of psychics and all that, but the old bat said I was never going to be a mom. Can you believe that?
What she didn't know was that I come from an amazing line of breeders, and you only have to look at a woman in my family to fertilize our eggs.

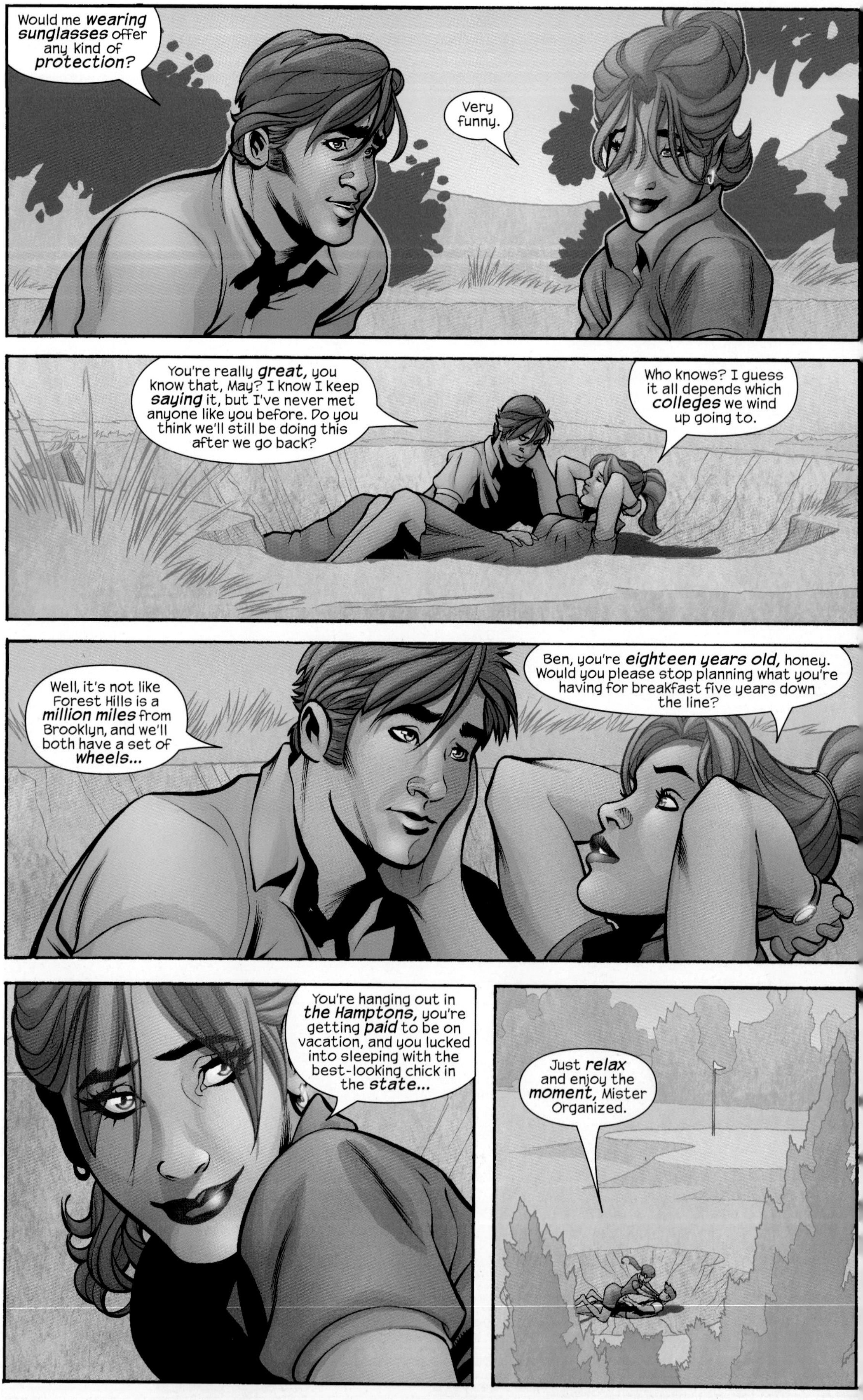

Would me wearing sunglasses offer any kind of protection?
Very funny.
You're really great, you know that, May? I know I keep saying it, but I've never met anyone like you before. Do you think we'll still be doing this after we go back?
Who knows? I guess it all depends which colleges we wind up going to.
Well, it's not like Forest Hills is a million miles from Brooklyn, and we'll both have a set of wheels...
Ben, you're eighteen years old, honey. Would you please stop planning what you're having for breakfast five years down the line?
You're hanging out in the Hamptons, you're getting paid to be on vacation, and you lucked into sleeping with the best-looking chick in the state...
Just relax and enjoy the moment, Mister Organized.

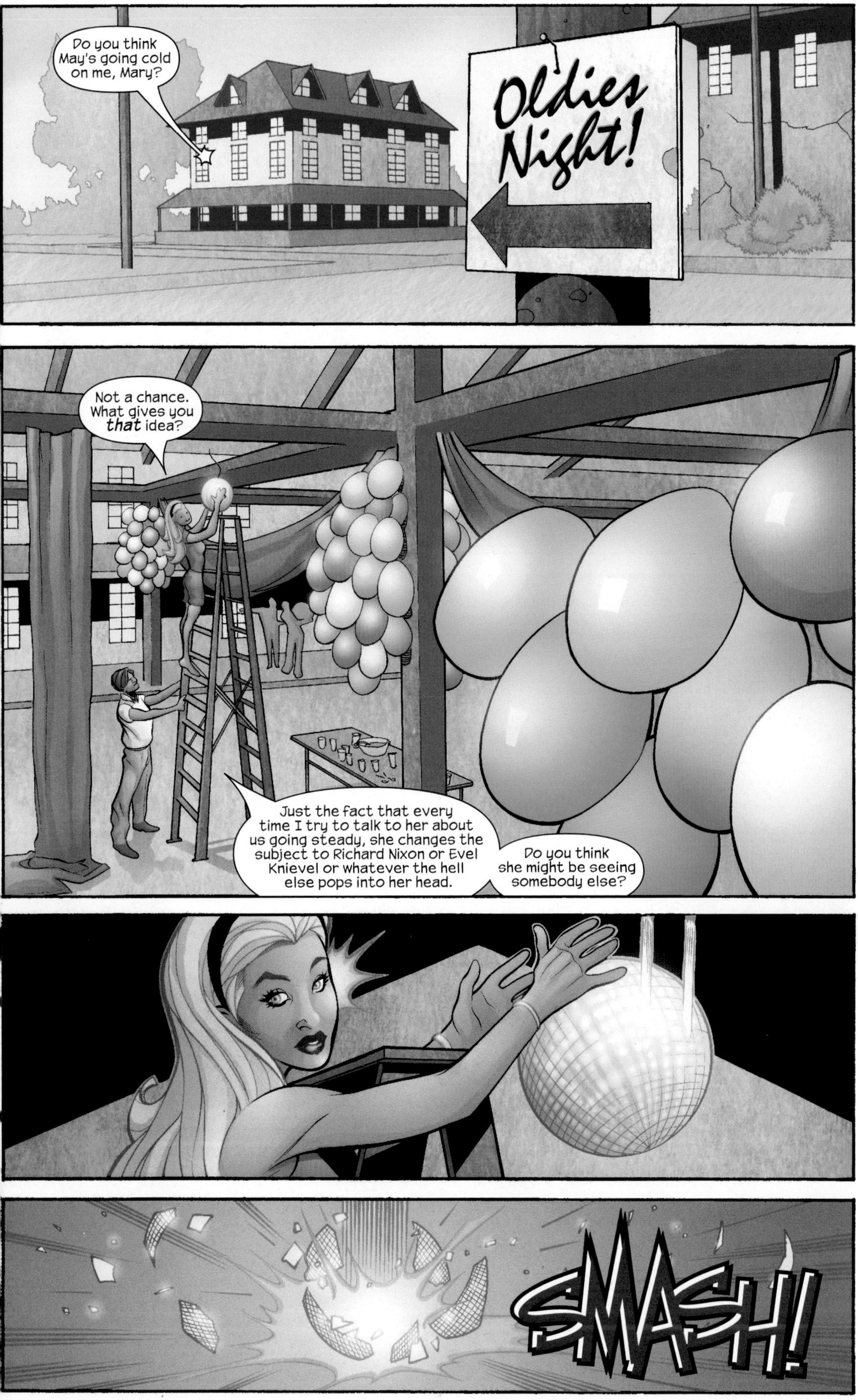
Do you think May's going cold on me, Mary?
Oldies Night!
Not a chance. What gives you *that* idea?
Just the fact that every time I try to talk to her about us going steady, she changes the subject to Richard Nixon or Evel Knievel or whatever the hell else pops into her head.
Do you think she might be seeing somebody else?
SMASH!

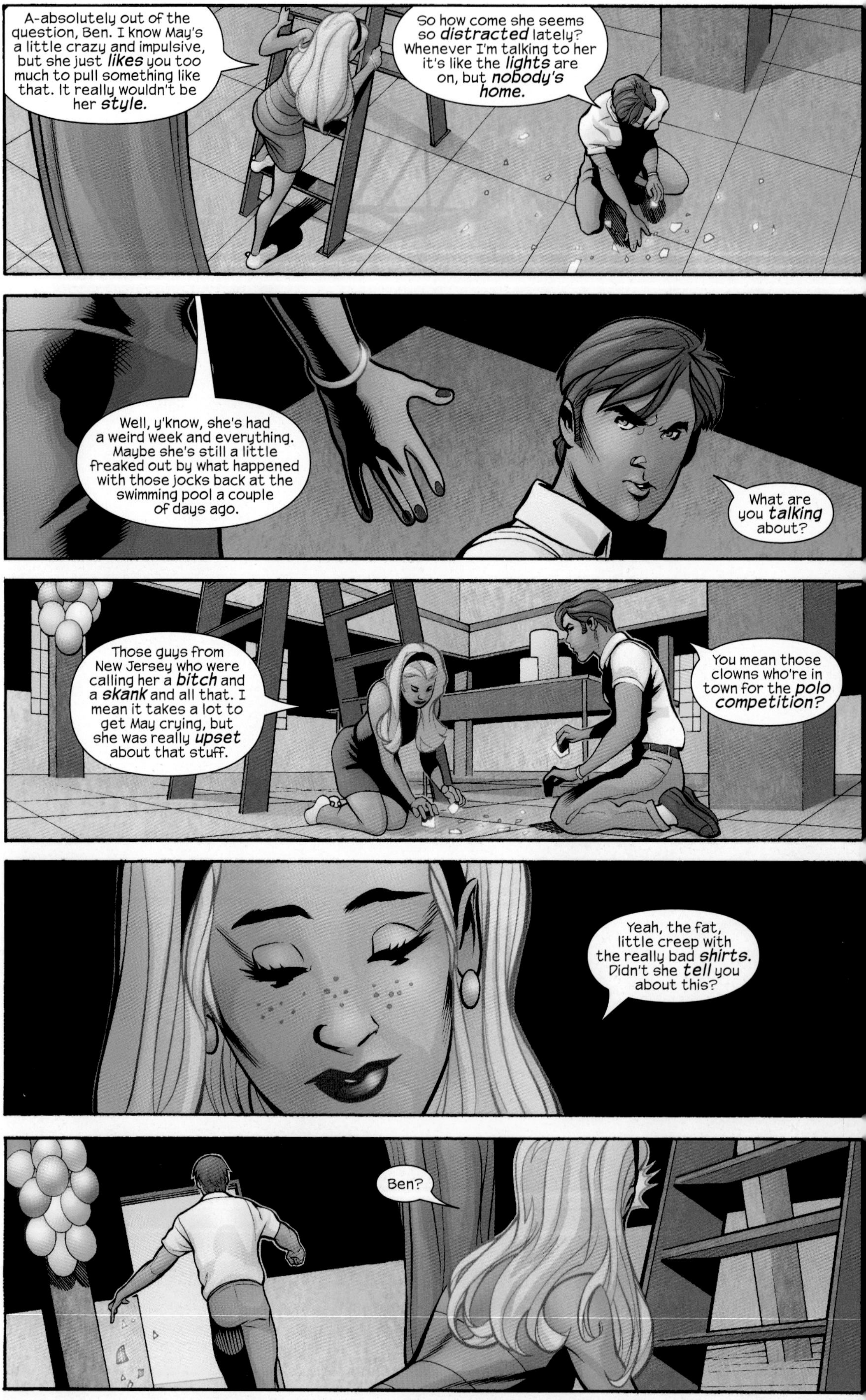
A-absolutely out of the question, Ben. I know May's a little crazy and impulsive, but she just *likes* you too much to pull something like that. It really wouldn't be her ***style.***
So how come she seems so ***distracted*** lately? Whenever I'm talking to her it's like the ***lights*** are on, but ***nobody's home.***
Well, y'know, she's had a weird week and everything. Maybe she's still a little freaked out by what happened with those jocks back at the swimming pool a couple of days ago.
What are you ***talking*** about?
Those guys from New Jersey who were calling her a ***bitch*** and a ***skank*** and all that. I mean it takes a lot to get May crying, but she was really ***upset*** about that stuff.
You mean those clowns who're in town for the ***polo competition?***
Yeah, the fat, little creep with the really bad ***shirts.*** Didn't she ***tell*** you about this?
Ben?

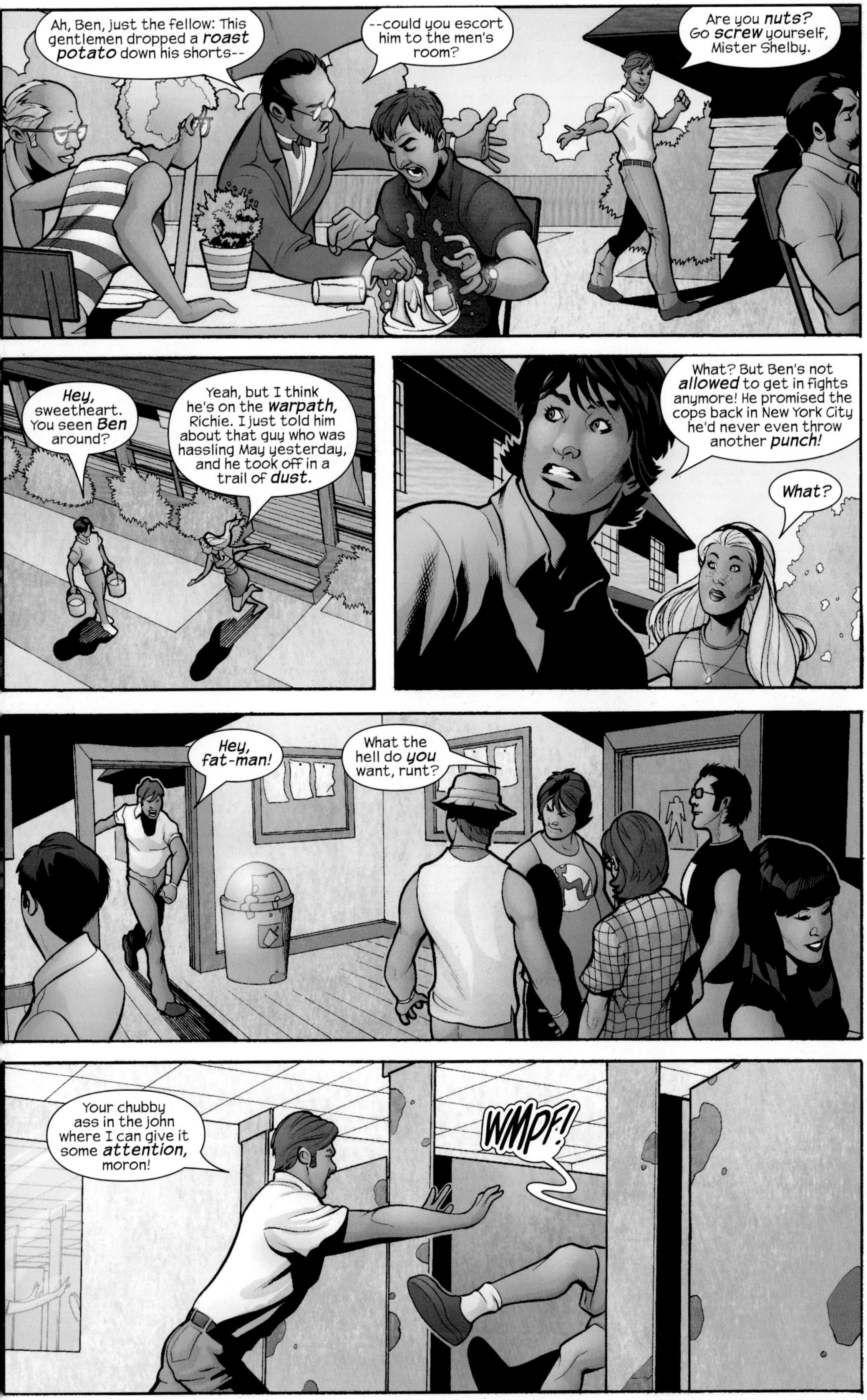
Ah, Ben, just the fellow: This gentlemen dropped a roast potato down his shorts--
--could you escort him to the men's room?
Are you nuts? Go screw yourself, Mister Shelby.
Hey, sweetheart. You seen Ben around?
Yeah, but I think he's on the warpath, Richie. I just told him about that guy who was hassling May yesterday, and he took off in a trail of dust.
What? But Ben's not allowed to get in fights anymore! He promised the cops back in New York City he'd never even throw another punch!
What?
Hey, fat-man!
What the hell do you want, runt?
Your chubby ass in the john where I can give it some attention, moron!
WMPF!

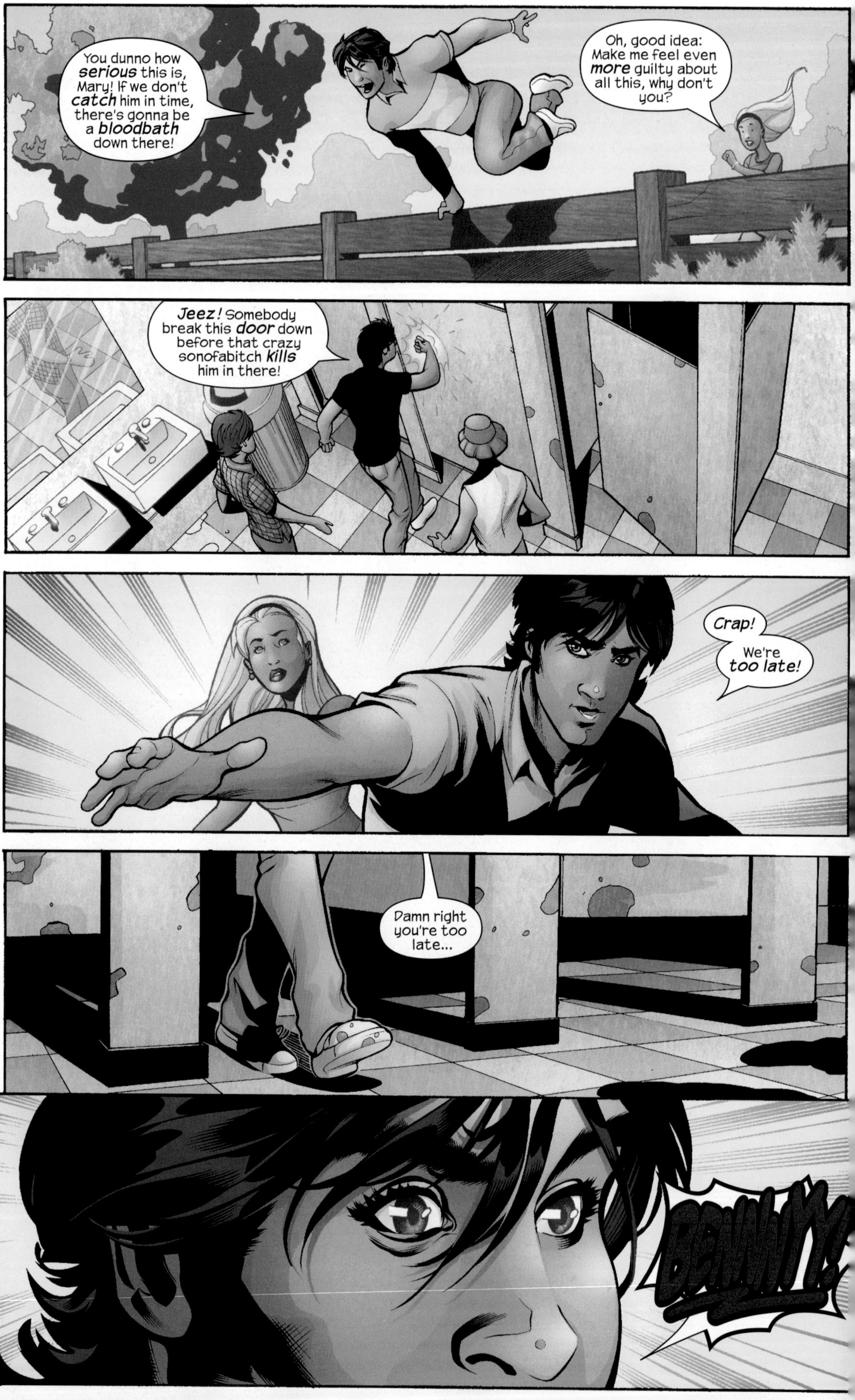
You dunno how serious this is, Mary! If we don't catch him in time, there's gonna be a bloodbath down there!
Oh, good idea: Make me feel even more guilty about all this, why don't you?
Jeez! Somebody break this door down before that crazy sonofabitch kills him in there!
Crap!
We're too late!
Damn right you're too late...
BENNNY!!

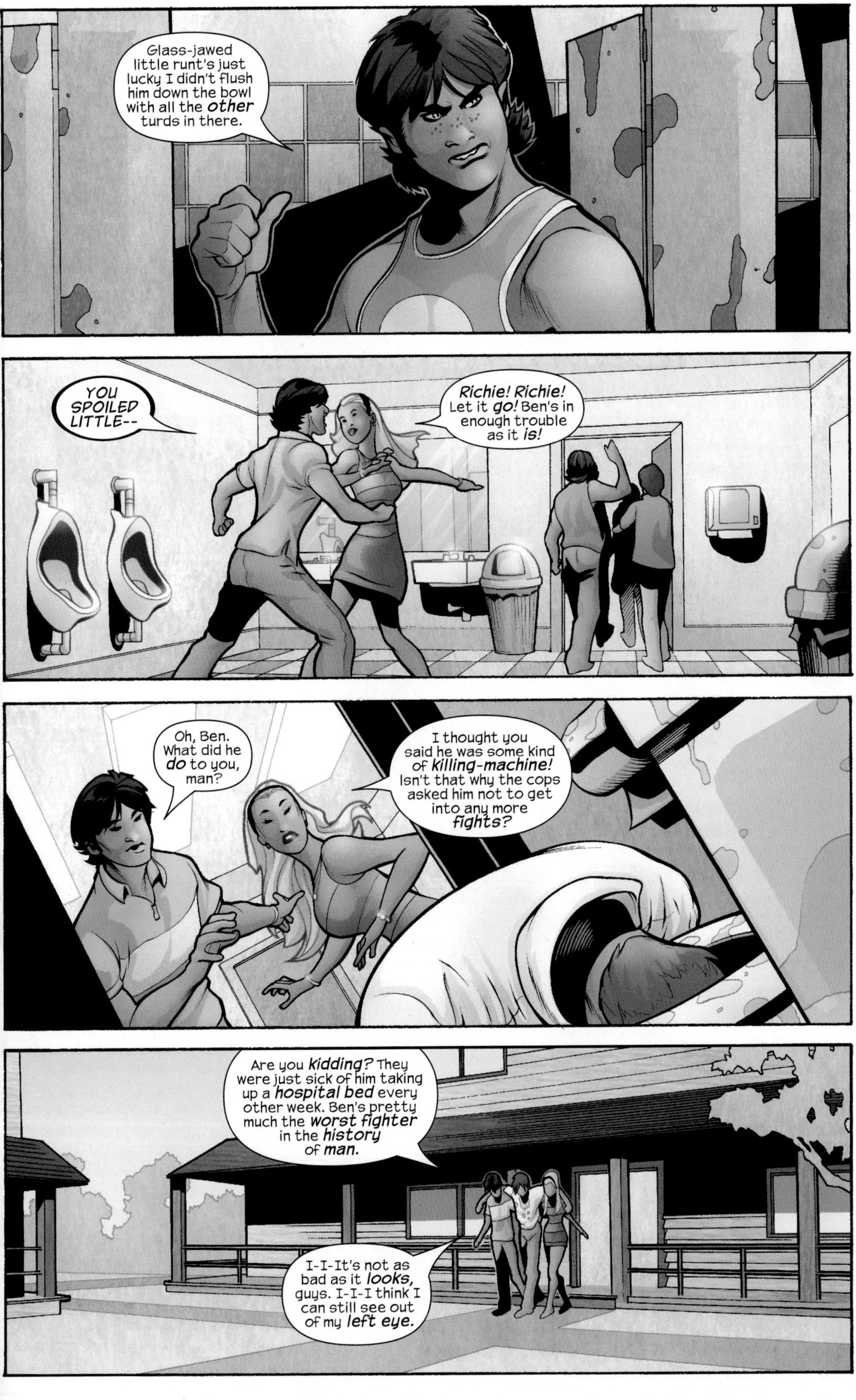
Glass-jawed little runt's just lucky I didn't flush him down the bowl with all the other turds in there.
YOU SPOILED LITTLE--
Richie! Richie! Let it go! Ben's in enough trouble as it is!
Oh, Ben. What did he do to you, man?
I thought you said he was some kind of killing-machine! Isn't that why the cops asked him not to get into any more fights?
Are you kidding? They were just sick of him taking up a hospital bed every other week. Ben's pretty much the worst fighter in the history of man.
I-I-It's not as bad as it looks, guys. I-I-I think I can still see out of my left eye.

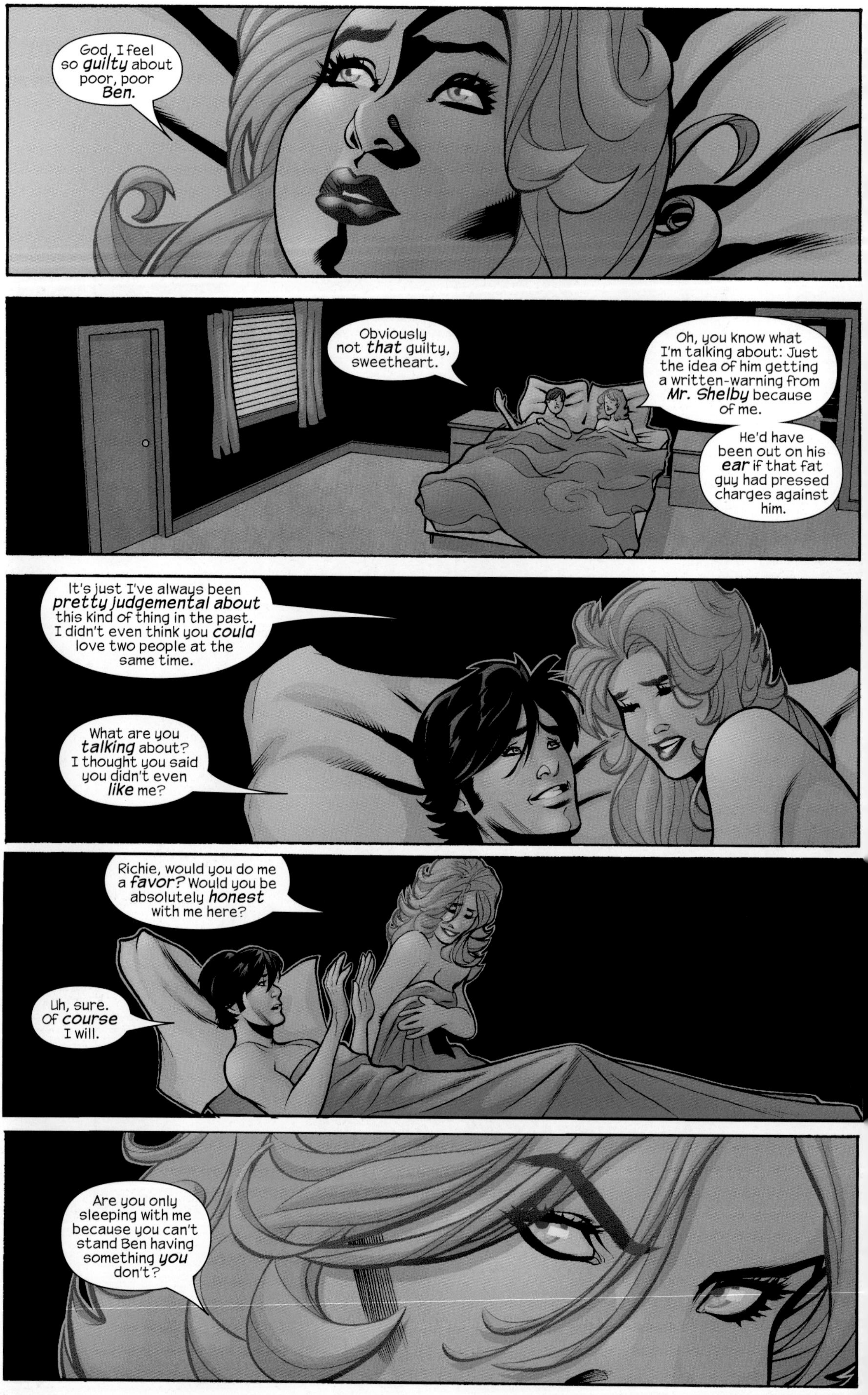

God, I feel so guilty about poor, poor Ben.
Obviously not that guilty, sweetheart.
Oh, you know what I'm talking about: Just the idea of him getting a written-warning from Mr. Shelby because of me.
He'd have been out on his ear if that fat guy had pressed charges against him.
It's just I've always been pretty judgemental about this kind of thing in the past. I didn't even think you could love two people at the same time.
What are you talking about? I thought you said you didn't even like me?
Richie, would you do me a favor? Would you be absolutely honest with me here?
Uh, sure. Of course I will.
Are you only sleeping with me because you can't stand Ben having something you don't?

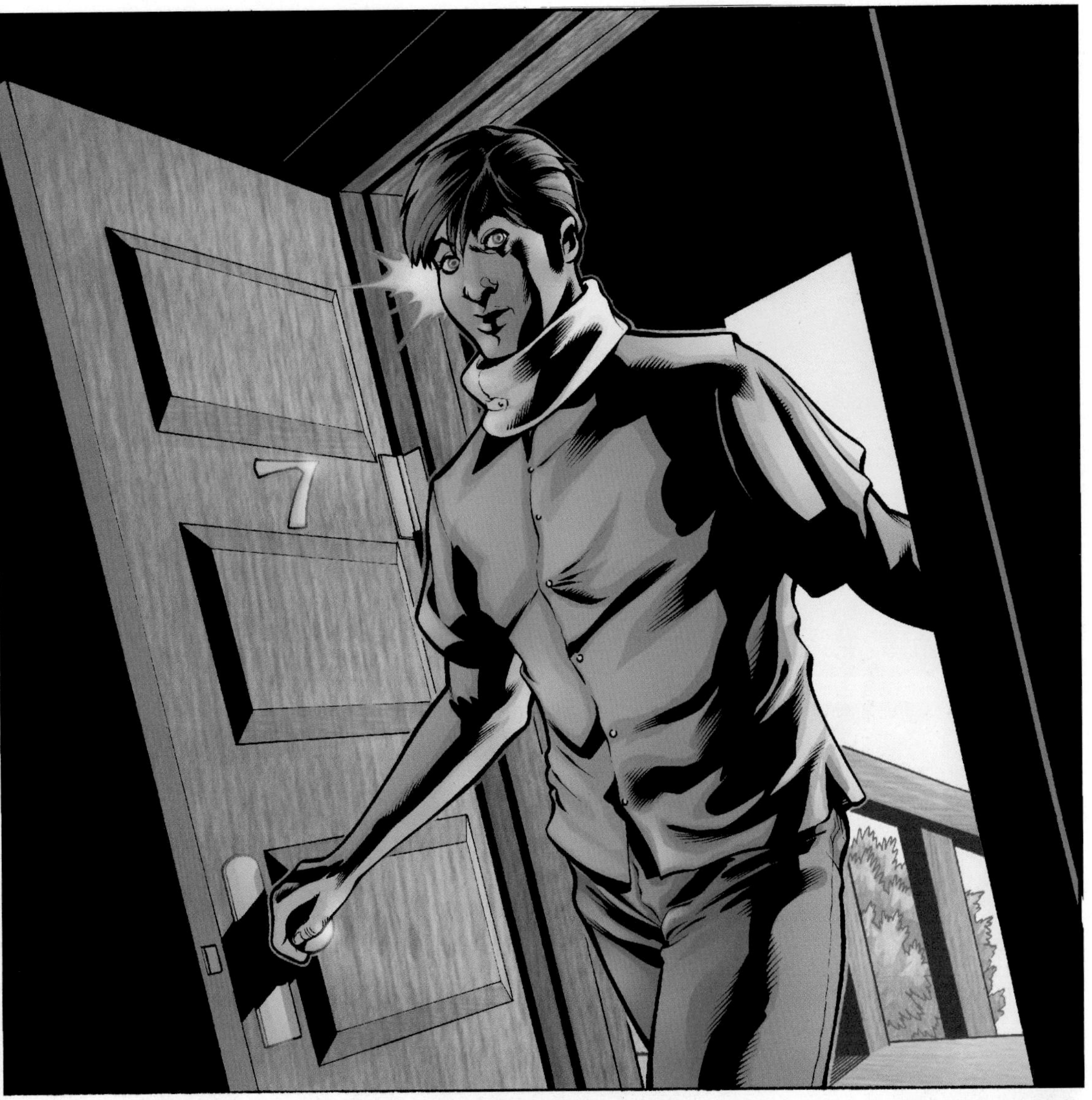

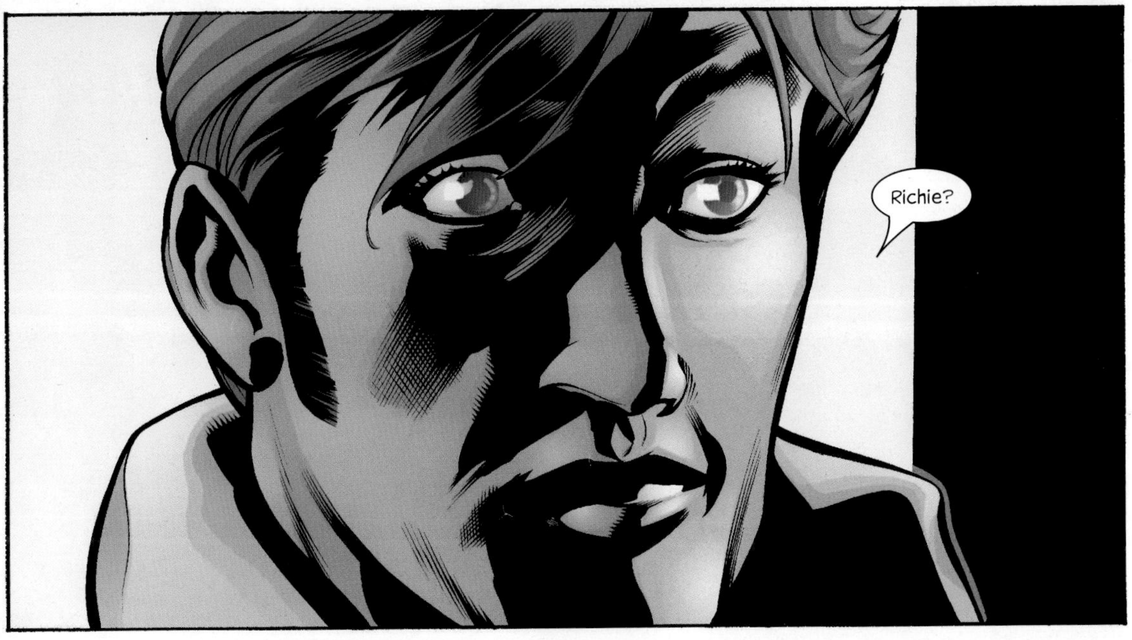
Richie?

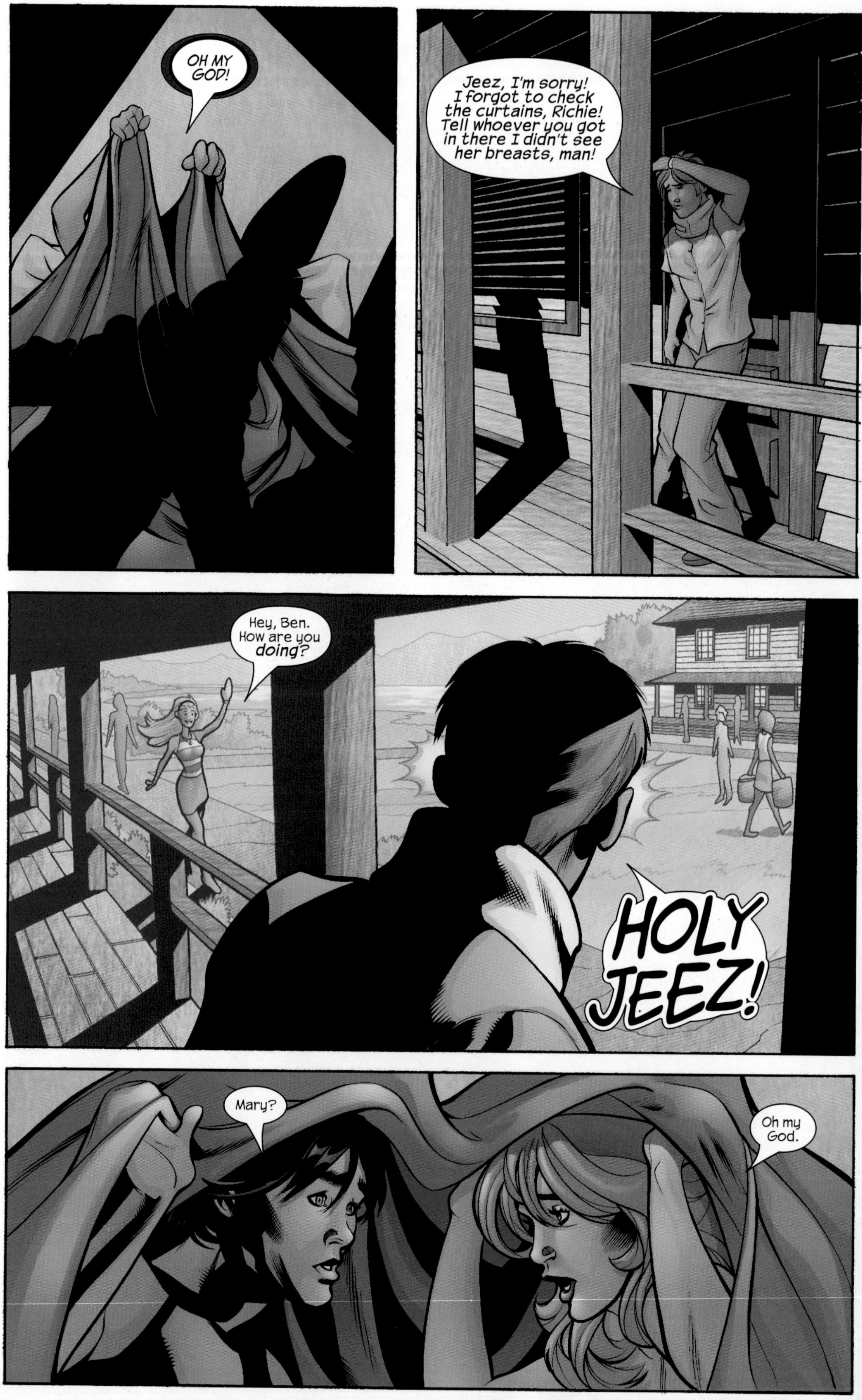
OH MY GOD!
Jeez, I'm sorry! I forgot to check the curtains, Richie! Tell whoever you got in there I didn't see her breasts, man!
Hey, Ben. How are you *doing*?
HOLY JEEZ!
Mary?
Oh my God.

Picked you up some cream for that eye, soldier. You want to head into the bathroom and I'll rub it on for you?

Uh, actually, I think we'd better go *someplace else* to stick it on because you *really, really* can't come inside here right now, Mary.

What are you *talking* about? Is everything *okay?*

Oh, sure, it's just that they, uh, found a wasp's nest in the *guys' locker room* and, uh, Richie and I said the team could get changed in *here* before the big game.

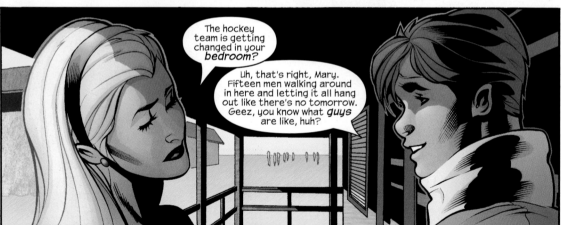

The hockey team is getting changed in your *bedroom?*

Uh, that's right, Mary. Fifteen men walking around in here and letting it all hang out like there's no tomorrow. Geez, you know what *guys* are like, huh?

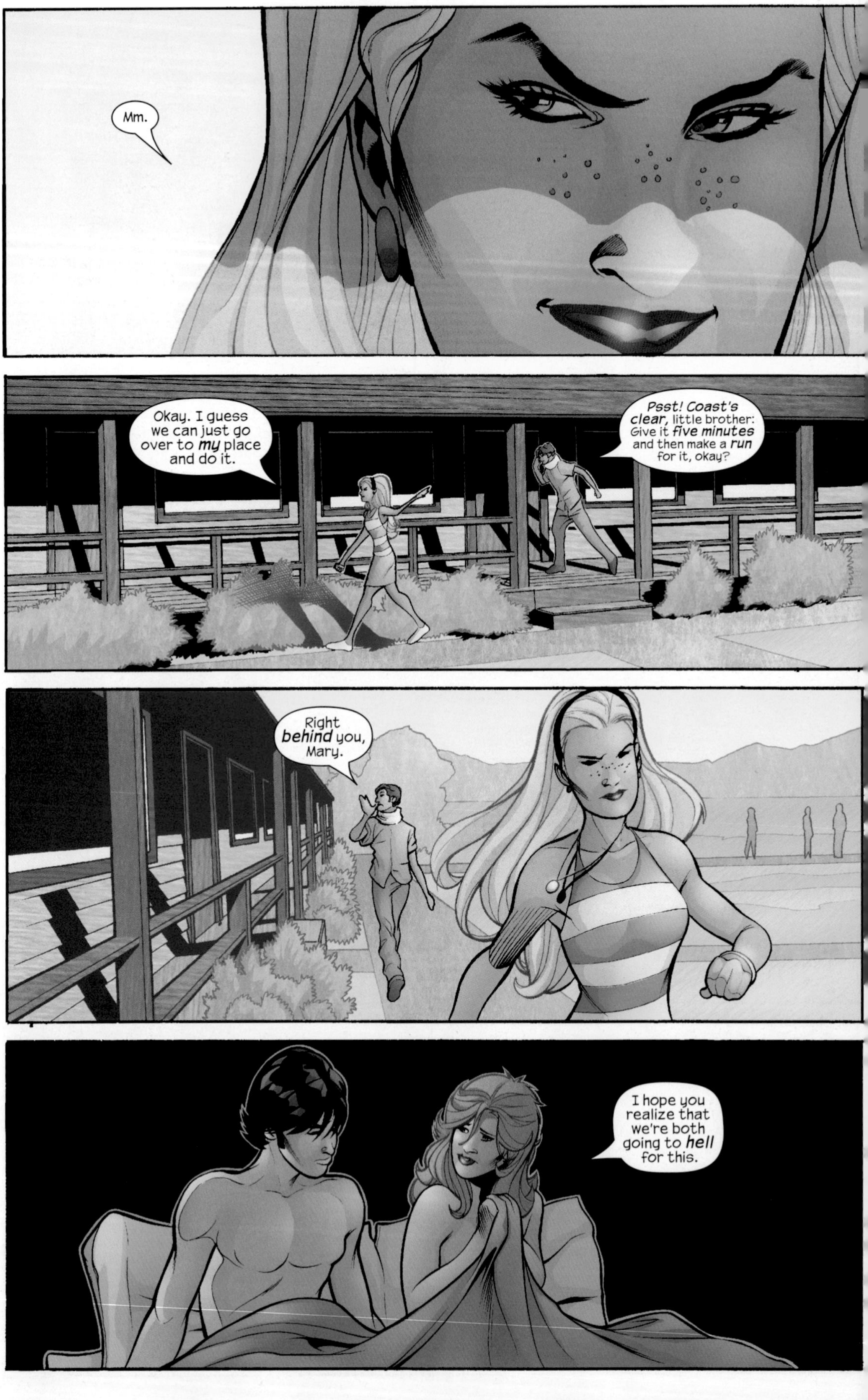
Mm.
Okay. I guess we can just go over to my place and do it.
Psst! Coast's clear, little brother: Give it five minutes and then make a run for it, okay?
Right behind you, Mary.
I hope you realize that we're both going to hell for this.

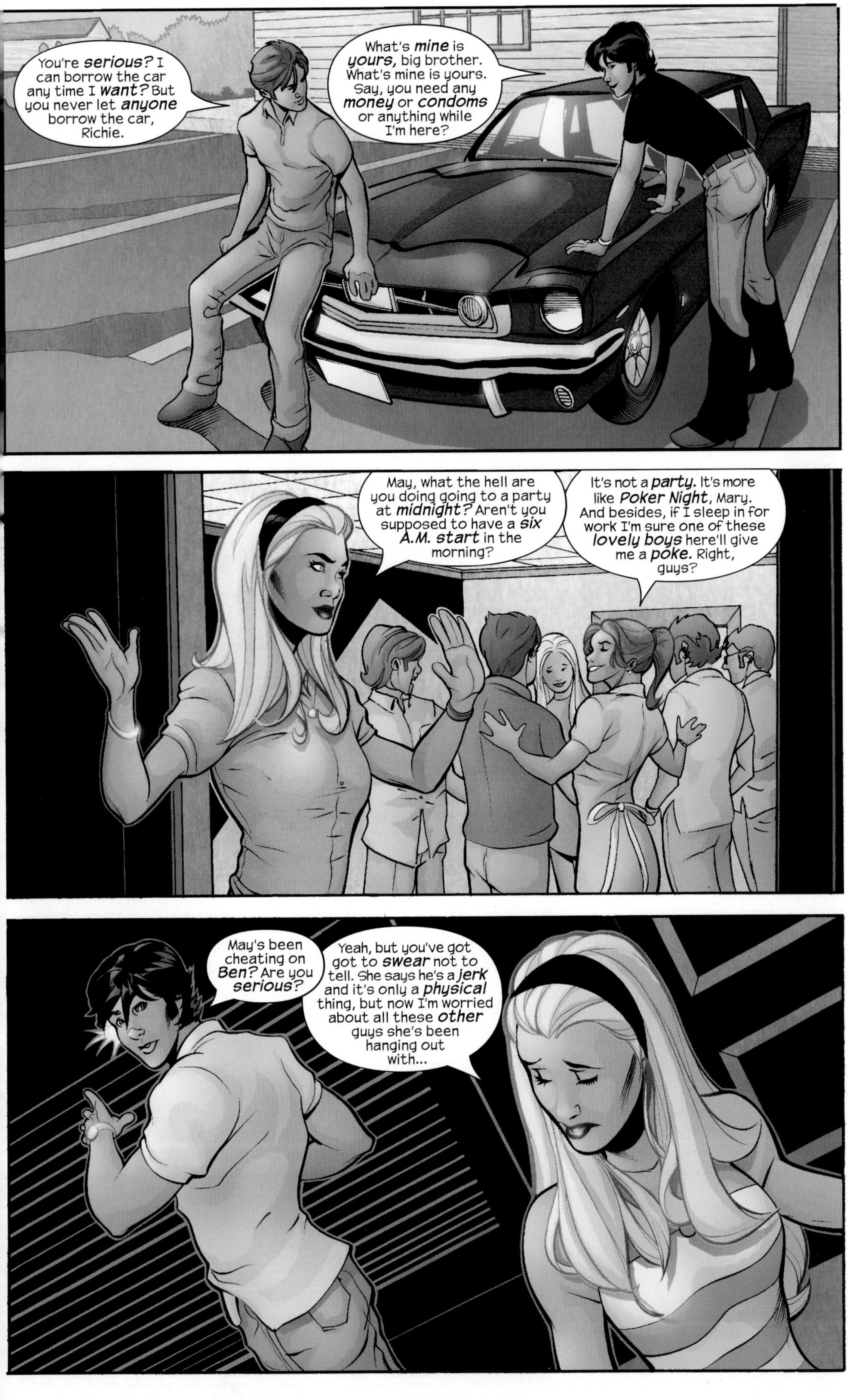
You're *serious?* I can borrow the car any time I *want?* But you never let *anyone* borrow the car, Richie.
What's *mine* is *yours,* big brother. What's mine is yours. Say, you need any *money* or *condoms* or anything while I'm here?
May, what the hell are you doing going to a party at *midnight?* Aren't you supposed to have a *six A.M. start* in the morning?
It's not a *party.* It's more like *Poker Night*, Mary. And besides, if I sleep in for work I'm sure one of these *lovely boys* here'll give me a *poke.* Right, guys?
May's been cheating on *Ben?* Are you *serious?*
Yeah, but you've got got to *swear* not to tell. She says he's a *jerk* and it's only a *physical* thing, but now I'm worried about all these *other* guys she's been hanging out with...

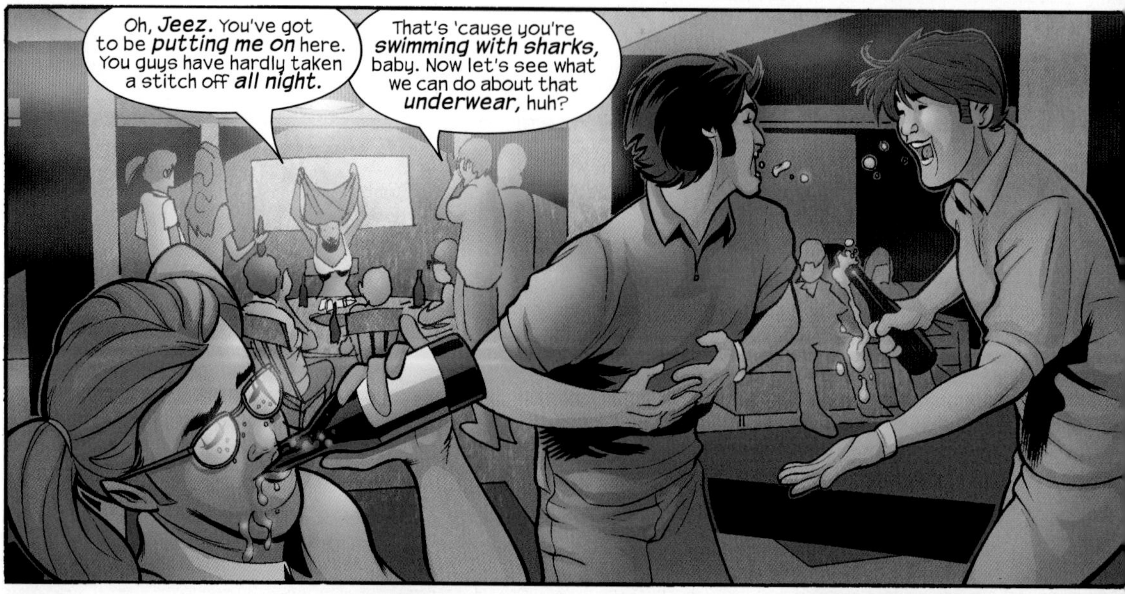
Oh, Jeez. You've got to be putting me on here. You guys have hardly taken a stitch off all night.
That's 'cause you're swimming with sharks, baby. Now let's see what we can do about that underwear, huh?

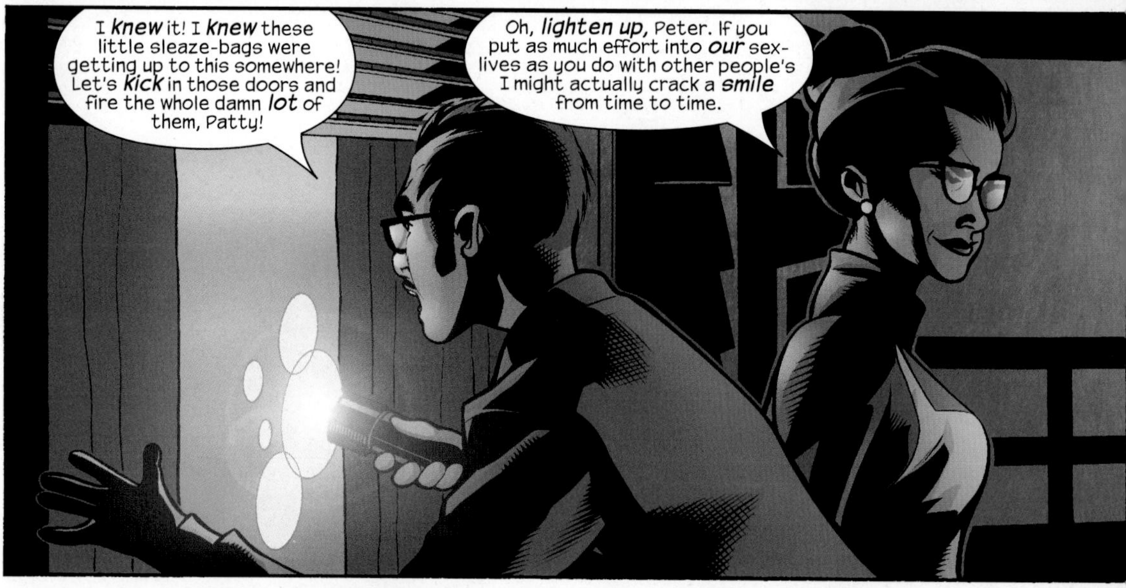
I knew it! I knew these little sleaze-bags were getting up to this somewhere! Let's kick in those doors and fire the whole damn lot of them, Patty!
Oh, lighten up, Peter. If you put as much effort into our sex-lives as you do with other people's I might actually crack a smile from time to time.

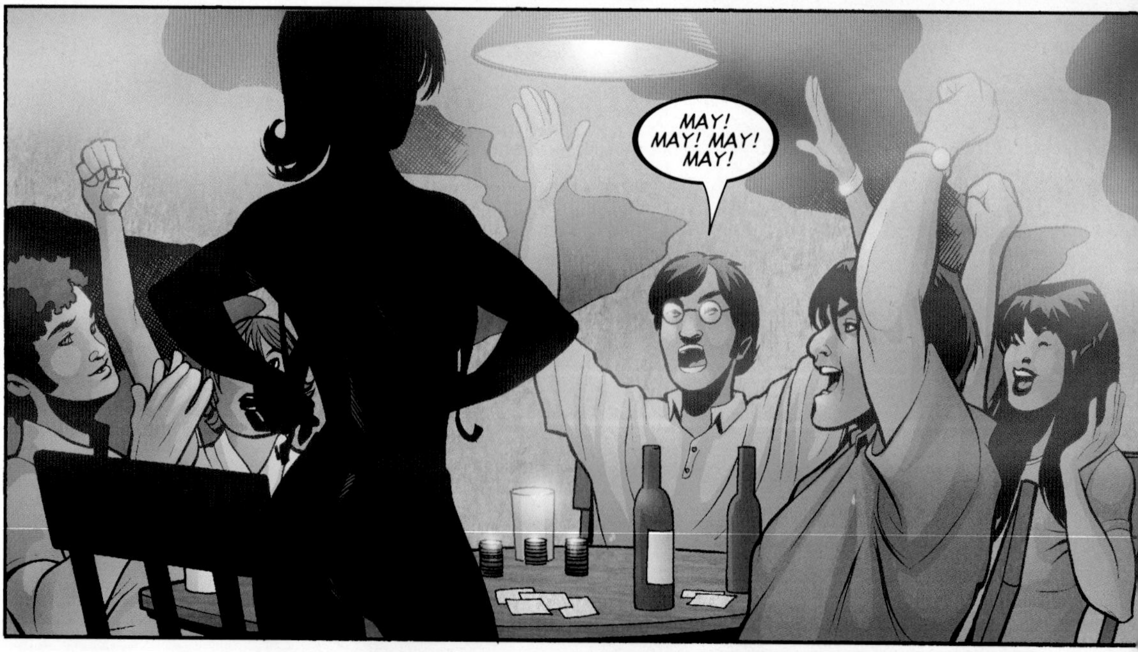
MAY! MAY! MAY! MAY!

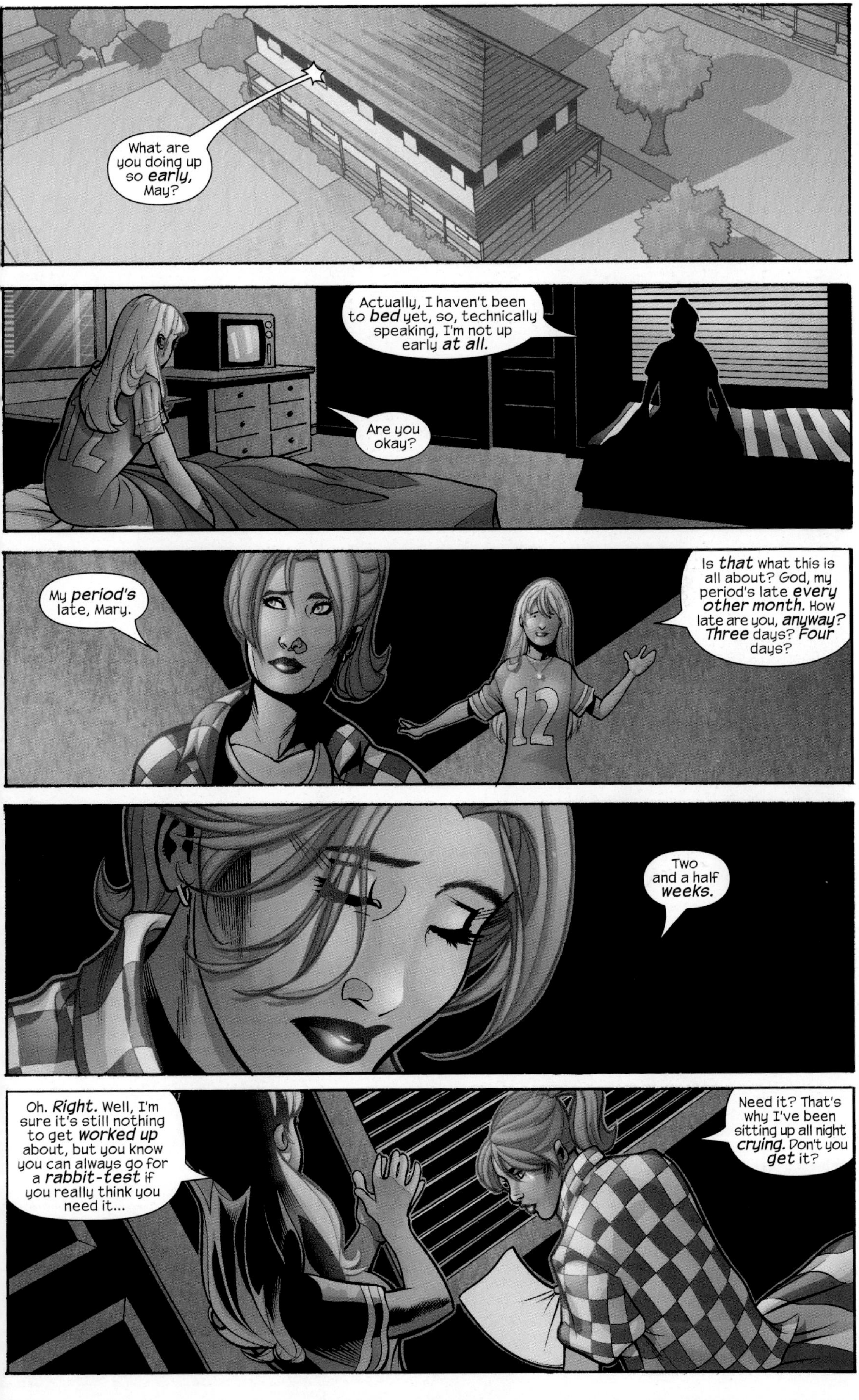

What are you doing up so early, May?
Actually, I haven't been to bed yet, so, technically speaking, I'm not up early at all.
Are you okay?
My period's late, Mary.
Is that what this is all about? God, my period's late every other month. How late are you, anyway? Three days? Four days?
Two and a half weeks.
Oh. Right. Well, I'm sure it's still nothing to get worked up about, but you know you can always go for a rabbit-test if you really think you need it...
Need it? That's why I've been sitting up all night crying. Don't you get it?

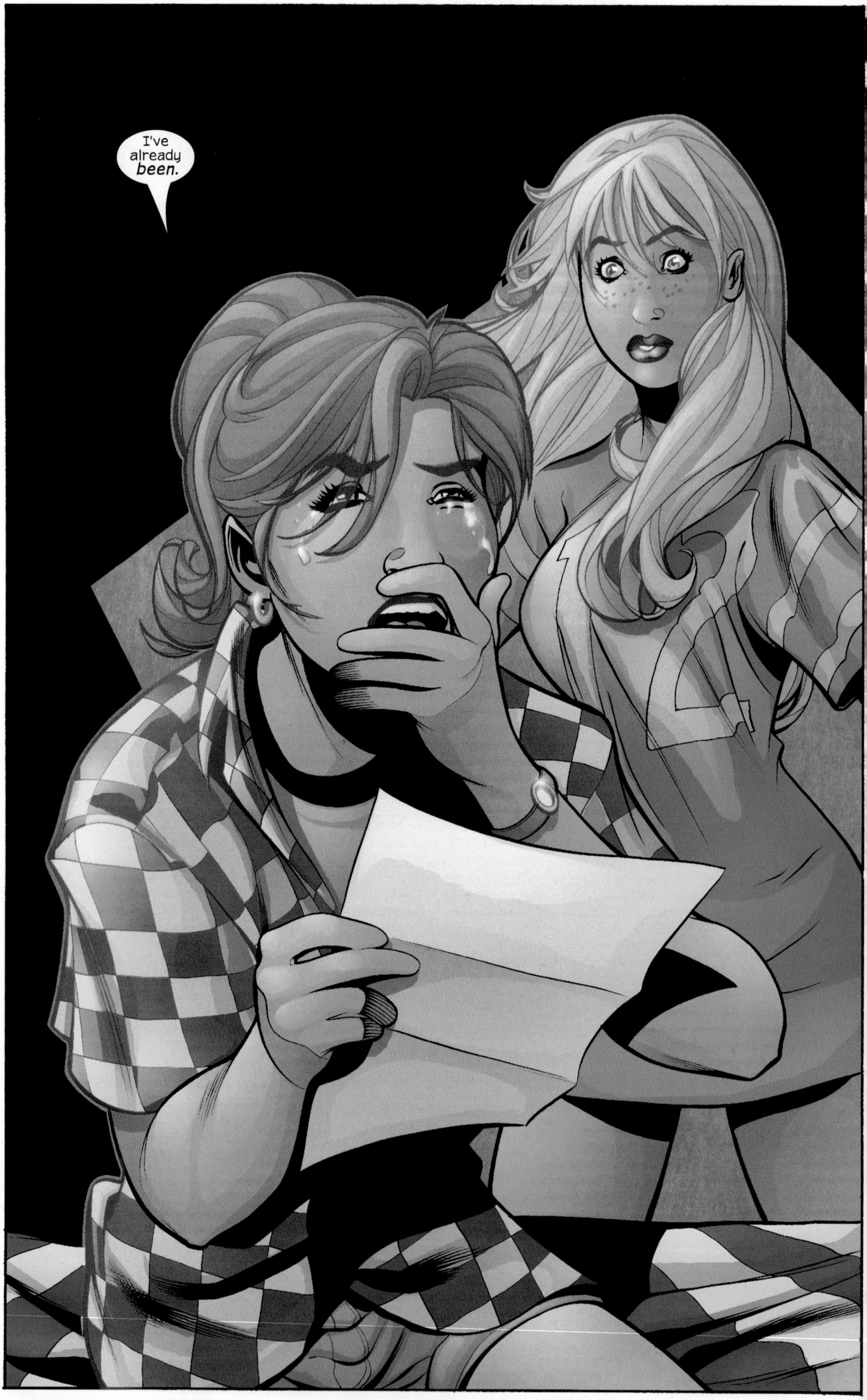
I've already been.

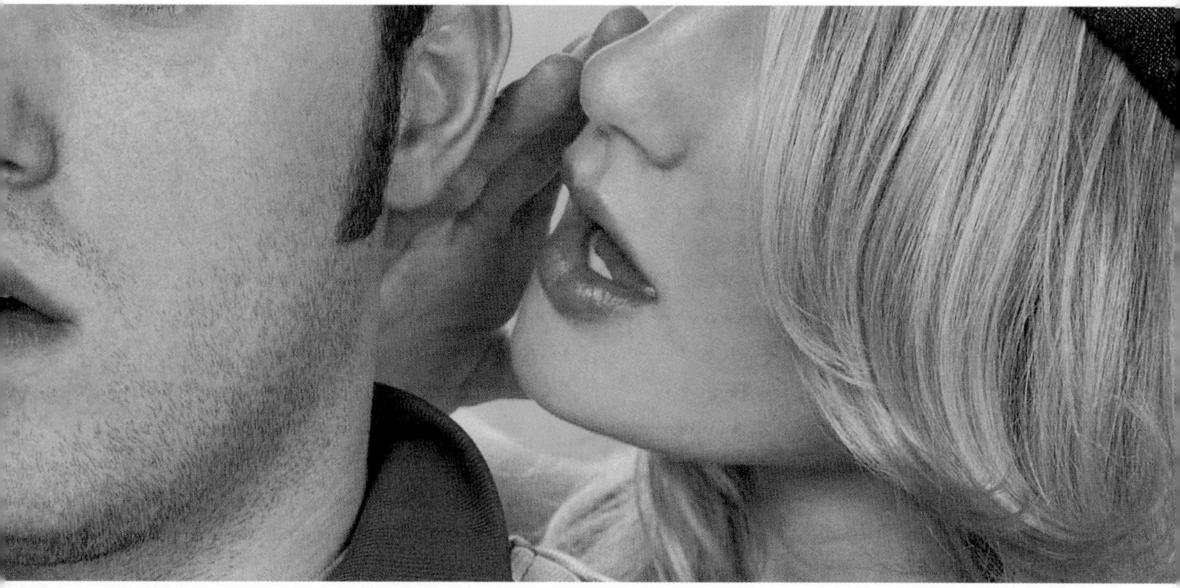

Trouble

part four of five

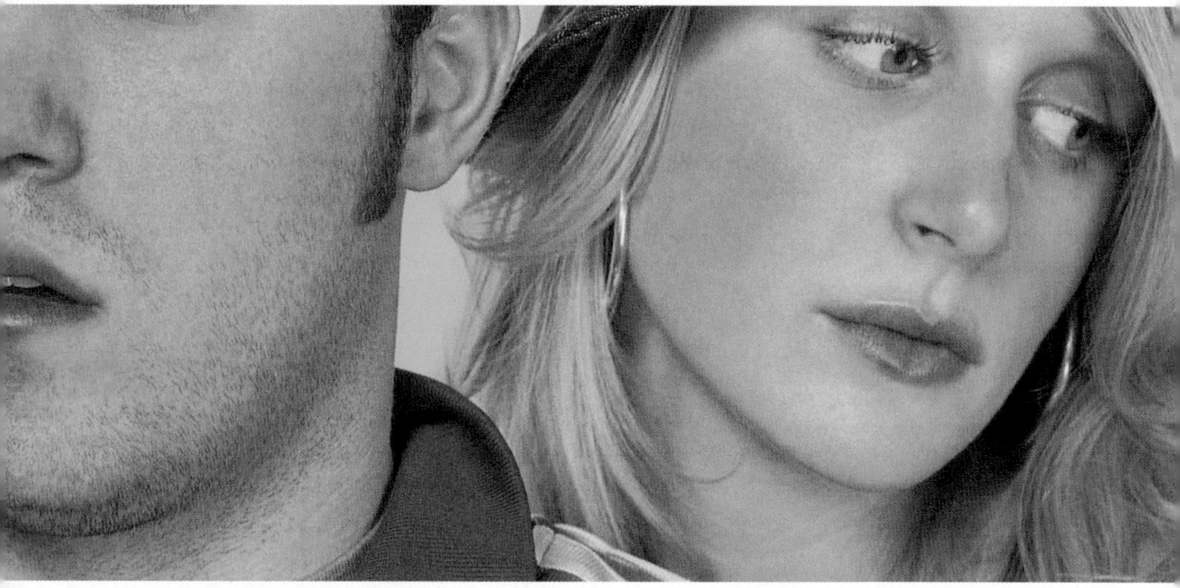

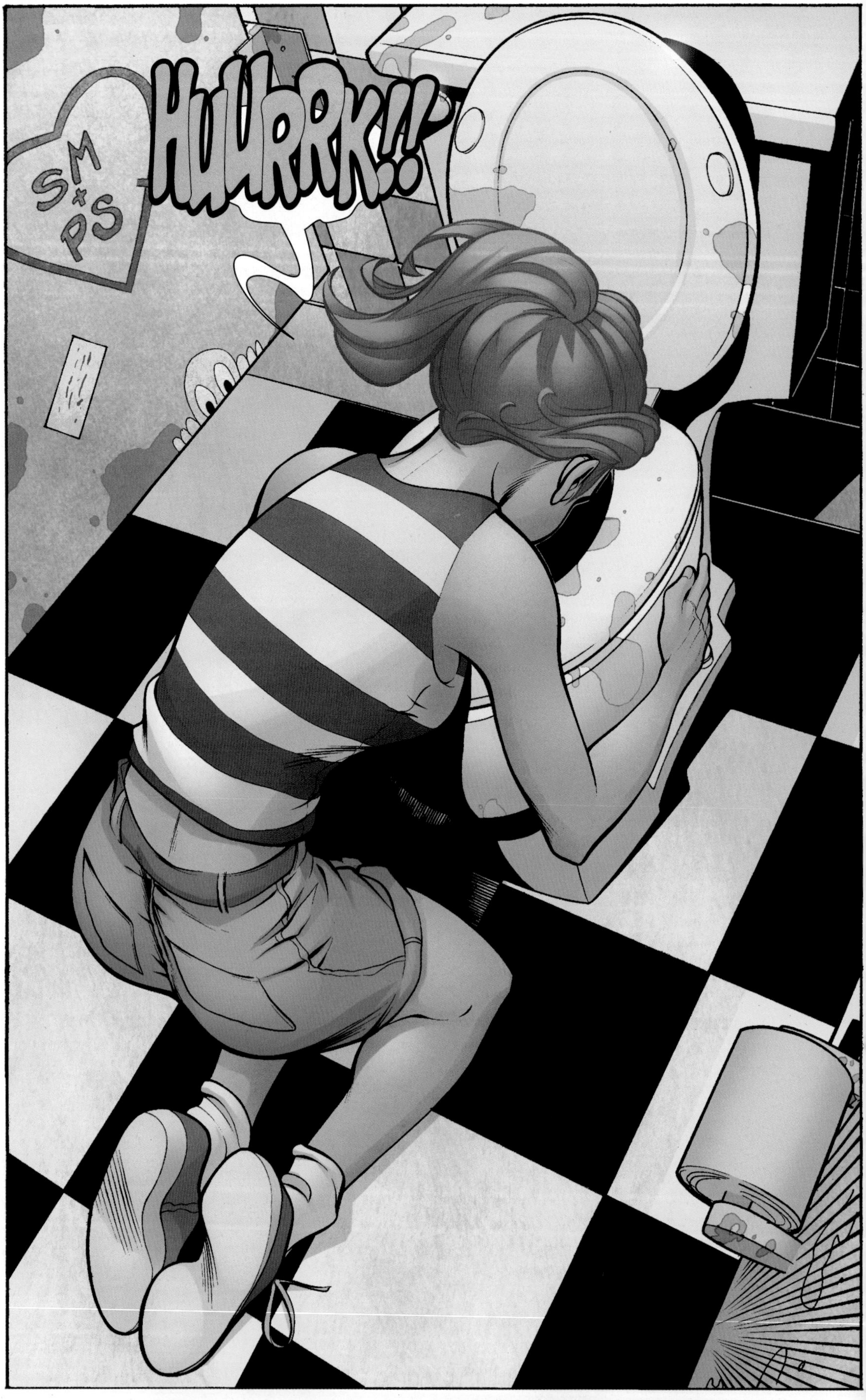
SM & PS
HUURRK!!

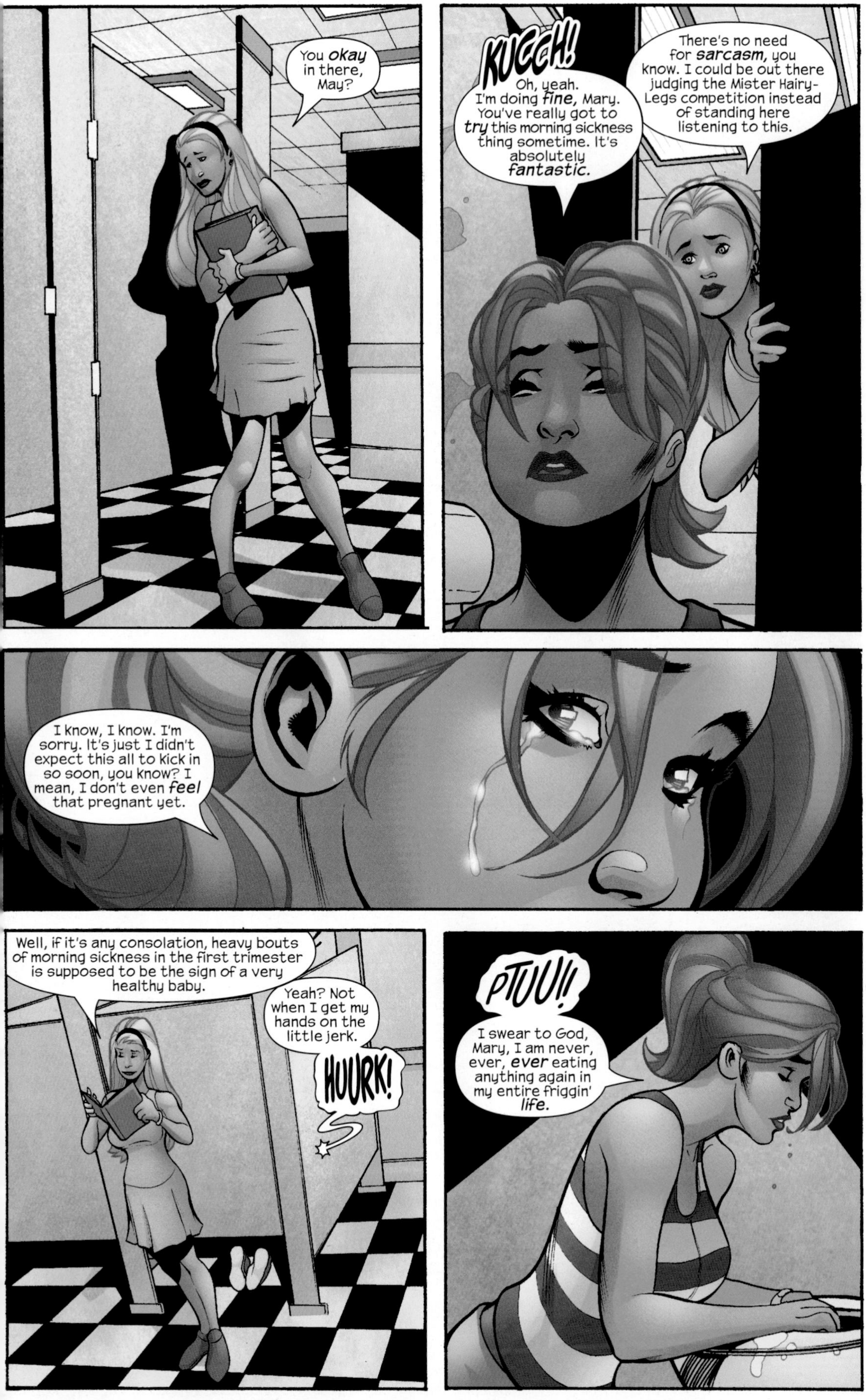
You okay in there, May?
KUCCH!
Oh, yeah. I'm doing fine, Mary. You've really got to try this morning sickness thing sometime. It's absolutely fantastic.
There's no need for sarcasm, you know. I could be out there judging the Mister Hairy-Legs competition instead of standing here listening to this.
I know, I know. I'm sorry. It's just I didn't expect this all to kick in so soon, you know? I mean, I don't even feel that pregnant yet.
Well, if it's any consolation, heavy bouts of morning sickness in the first trimester is supposed to be the sign of a very healthy baby.
Yeah? Not when I get my hands on the little jerk.
HUURK!
PTUU!!
I swear to God, Mary, I am never, ever, ever eating anything again in my entire friggin' life.

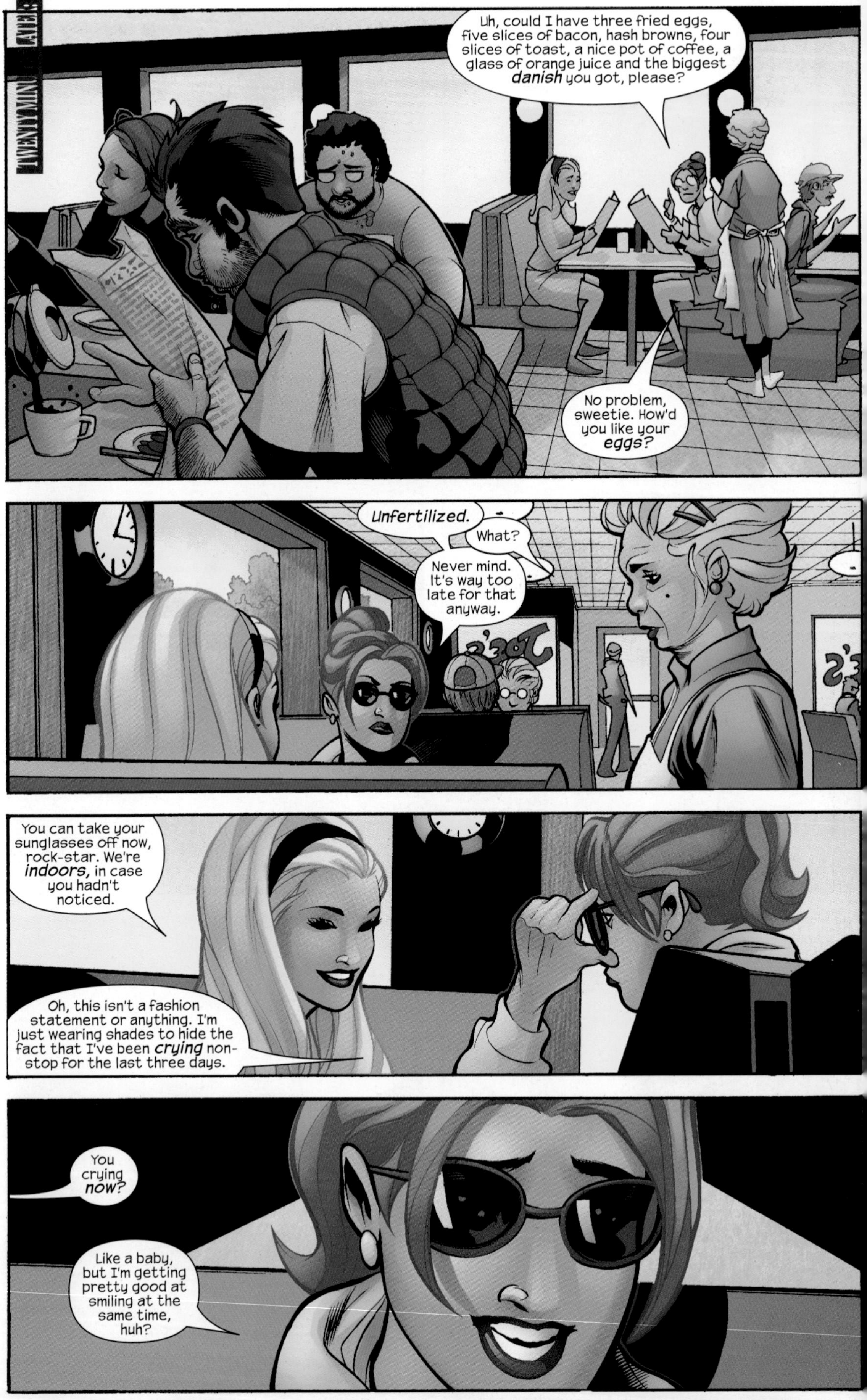
TWENTY MINU LATER:
Uh, could I have three fried eggs, five slices of bacon, hash browns, four slices of toast, a nice pot of coffee, a glass of orange juice and the biggest danish you got, please?
No problem, sweetie. How'd you like your eggs?
Unfertilized.
What?
Never mind. It's way too late for that anyway.
You can take your sunglasses off now, rock-star. We're indoors, in case you hadn't noticed.
Oh, this isn't a fashion statement or anything. I'm just wearing shades to hide the fact that I've been crying non-stop for the last three days.
You crying now?
Like a baby, but I'm getting pretty good at smiling at the same time, huh?

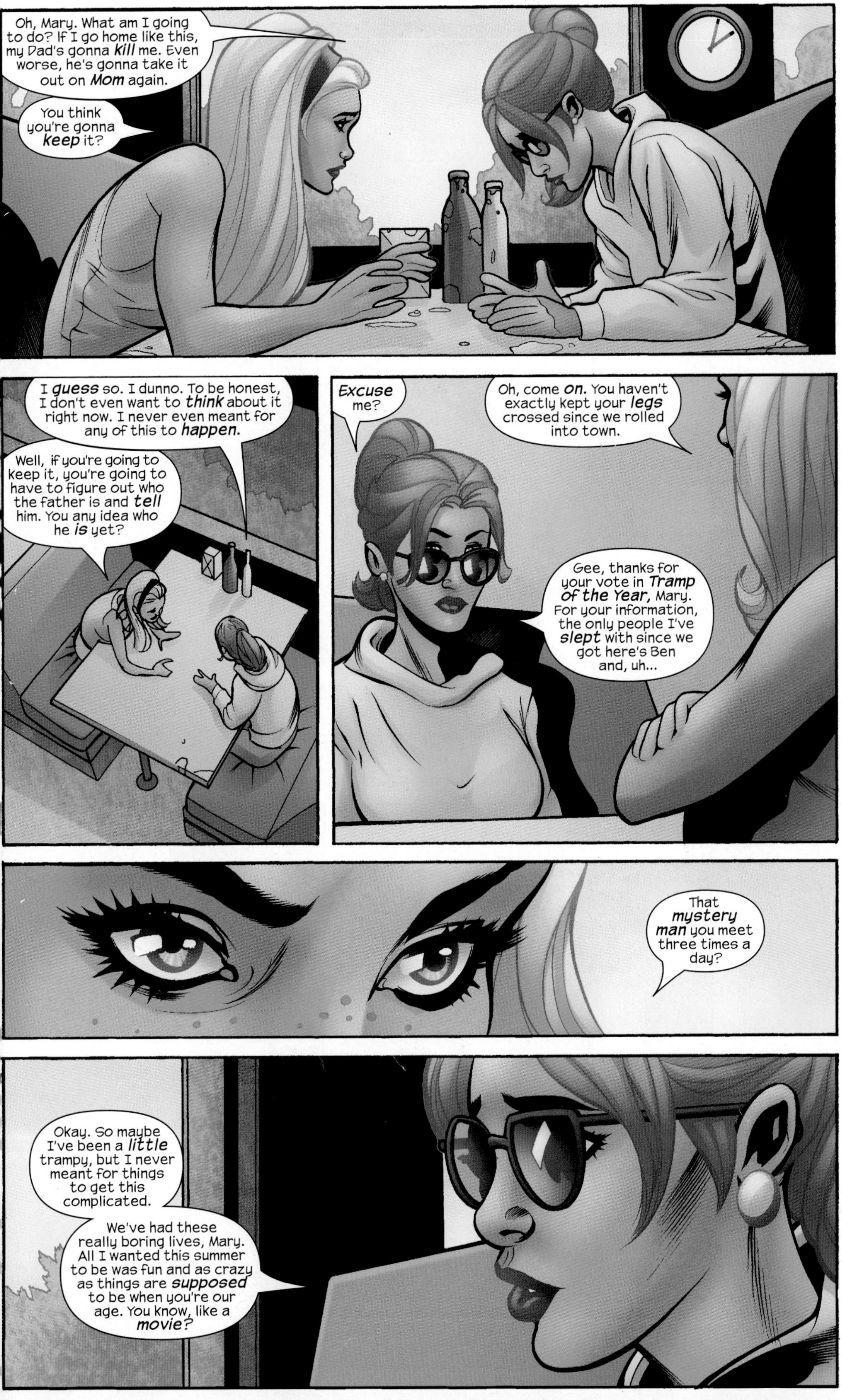
Oh, Mary. What am I going to do? If I go home like this, my Dad's gonna kill me. Even worse, he's gonna take it out on Mom again.
You think you're gonna keep it?
I guess so. I dunno. To be honest, I don't even want to think about it right now. I never even meant for any of this to happen.
Well, if you're going to keep it, you're going to have to figure out who the father is and tell him. You any idea who he is yet?
Excuse me?
Oh, come on. You haven't exactly kept your legs crossed since we rolled into town.
Gee, thanks for your vote in Tramp of the Year, Mary. For your information, the only people I've slept with since we got here's Ben and, uh...
That mystery man you meet three times a day?
Okay. So maybe I've been a little trampy, but I never meant for things to get this complicated.
We've had these really boring lives, Mary. All I wanted this summer to be was fun and as crazy as things are supposed to be when you're our age. You know, like a movie?

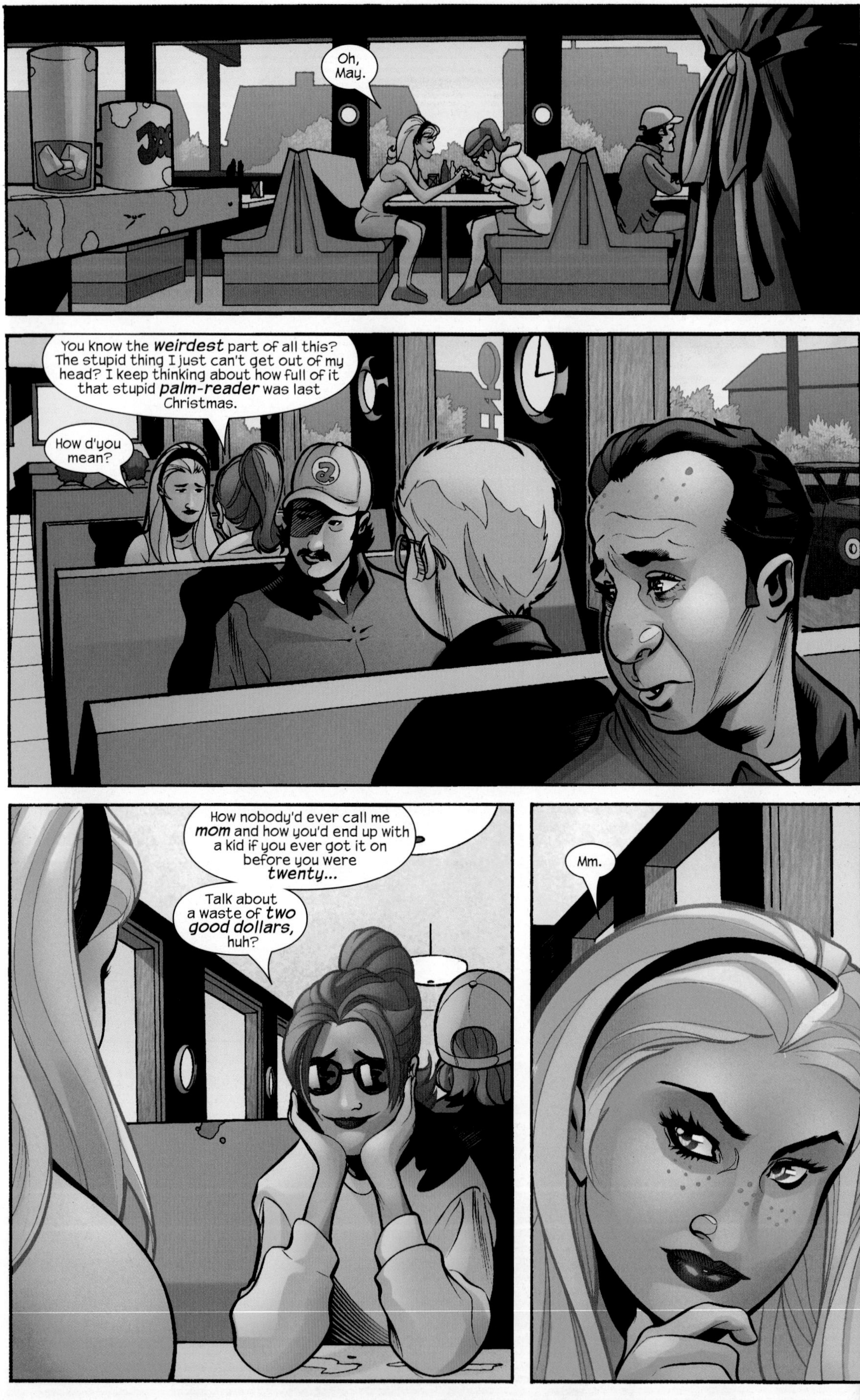
Oh, May.
You know the weirdest part of all this? The stupid thing I just can't get out of my head? I keep thinking about how full of it that stupid palm-reader was last Christmas.
How d'you mean?
How nobody'd ever call me mom and how you'd end up with a kid if you ever got it on before you were twenty...
Talk about a waste of two good dollars, huh?
Mm.

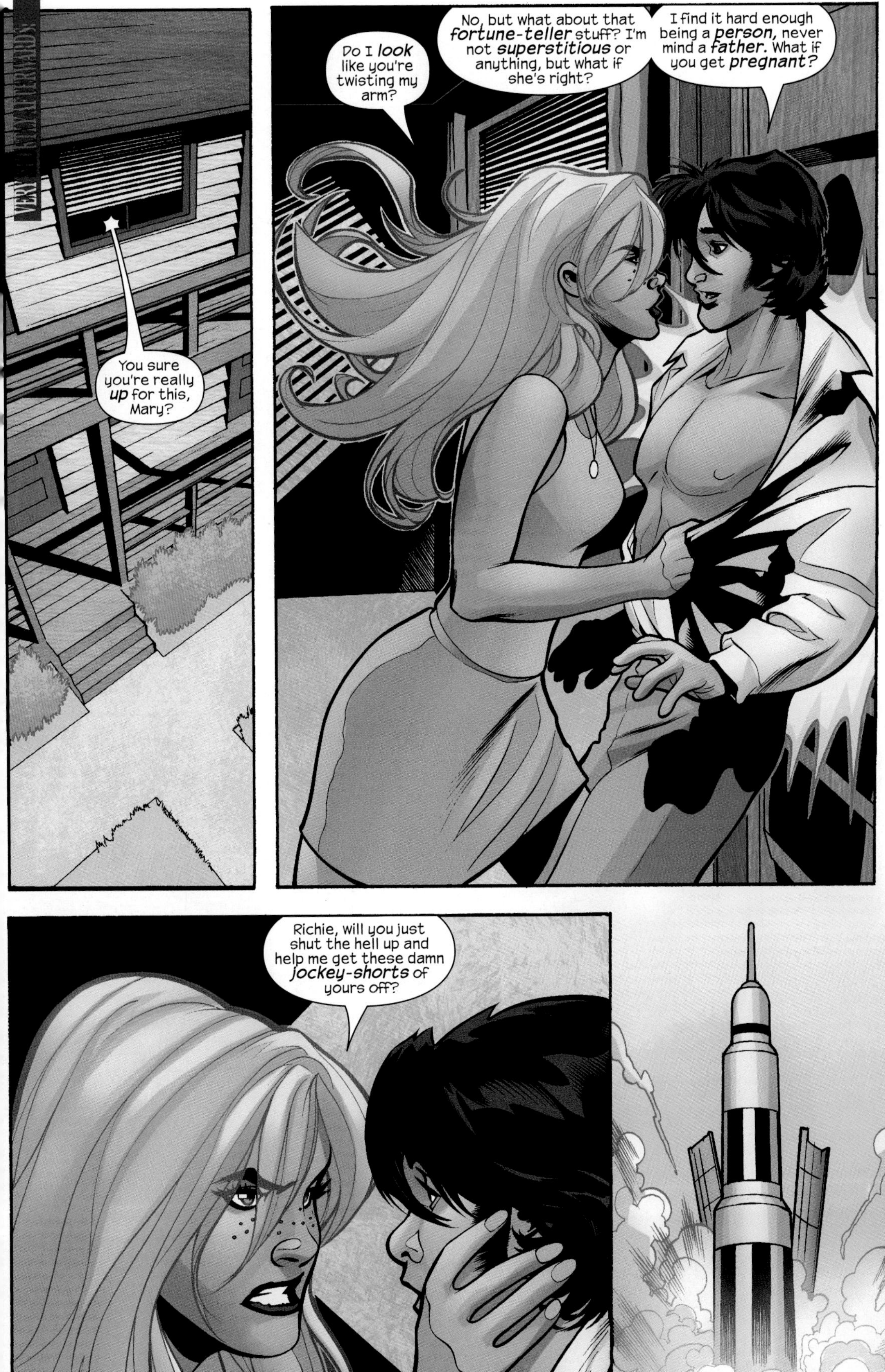

You sure you're really up for this, Mary?
Do I look like you're twisting my arm?
No, but what about that fortune-teller stuff? I'm not superstitious or anything, but what if she's right?
I find it hard enough being a person, never mind a father. What if you get pregnant?
Richie, will you just shut the hell up and help me get these damn jockey-shorts of yours off?

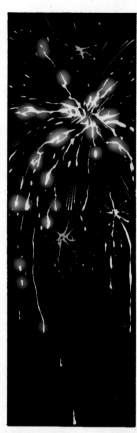

Mary, p-please! We've been at it for *hours* and Shelby's got me starting at 6AM tomorrow morning and...

MARYYY!!!

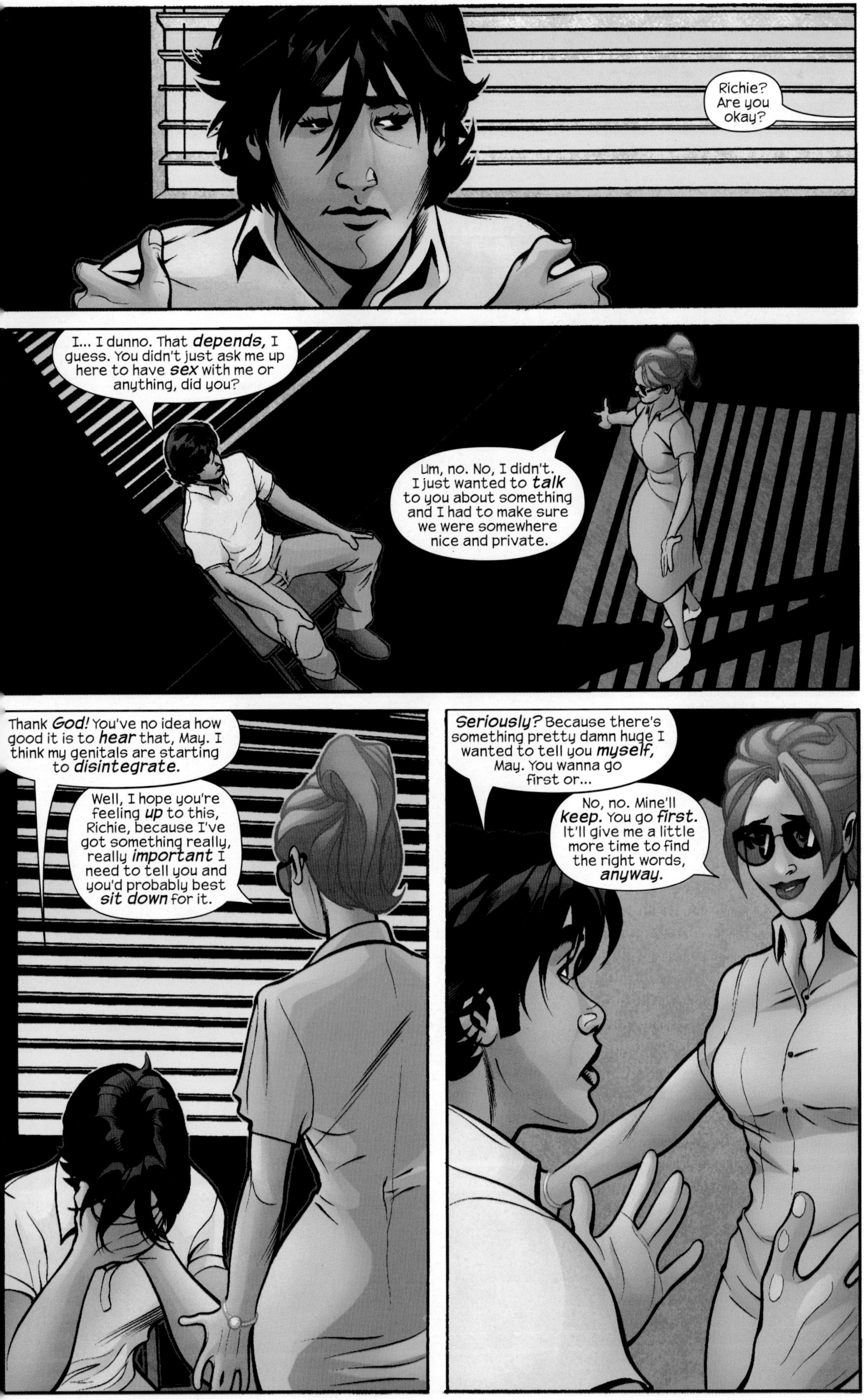

Richie? Are you okay?
I... I dunno. That depends, I guess. You didn't just ask me up here to have sex with me or anything, did you?
Um, no. No, I didn't. I just wanted to talk to you about something and I had to make sure we were somewhere nice and private.
Thank God! You've no idea how good it is to hear that, May. I think my genitals are starting to disintegrate.
Well, I hope you're feeling up to this, Richie, because I've got something really, really important I need to tell you and you'd probably best sit down for it.
Seriously? Because there's something pretty damn huge I wanted to tell you myself, May. You wanna go first or...
No, no. Mine'll keep. You go first. It'll give me a little more time to find the right words, anyway.

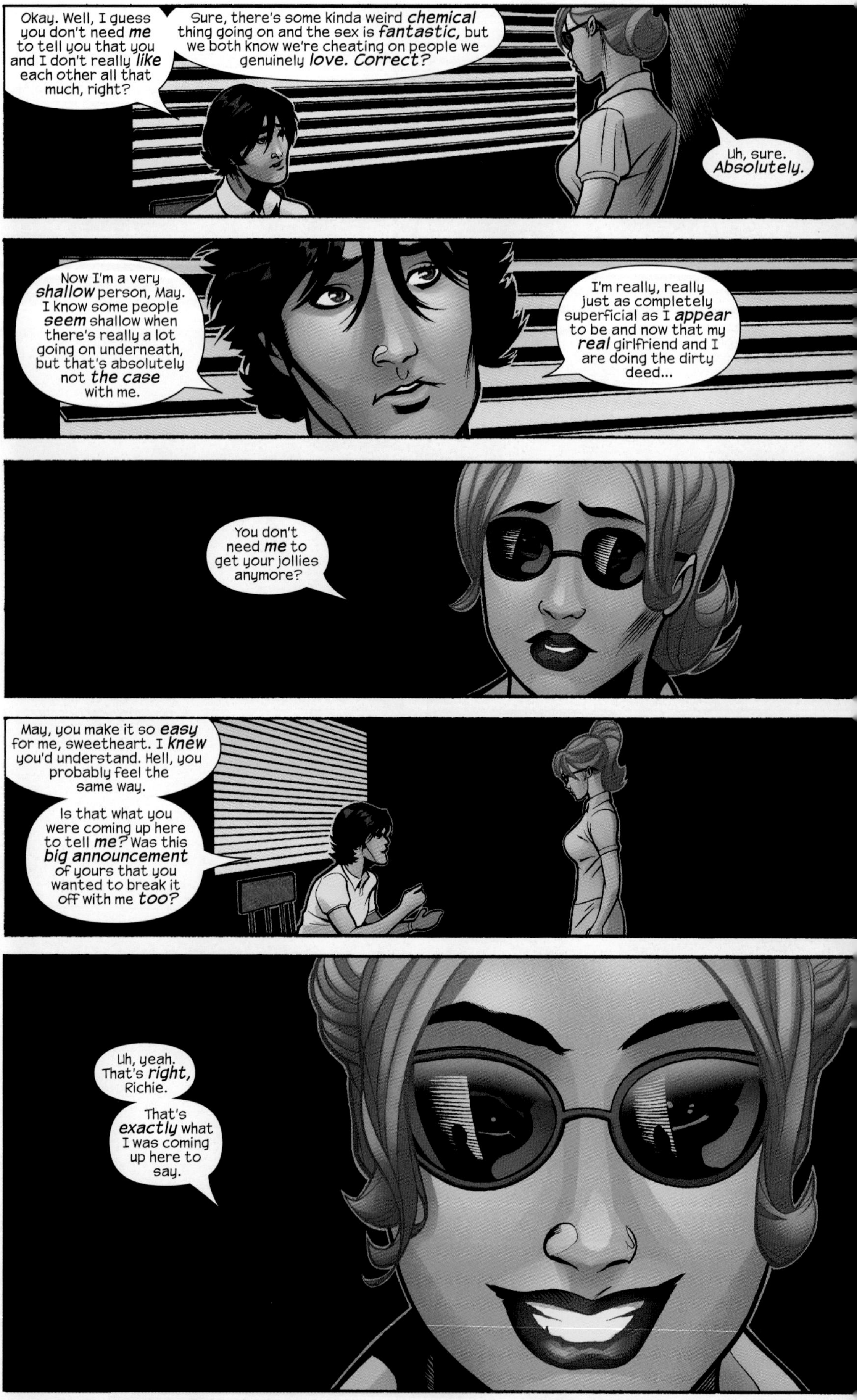
Okay. Well, I guess you don't need me to tell you that you and I don't really like each other all that much, right?
Sure, there's some kinda weird chemical thing going on and the sex is fantastic, but we both know we're cheating on people we genuinely love. Correct?
Uh, sure. Absolutely.
Now I'm a very shallow person, May. I know some people seem shallow when there's really a lot going on underneath, but that's absolutely not the case with me.
I'm really, really just as completely superficial as I appear to be and now that my real girlfriend and I are doing the dirty deed...
You don't need me to get your jollies anymore?
May, you make it so easy for me, sweetheart. I knew you'd understand. Hell, you probably feel the same way.
Is that what you were coming up here to tell me? Was this big announcement of yours that you wanted to break it off with me too?
Uh, yeah. That's right, Richie.
That's exactly what I was coming up here to say.

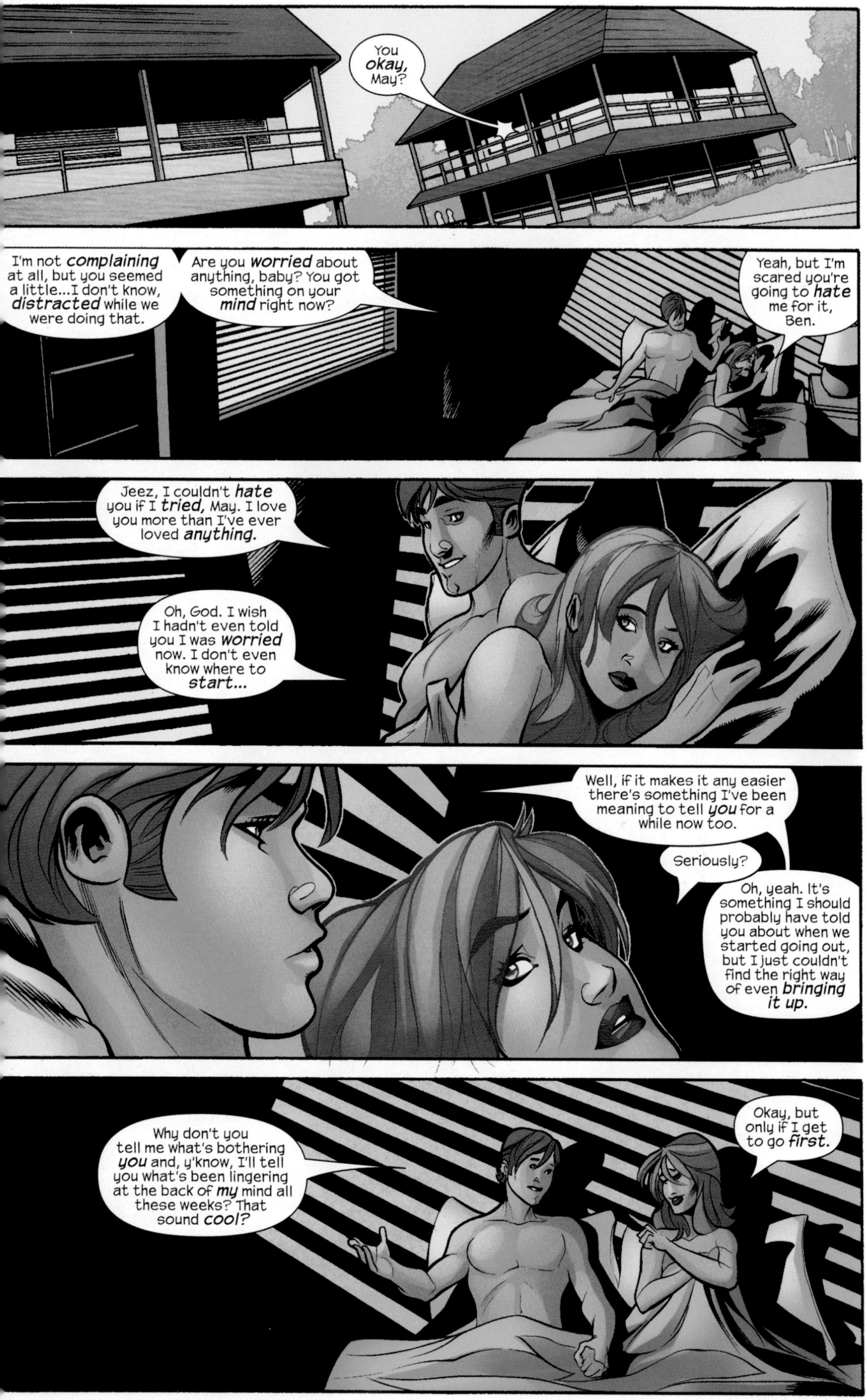

You okay, May?
I'm not complaining at all, but you seemed a little...I don't know, distracted while we were doing that.
Are you worried about anything, baby? You got something on your mind right now?
Yeah, but I'm scared you're going to hate me for it, Ben.
Jeez, I couldn't hate you if I tried, May. I love you more than I've ever loved anything.
Oh, God. I wish I hadn't even told you I was worried now. I don't even know where to start...
Well, if it makes it any easier there's something I've been meaning to tell you for a while now too.
Seriously?
Oh, yeah. It's something I should probably have told you about when we started going out, but I just couldn't find the right way of even bringing it up.
Why don't you tell me what's bothering you and, y'know, I'll tell you what's been lingering at the back of my mind all these weeks? That sound cool?
Okay, but only if I get to go first.

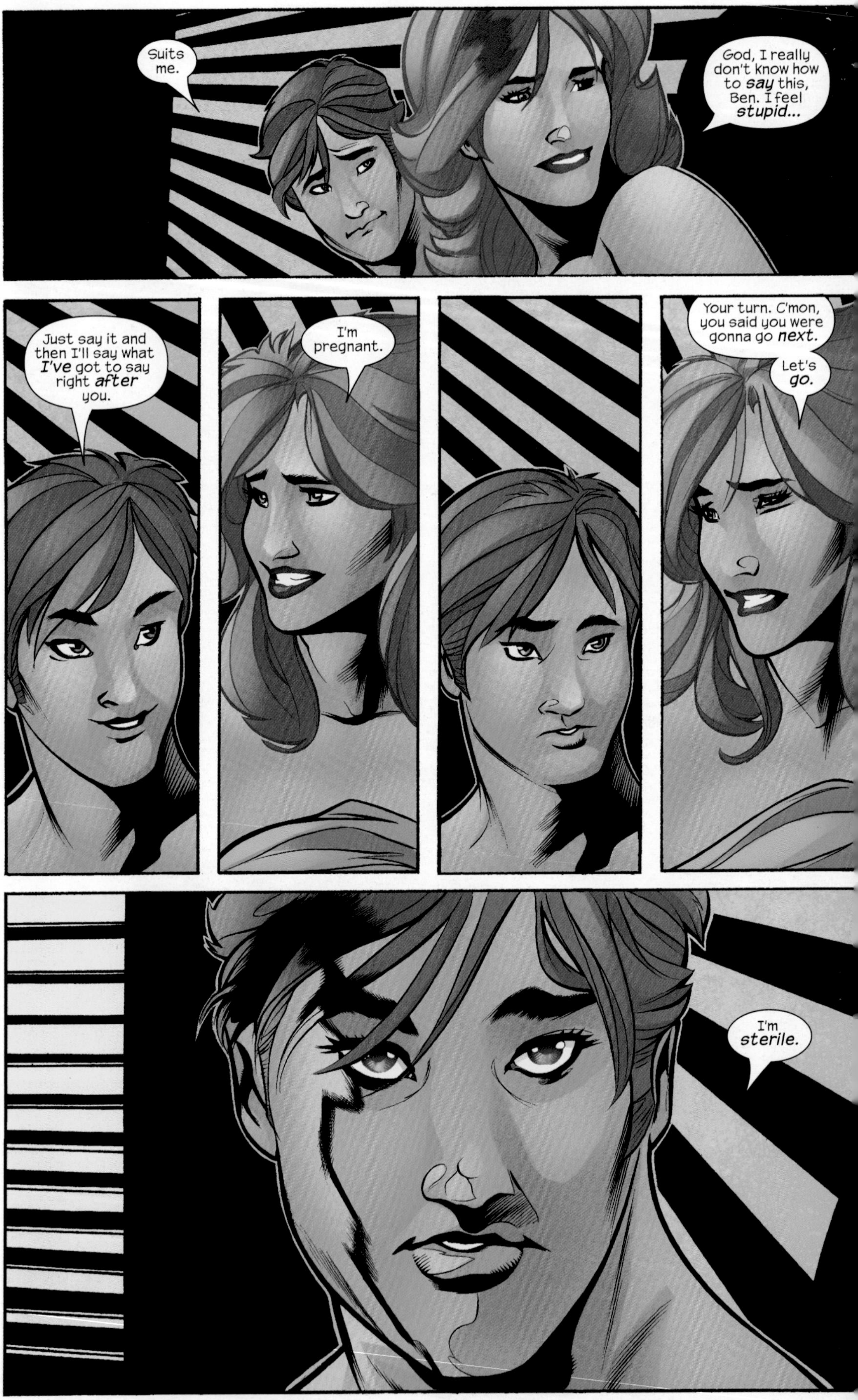
Suits me.
God, I really don't know how to *say* this, Ben. I feel *stupid...*
Just say it and then I'll say what *I've* got to say right *after* you.
I'm pregnant.
Your turn. C'mon, you said you were gonna go *next.*
Let's *go.*
I'm *sterile.*

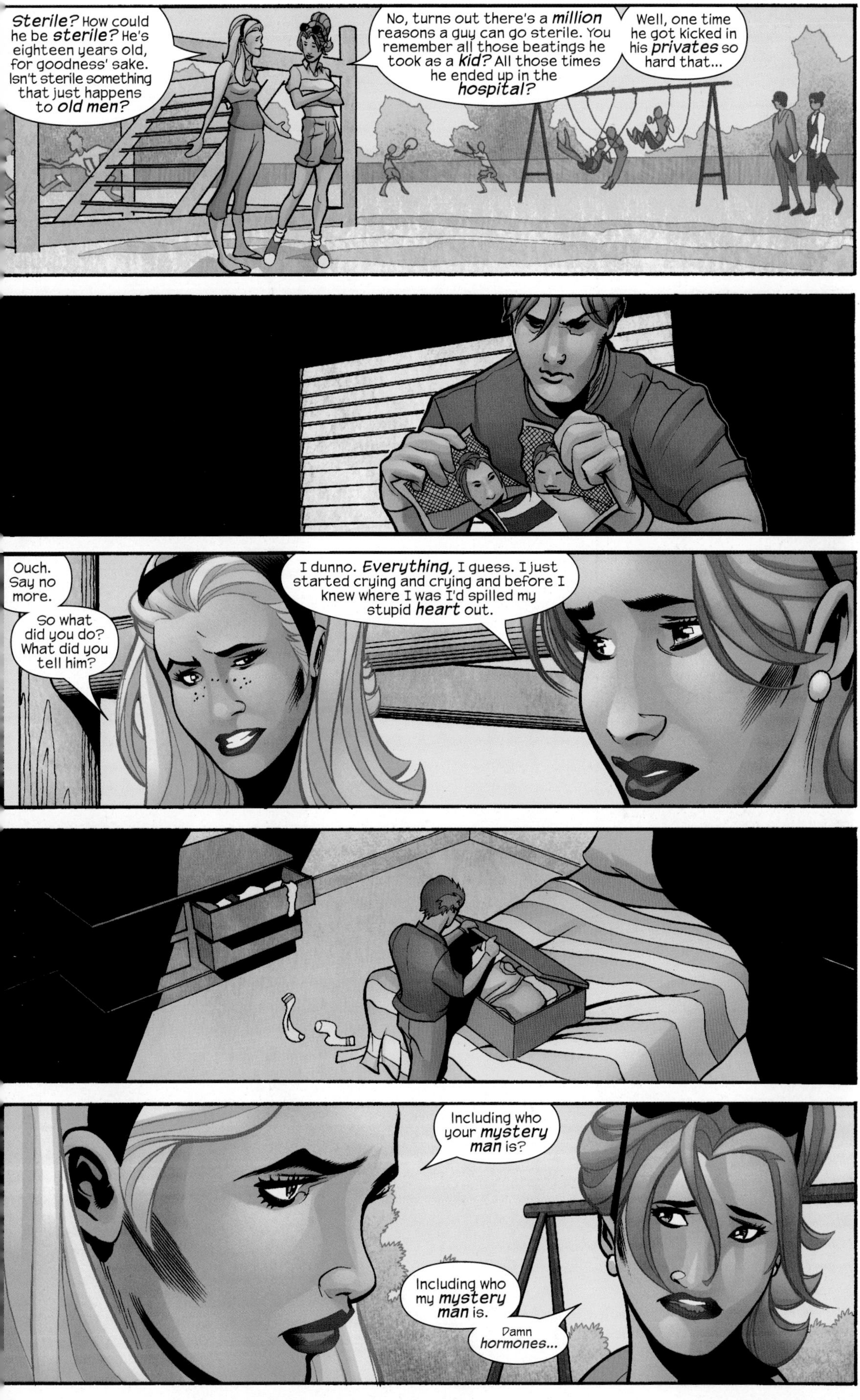
Sterile? How could he be sterile? He's eighteen years old, for goodness' sake. Isn't sterile something that just happens to old men?
No, turns out there's a million reasons a guy can go sterile. You remember all those beatings he took as a kid? All those times he ended up in the hospital?
Well, one time he got kicked in his privates so hard that...
Ouch. Say no more.
So what did you do? What did you tell him?
I dunno. Everything, I guess. I just started crying and crying and before I knew where I was I'd spilled my stupid heart out.
Including who your mystery man is?
Including who my mystery man is.
Damn hormones...

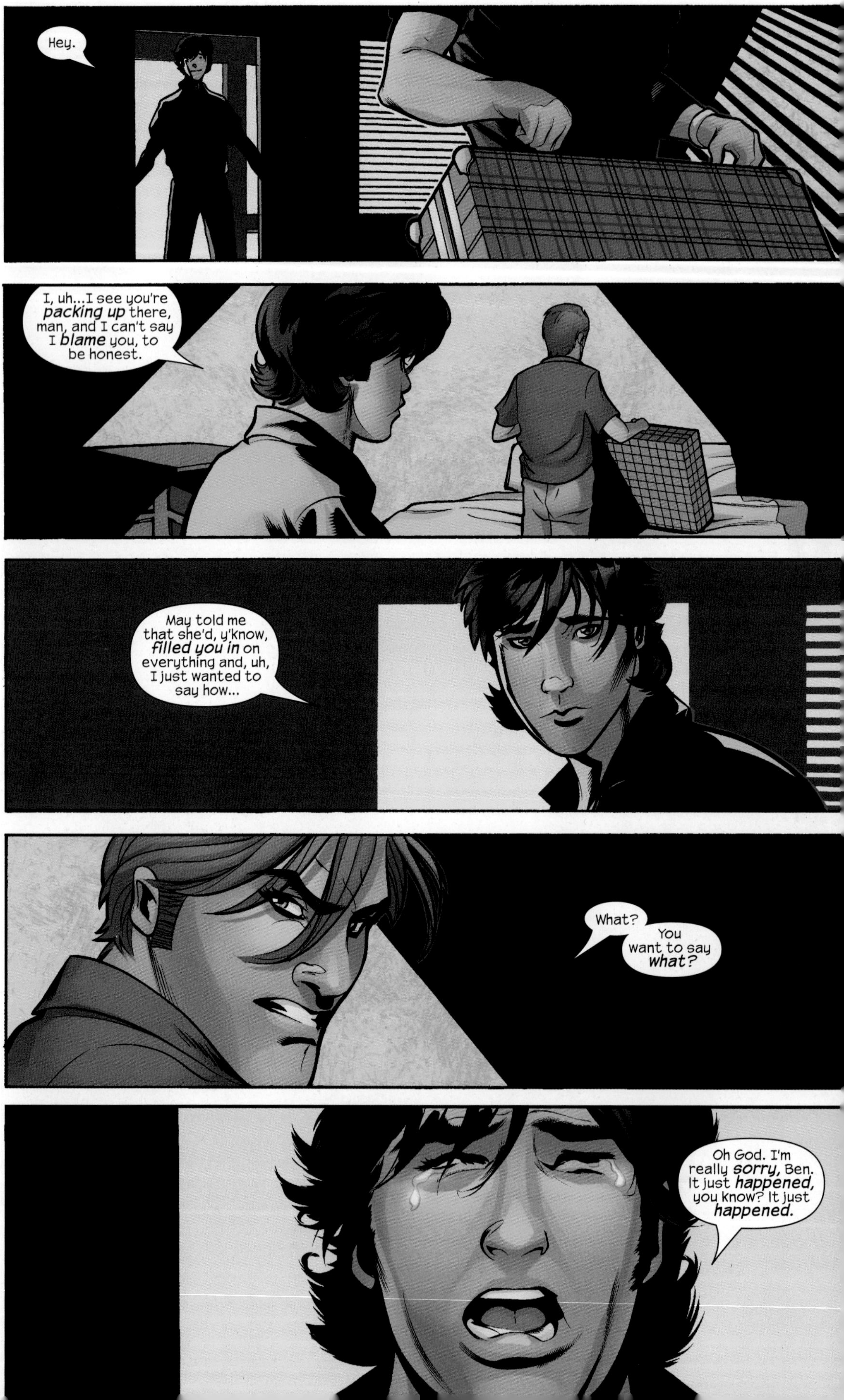
Hey.
I, uh...I see you're packing up there, man, and I can't say I blame you, to be honest.
May told me that she'd, y'know, filled you in on everything and, uh, I just wanted to say how...
What?
You want to say what?
Oh God. I'm really sorry, Ben. It just happened, you know? It just happened.

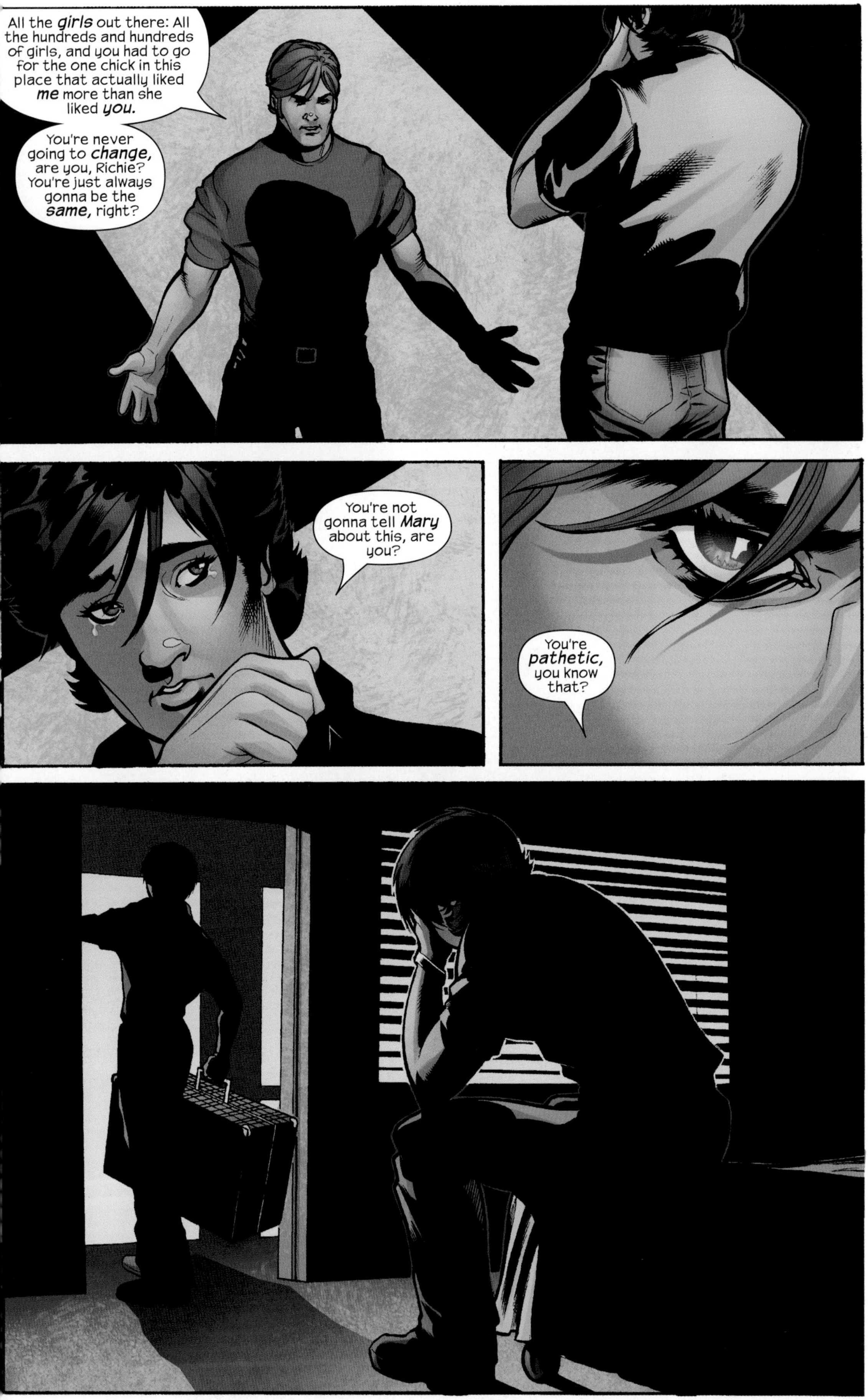
All the girls out there: All the hundreds and hundreds of girls, and you had to go for the one chick in this place that actually liked me more than she liked you.
You're never going to change, are you, Richie? You're just always gonna be the same, right?
You're not gonna tell Mary about this, are you?
You're pathetic, you know that?

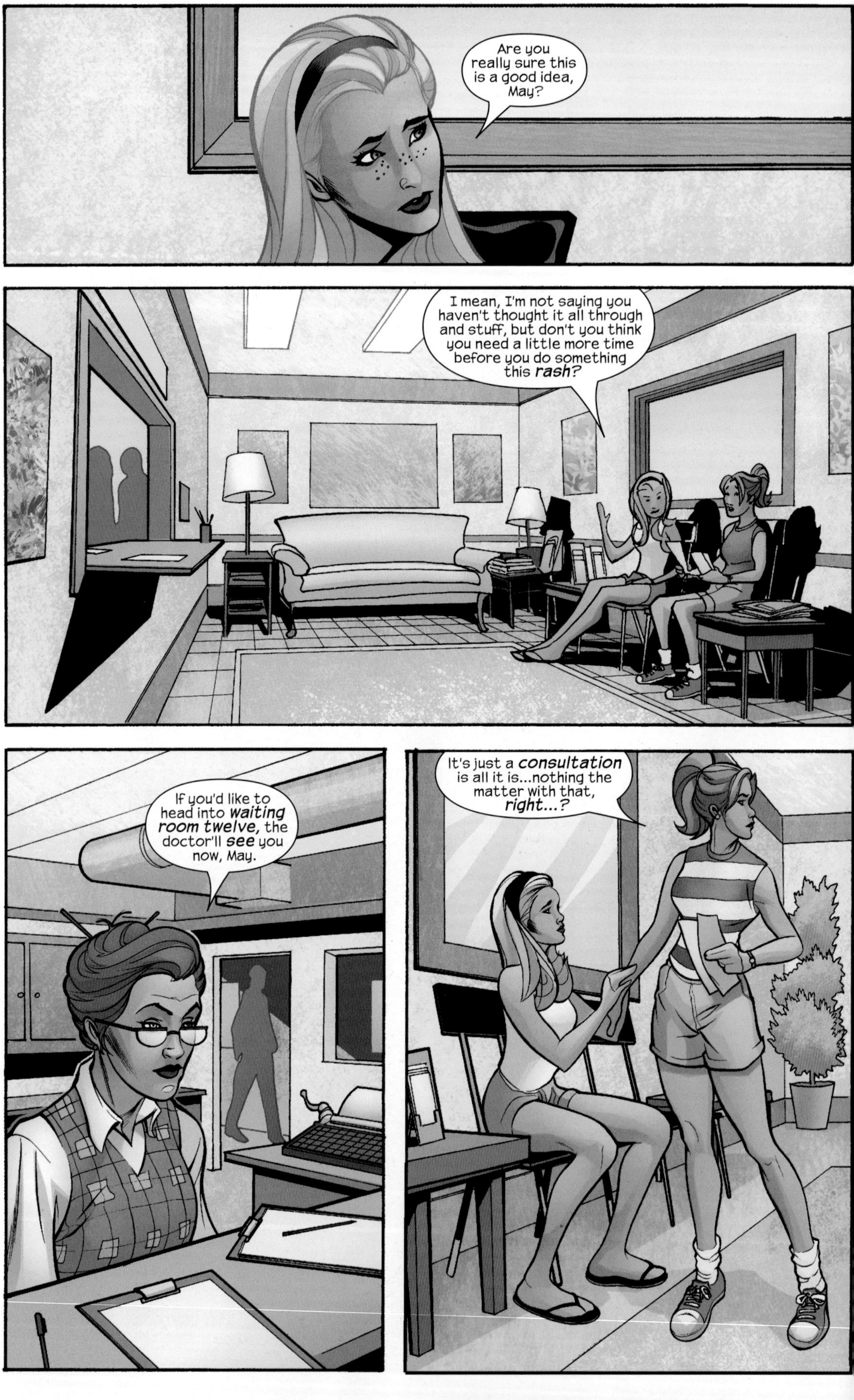
Are you really sure this is a good idea, May?
I mean, I'm not saying you haven't thought it all through and stuff, but don't you think you need a little more time before you do something this rash?
If you'd like to head into waiting room twelve, the doctor'll see you now, May.
It's just a consultation is all it is...nothing the matter with that, right...?

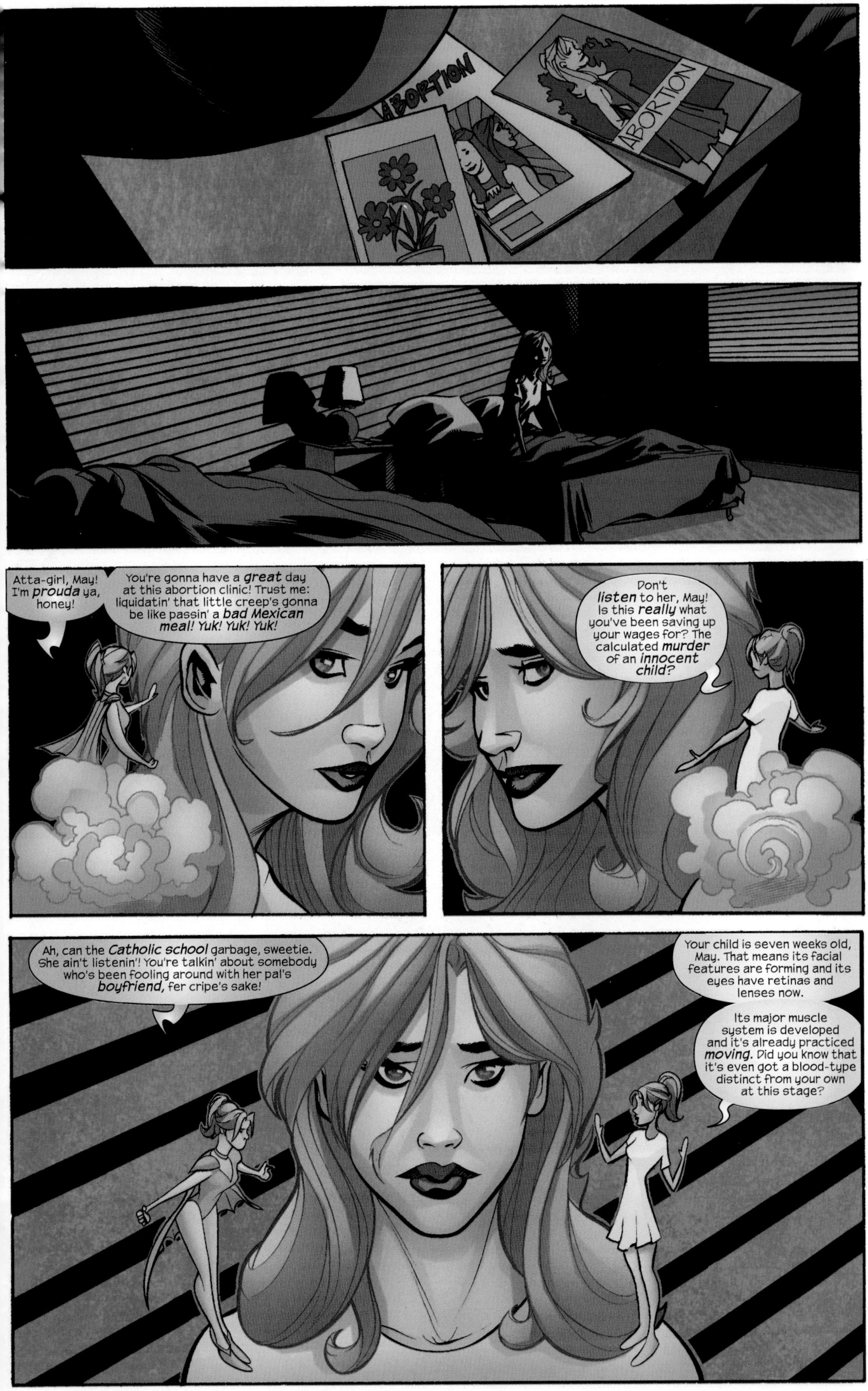
ABORTION
ABORTION
Atta-girl, May! I'm *prouda* ya, honey!
You're gonna have a *great* day at this abortion clinic! Trust me: liquidatin' that little creep's gonna be like passin' a *bad Mexican meal! Yuk! Yuk! Yuk!*
Don't *listen* to her, May! Is this *really* what you've been saving up your wages for? The calculated *murder* of an *innocent child?*
Ah, can the *Catholic school* garbage, sweetie. She ain't listenin'! You're talkin' about somebody who's been fooling around with her pal's *boyfriend,* fer cripe's sake!
Your child is seven weeks old, May. That means its facial features are forming and its eyes have retinas and lenses now.
Its major muscle system is developed and it's already practiced *moving.* Did you know that it's even got a blood-type distinct from your own at this stage?

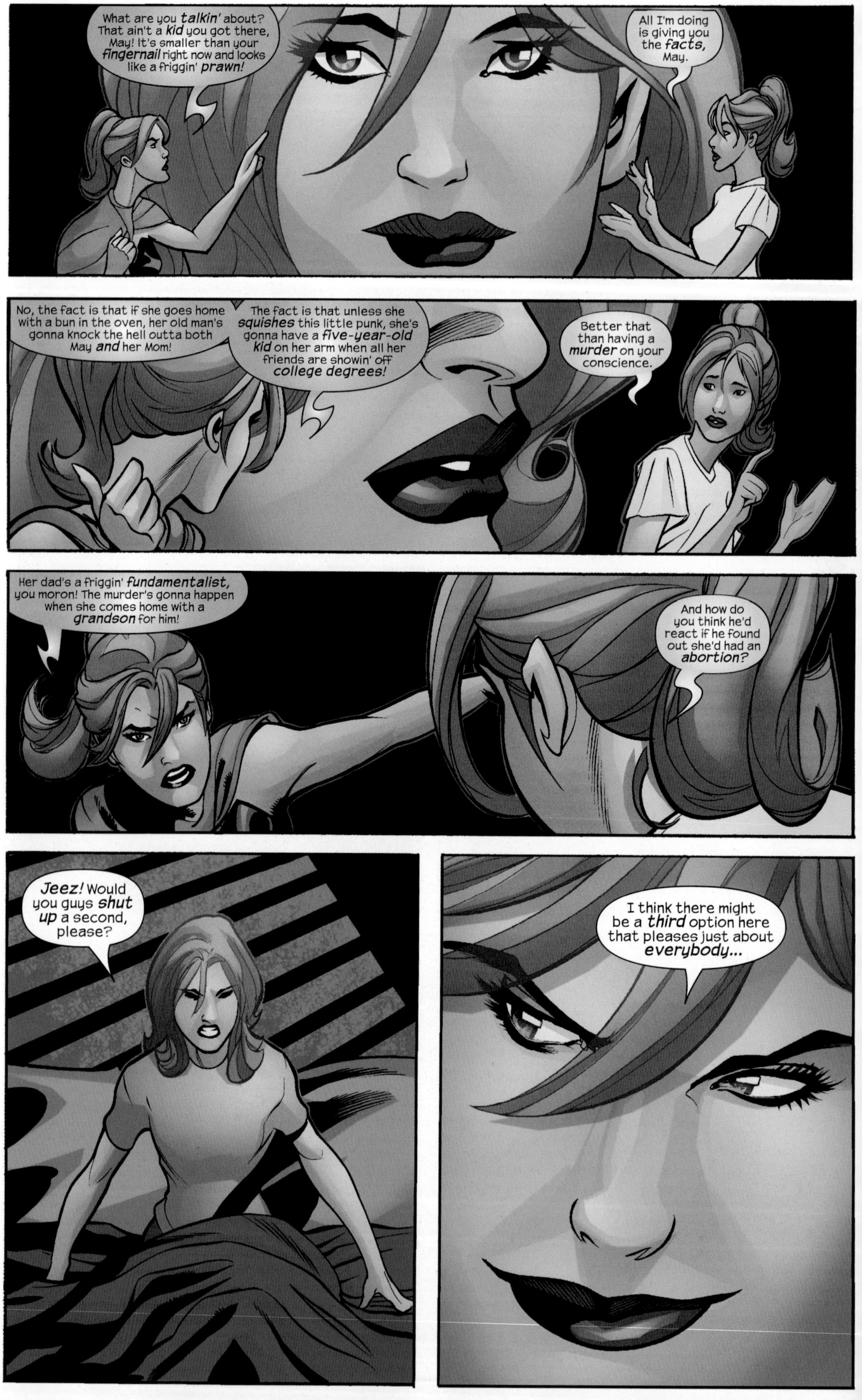
What are you talkin' about? That ain't a kid you got there, May! It's smaller than your fingernail right now and looks like a friggin' prawn!
All I'm doing is giving you the facts, May.
No, the fact is that if she goes home with a bun in the oven, her old man's gonna knock the hell outta both May and her Mom!
The fact is that unless she squishes this little punk, she's gonna have a five-year-old kid on her arm when all her friends are showin' off college degrees!
Better that than having a murder on your conscience.
Her dad's a friggin' fundamentalist, you moron! The murder's gonna happen when she comes home with a grandson for him!
And how do you think he'd react if he found out she'd had an abortion?
Jeez! Would you guys shut up a second, please?
I think there might be a third option here that pleases just about everybody...

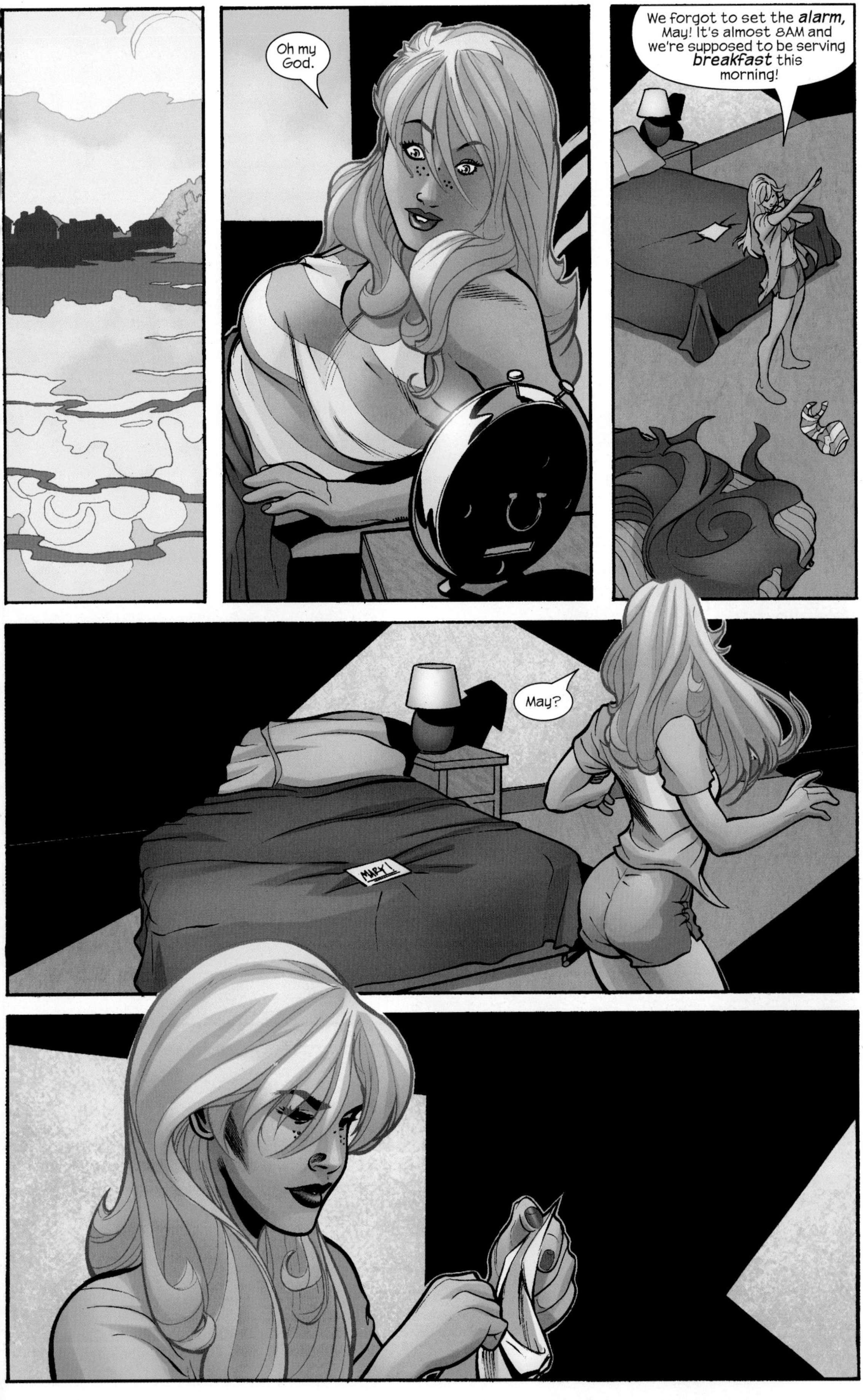
Oh my God.
We forgot to set the alarm, May! It's almost 8AM and we're supposed to be serving breakfast this morning!
May?
MARY!

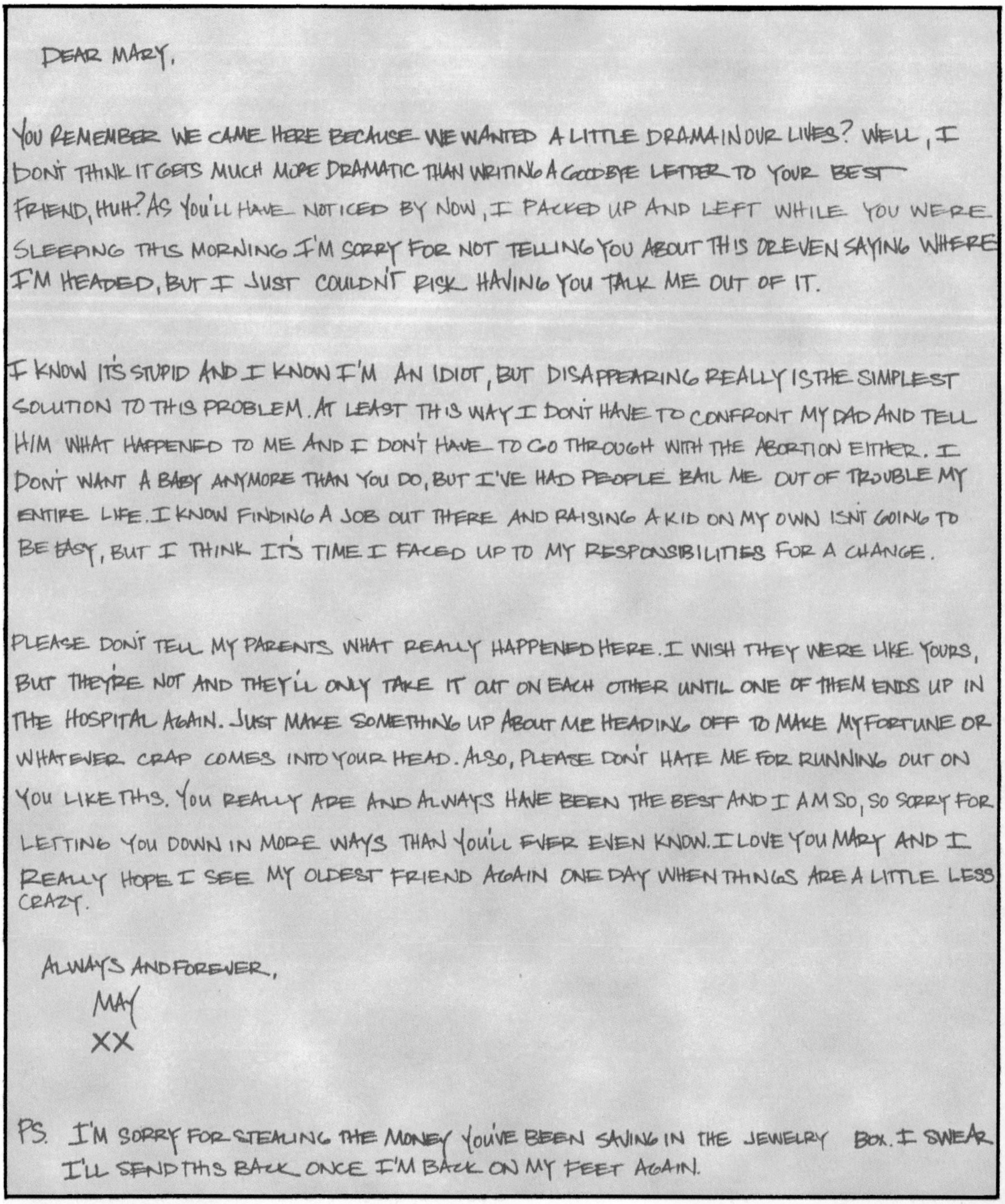

Dear Mary,

You remember we came here because we wanted a little drama in our lives? Well, I don't think it gets much more dramatic than writing a goodbye letter to your best friend, huh? As you'll have noticed by now, I packed up and left while you were sleeping this morning. I'm sorry for not telling you about this or even saying where I'm headed, but I just couldn't risk having you talk me out of it.

I know it's stupid and I know I'm an idiot, but disappearing really is the simplest solution to this problem. At least this way I don't have to confront my dad and tell him what happened to me and I don't have to go through with the abortion either. I don't want a baby anymore than you do, but I've had people bail me out of trouble my entire life. I know finding a job out there and raising a kid on my own isn't going to be easy, but I think it's time I faced up to my responsibilities for a change.

Please don't tell my parents what really happened here. I wish they were like yours, but they're not and they'll only take it out on each other until one of them ends up in the hospital again. Just make something up about me heading off to make my fortune or whatever crap comes into your head. Also, please don't hate me for running out on you like this. You really are and always have been the best and I am so, so sorry for letting you down in more ways than you'll ever even know. I love you Mary and I really hope I see my oldest friend again one day when things are a little less crazy.

Always and forever,
May
XX

PS. I'm sorry for stealing the money you've been saving in the jewelry box. I swear I'll send this back once I'm back on my feet again.

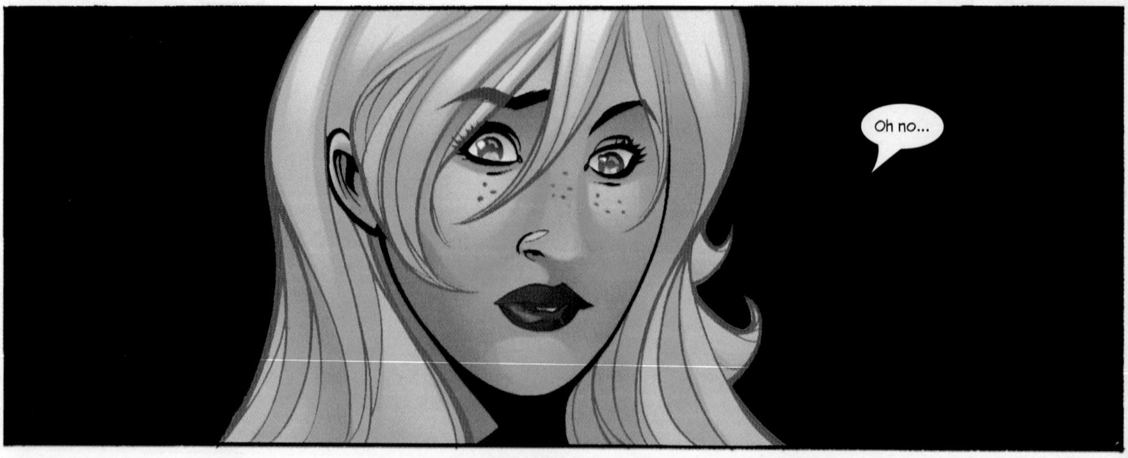
Oh no...

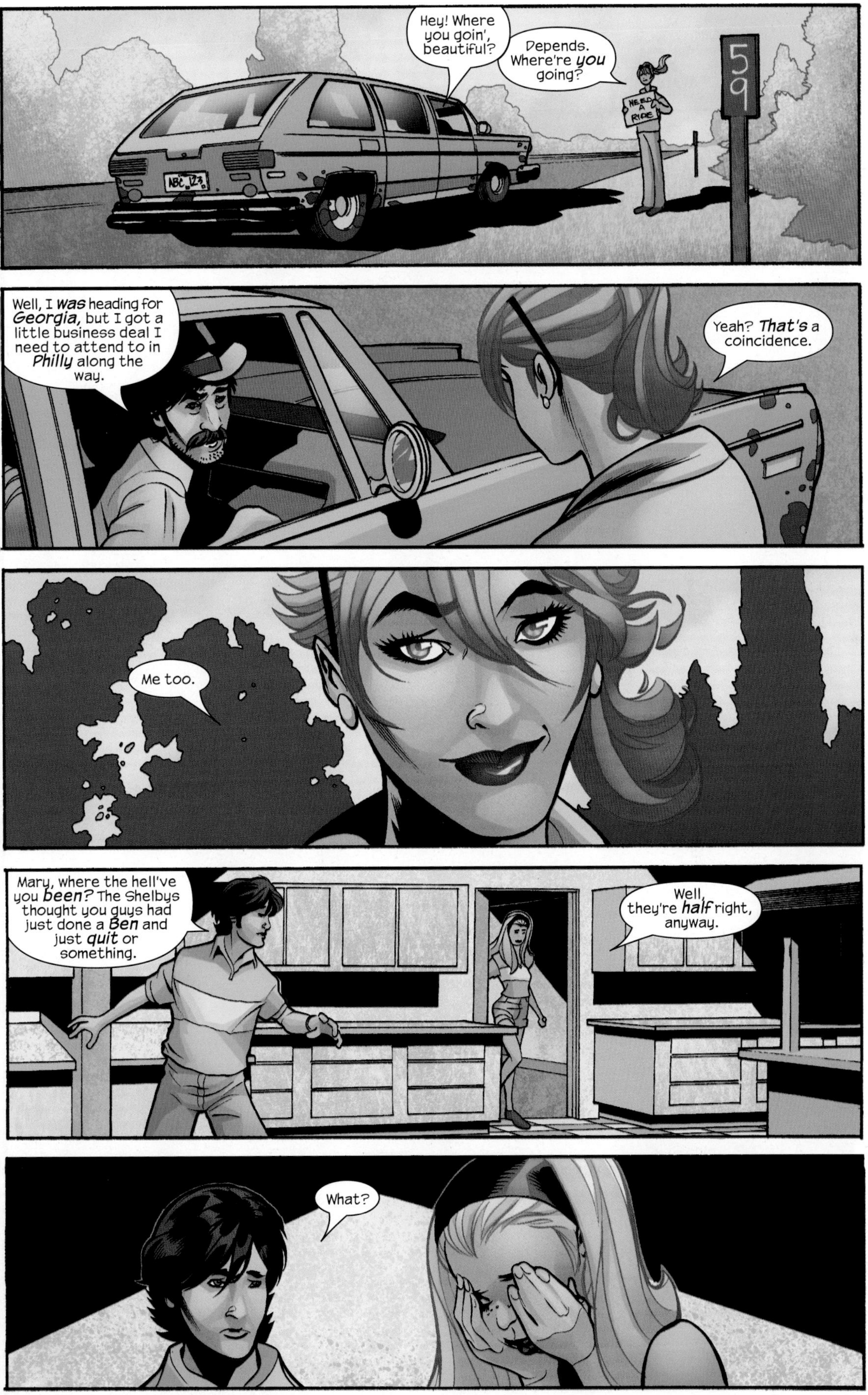
Hey! Where you goin', beautiful?
Depends. Where're you going?
NEED A RIDE
59
ABC 123
Well, I was heading for Georgia, but I got a little business deal I need to attend to in Philly along the way.
Yeah? That's a coincidence.
Me too.
Mary, where the hell've you been? The Shelbys thought you guys had just done a Ben and just quit or something.
Well, they're half right, anyway.
What?

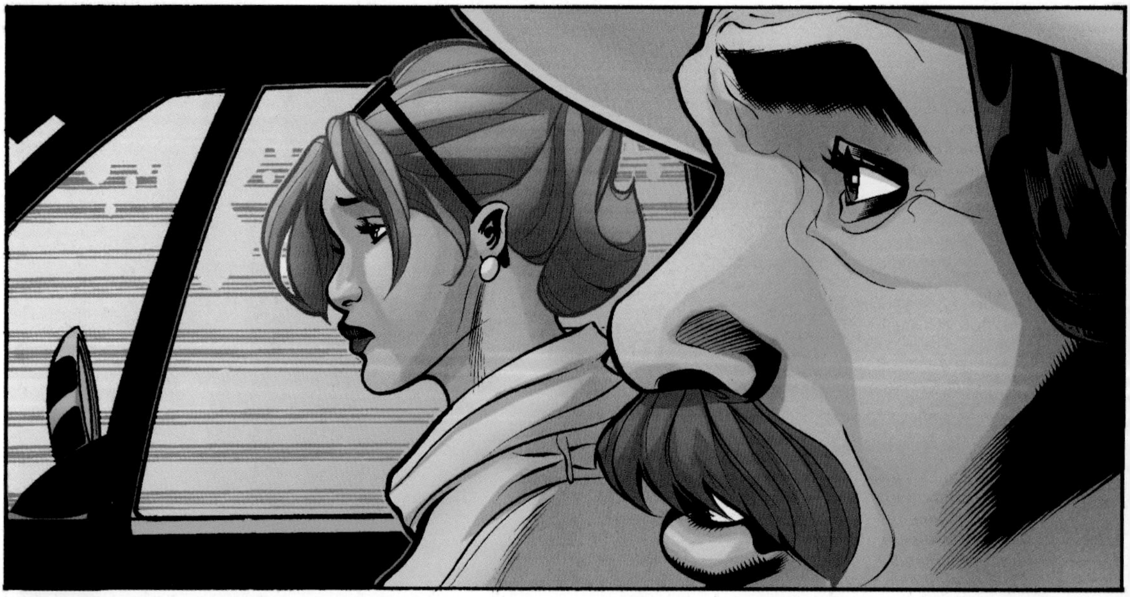

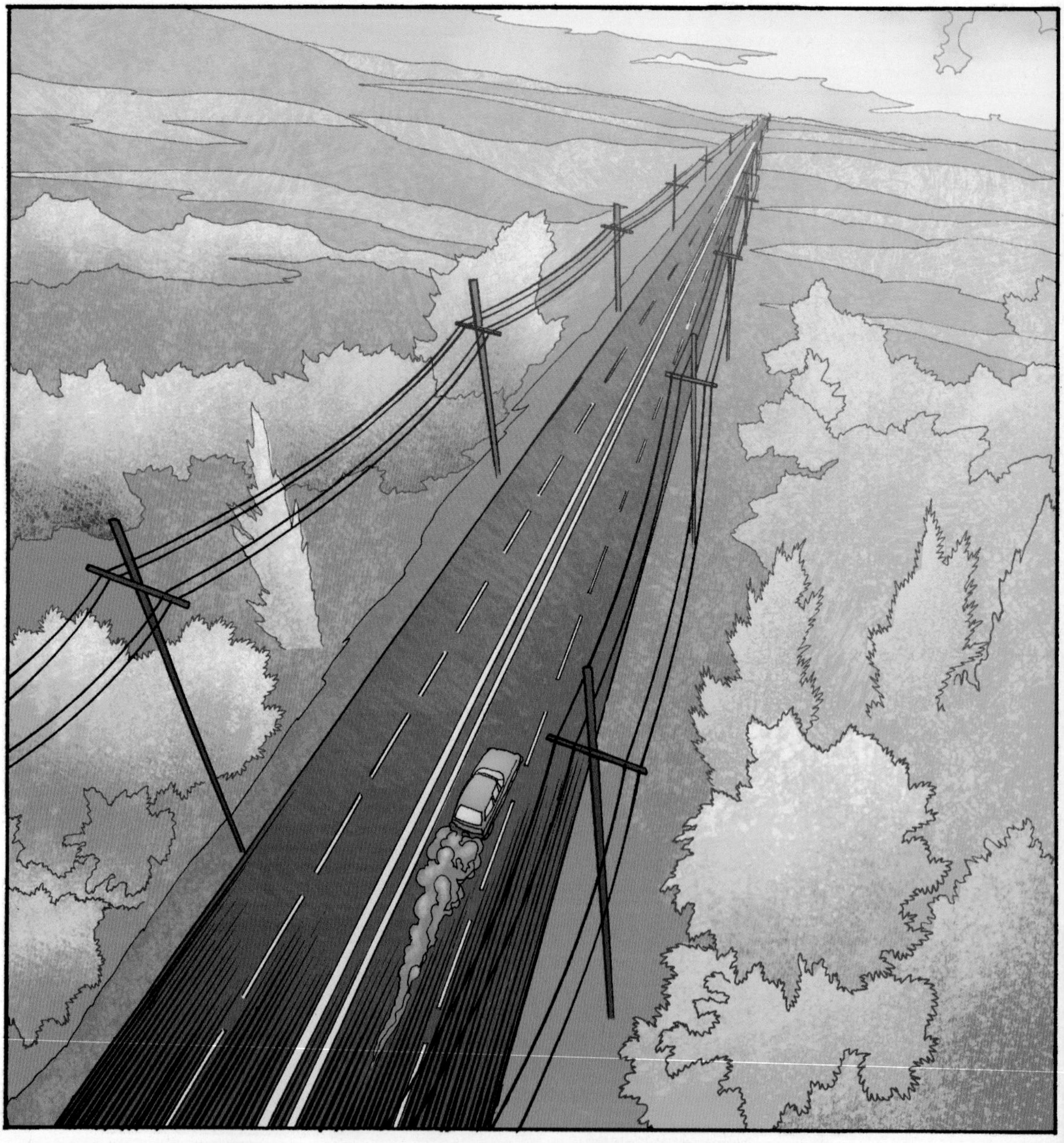

Trouble

part five of five

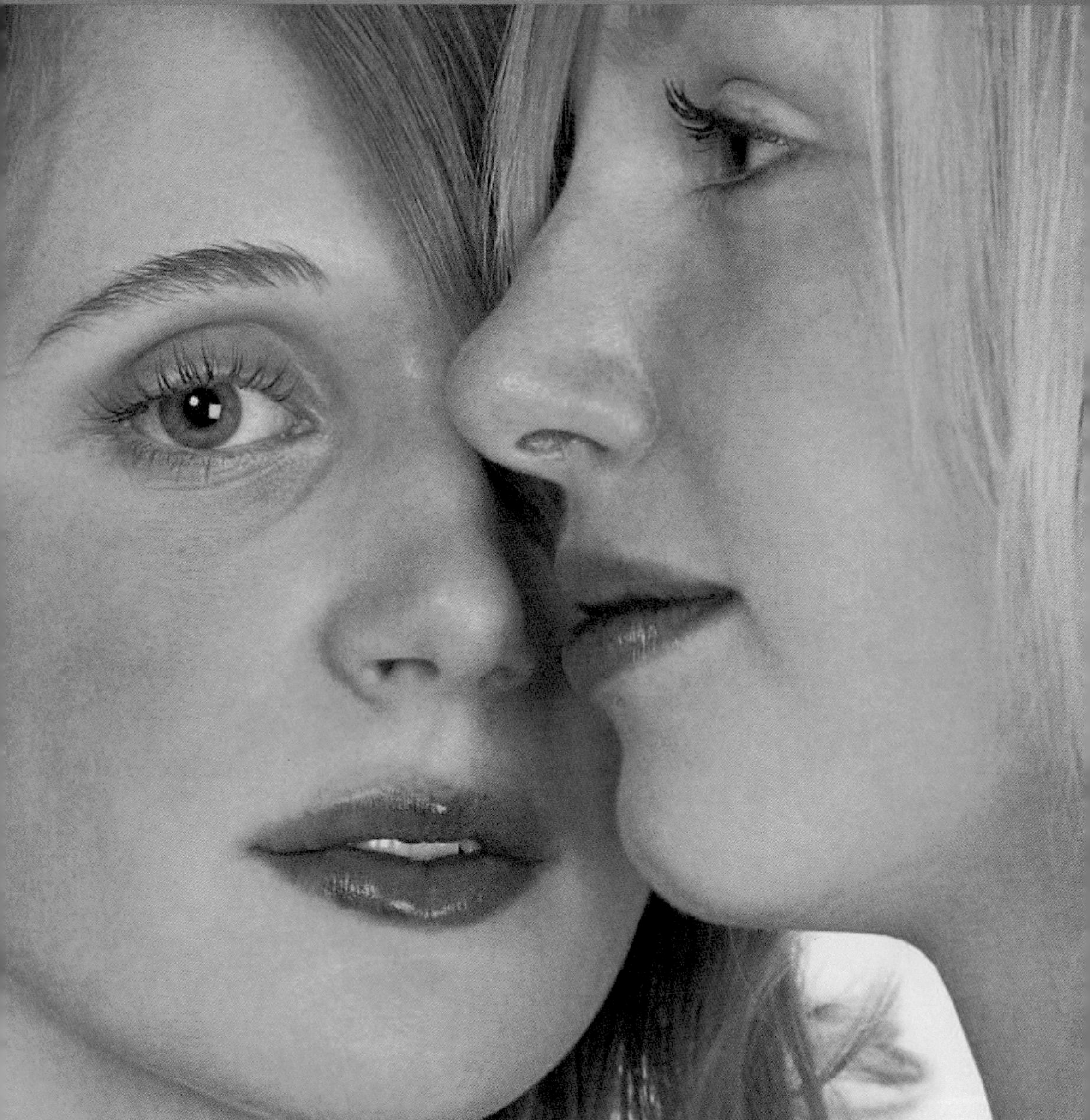

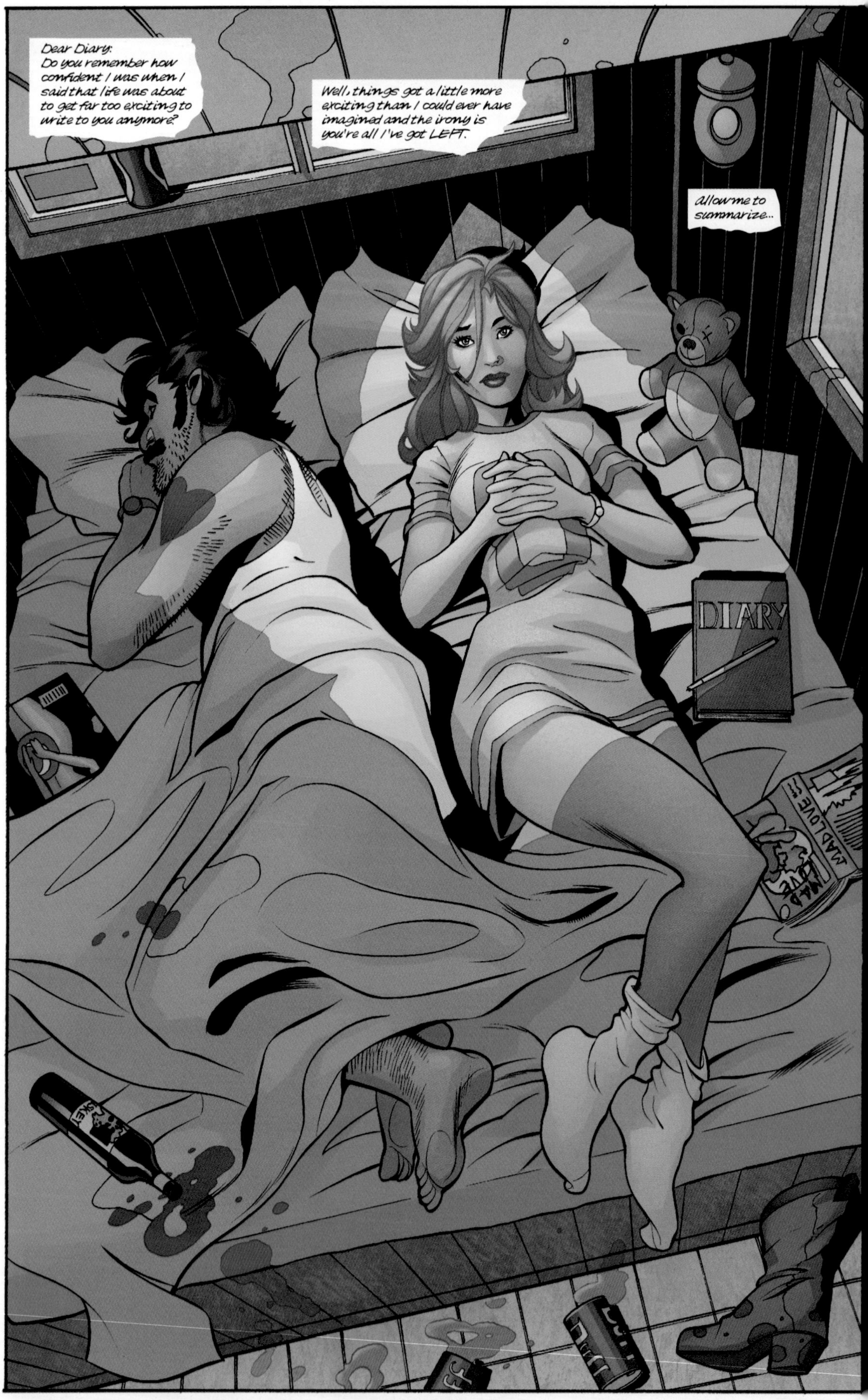
Dear Diary:
Do you remember how confident I was when I said that life was about to get far too exciting to write to you anymore?
Well, things got a little more exciting than I could ever have imagined and the irony is you're all I've got LEFT.
Allow me to summarize...
DIARY
MAD LOVE

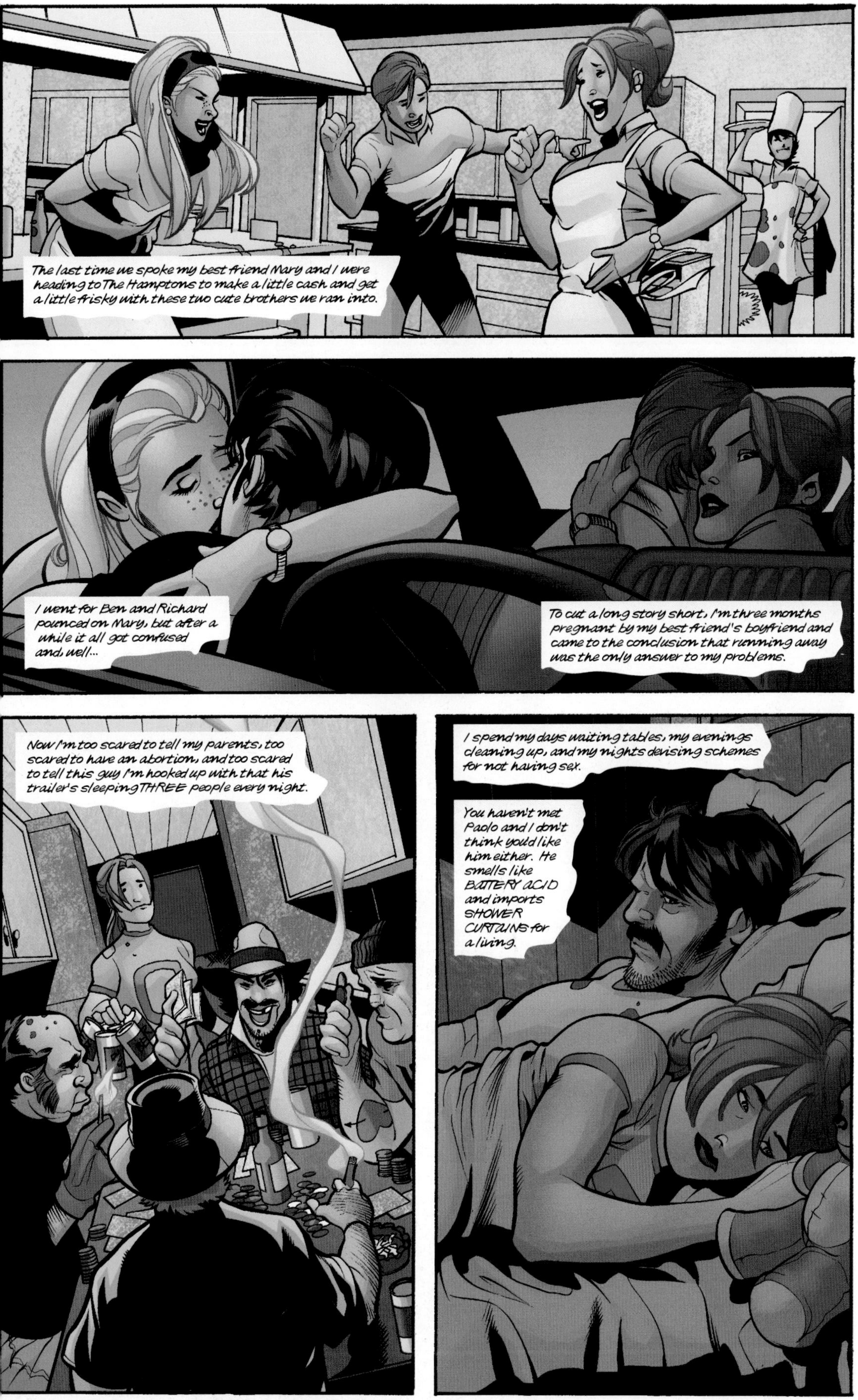
The last time we spoke my best friend Mary and I were heading to The Hamptons to make a little cash and get a little frisky with these two cute brothers we ran into.
I went for Ben and Richard pounced on Mary, but after a while it all got confused and, well...
To cut a long story short, I'm three months pregnant by my best friend's boyfriend and came to the conclusion that running away was the only answer to my problems.
Now I'm too scared to tell my parents, too scared to have an abortion, and too scared to tell this guy I'm hooked up with that his trailer's sleeping THREE people every night.
I spend my days waiting tables, my evenings cleaning up, and my nights devising schemes for not having sex.
You haven't met Paolo and I don't think you'd like him either. He smells like BATTERY ACID and imports SHOWER CURTAINS for a living.

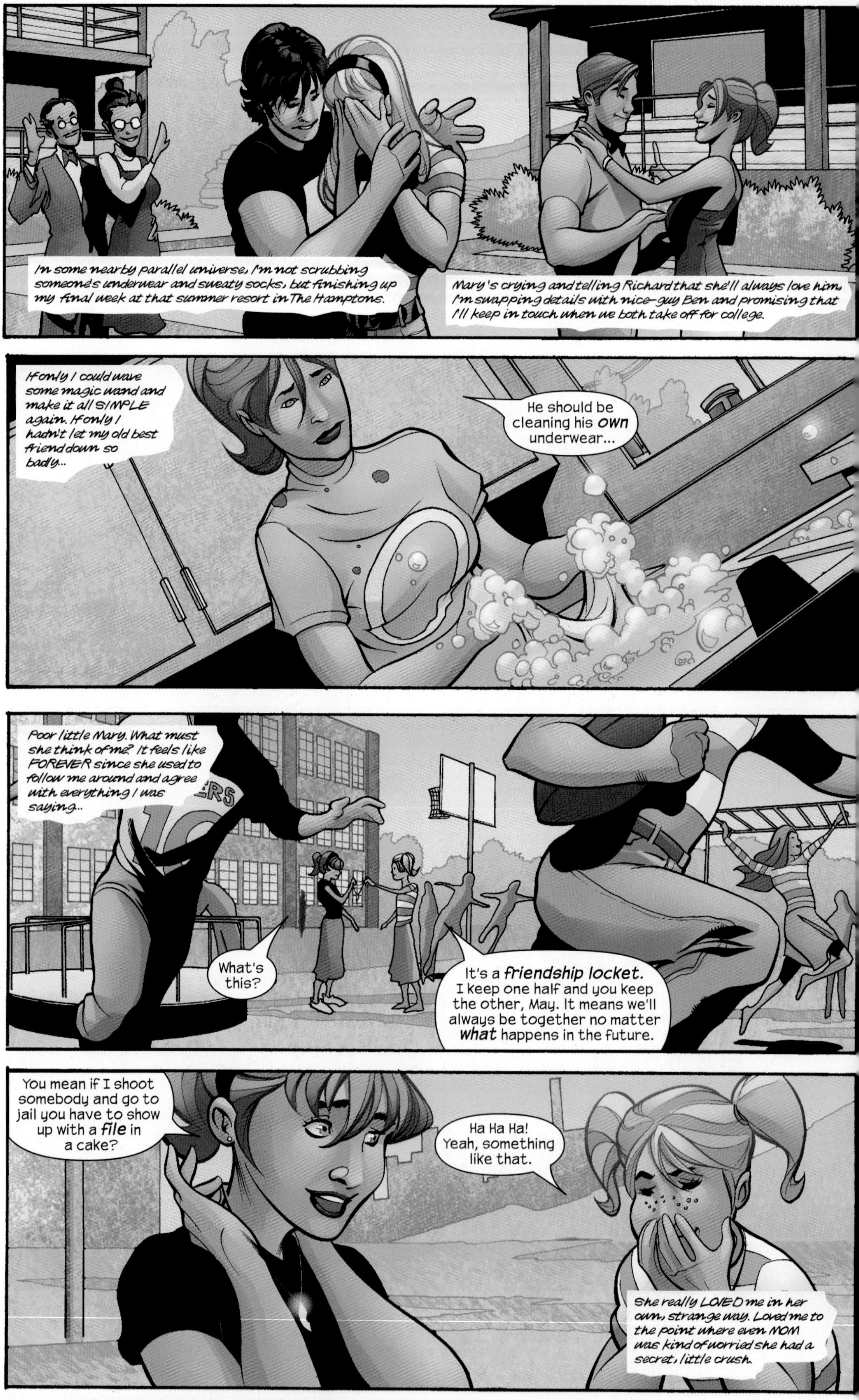
In some nearby parallel universe, I'm not scrubbing someone's underwear and sweaty socks, but finishing up my final week at that summer resort in The Hamptons.
Mary's crying and telling Richard that she'll always love him. I'm swapping details with nice-guy Ben and promising that I'll keep in touch when we both take off for college.
If only I could wave some magic wand and make it all SIMPLE again. If only I hadn't let my old best friend down so badly...
He should be cleaning his OWN underwear...
Poor little Mary. What must she think of me? It feels like FOREVER since she used to follow me around and agree with everything I was saying...
What's this?
It's a friendship locket. I keep one half and you keep the other, May. It means we'll always be together no matter what happens in the future.
You mean if I shoot somebody and go to jail you have to show up with a file in a cake?
Ha Ha Ha! Yeah, something like that.
She really LOVED me in her own, strange way. Loved me to the point where even MOM was kind of worried she had a secret, little crush.

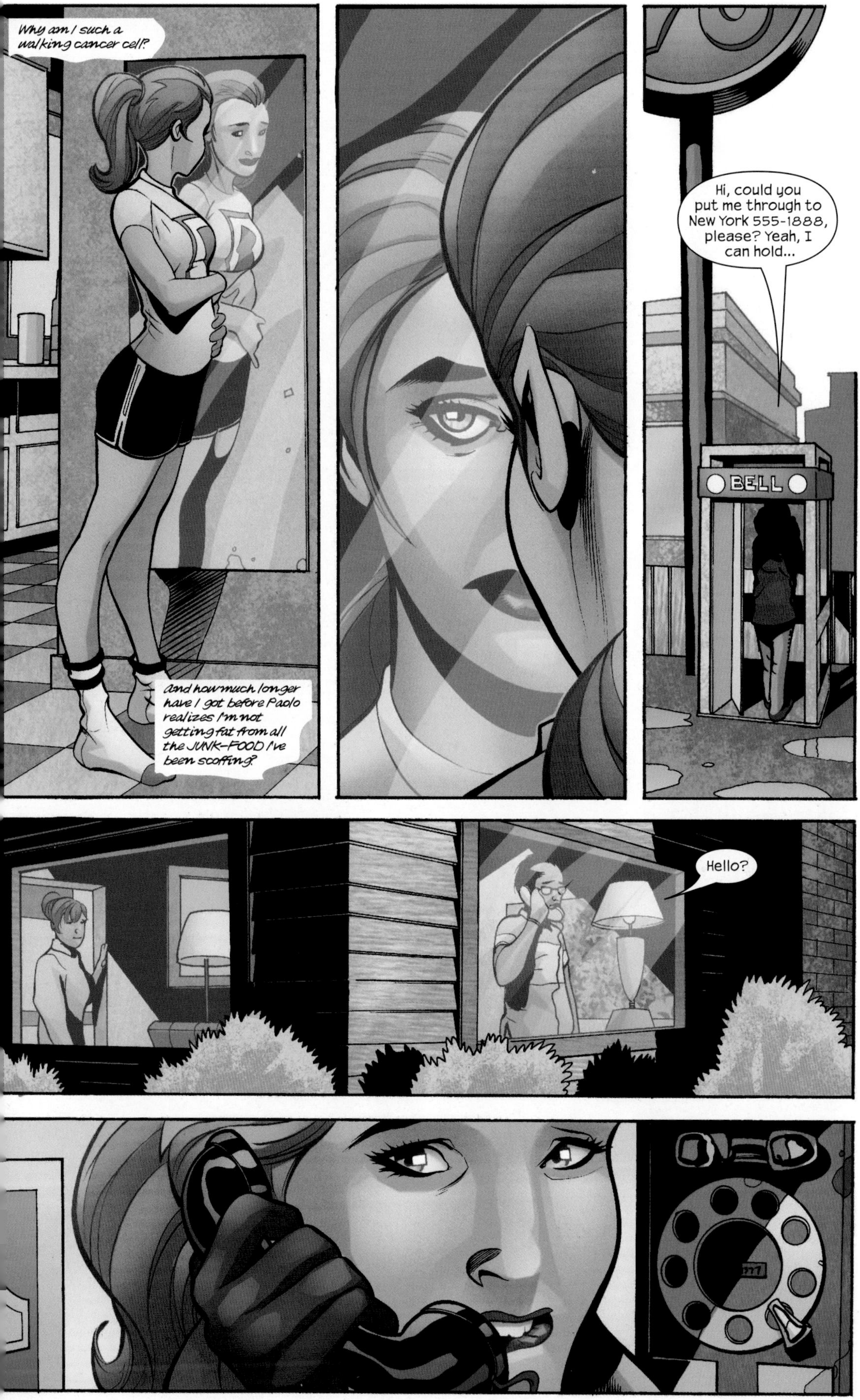
Why am I such a walking cancer cell?
And how much longer have I got before Paolo realizes I'm not getting fat from all the JUNK-FOOD I've been scoffing?
Hi, could you put me through to New York 555-1888, please? Yeah, I can hold...
BELL
Hello?

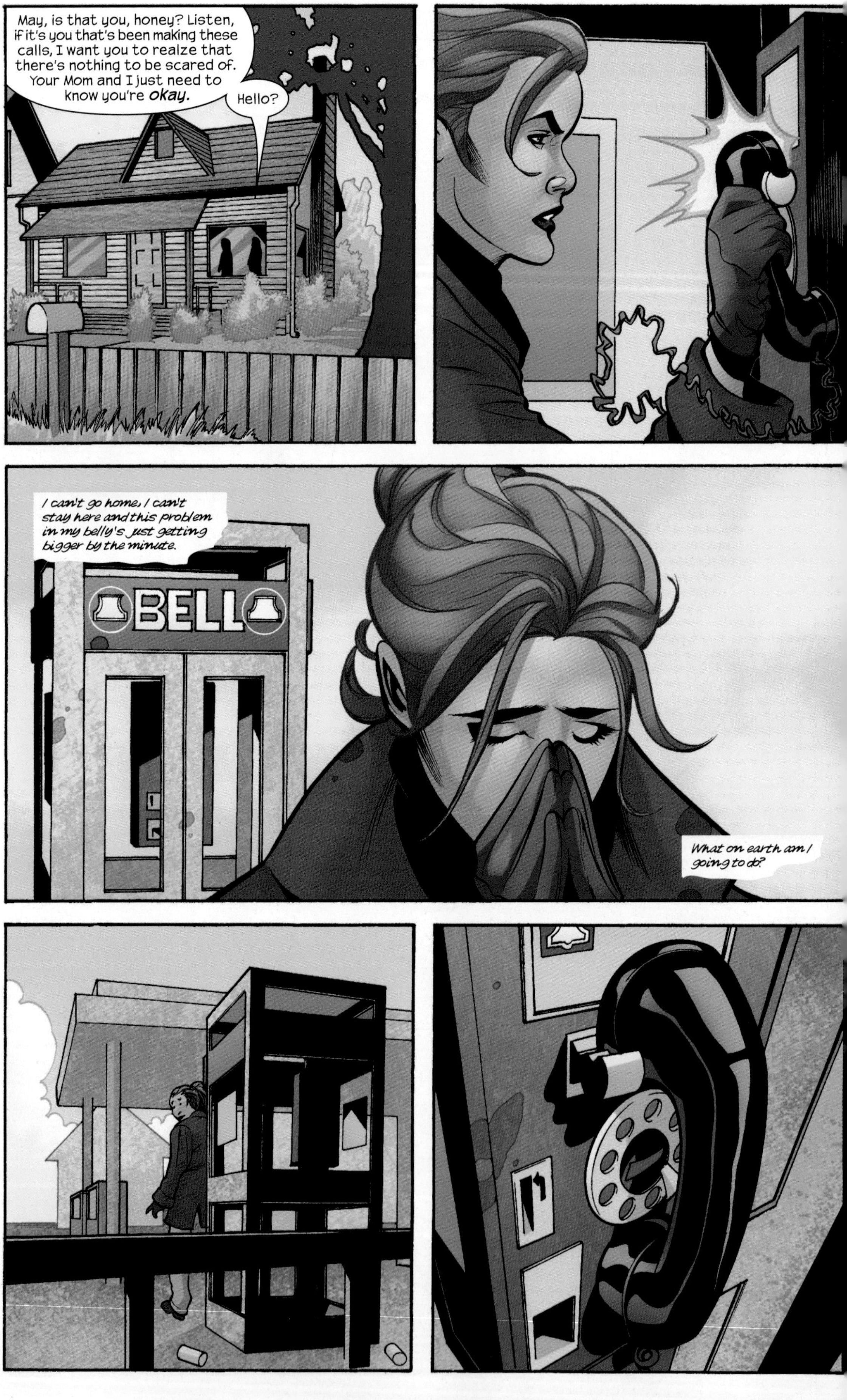
May, is that you, honey? Listen, if it's you that's been making these calls, I want you to realze that there's nothing to be scared of. Your Mom and I just need to know you're okay.
Hello?
I can't go home, I can't stay here and this problem in my belly's just getting bigger by the minute.
BELL
What on earth am I going to do?

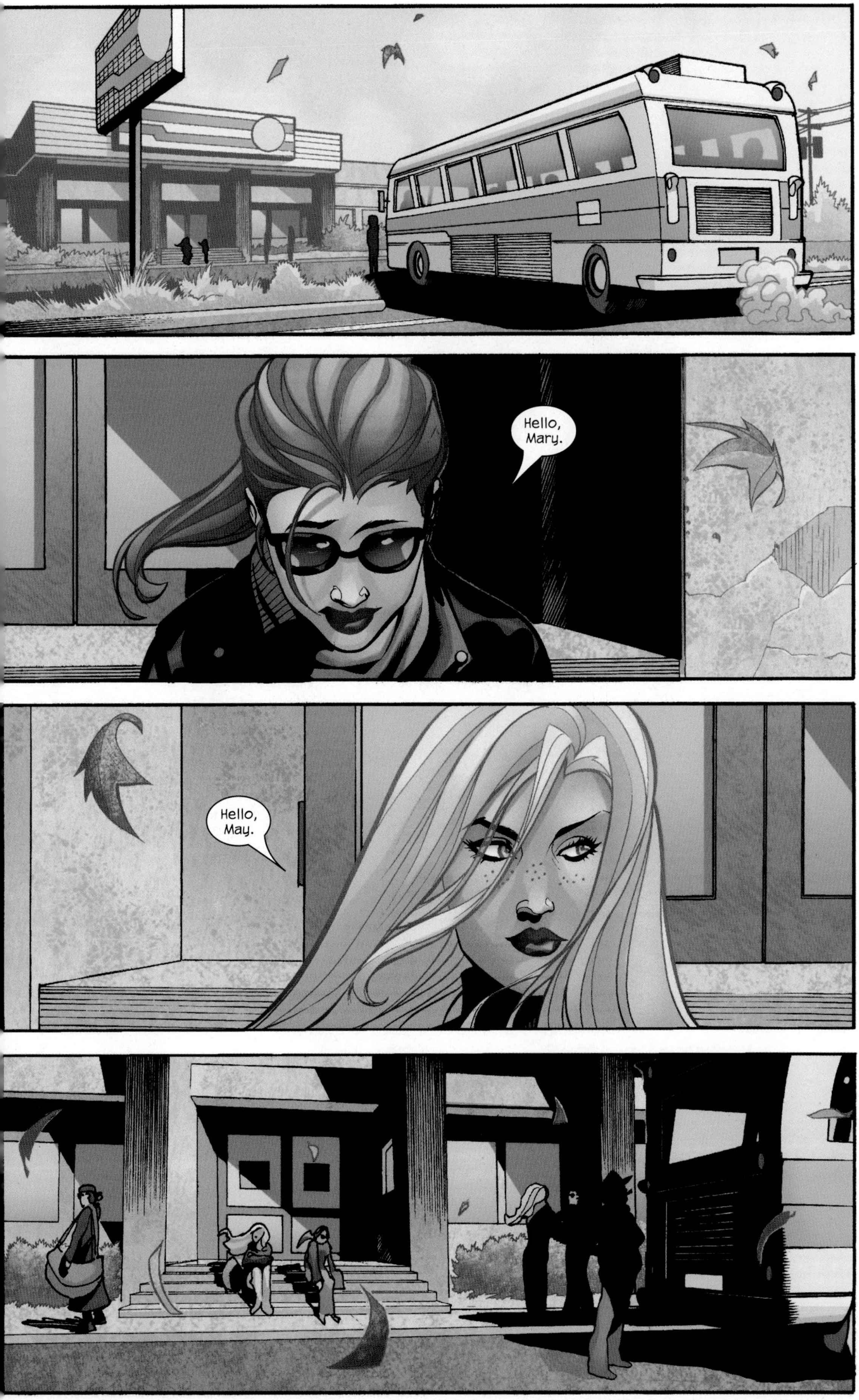
Hello, Mary.
Hello, May.

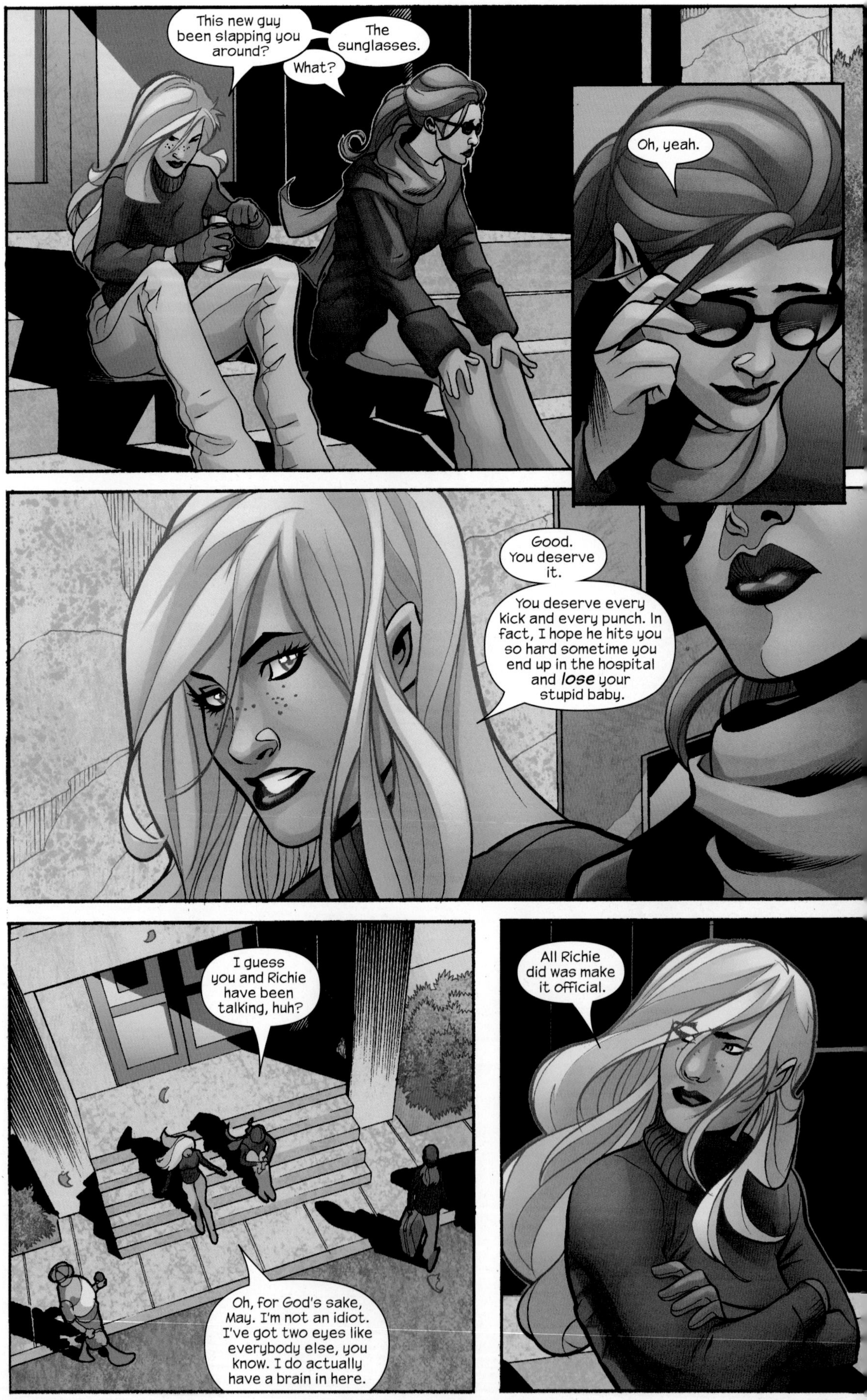
This new guy been slapping you around?
The sunglasses.
What?
Oh, yeah.
Good. You deserve it.
You deserve every kick and every punch. In fact, I hope he hits you so hard sometime you end up in the hospital and *lose* your stupid baby.
I guess you and Richie have been talking, huh?
Oh, for God's sake, May. I'm not an idiot. I've got two eyes like everybody else, you know. I do actually have a brain in here.
All Richie did was make it official.

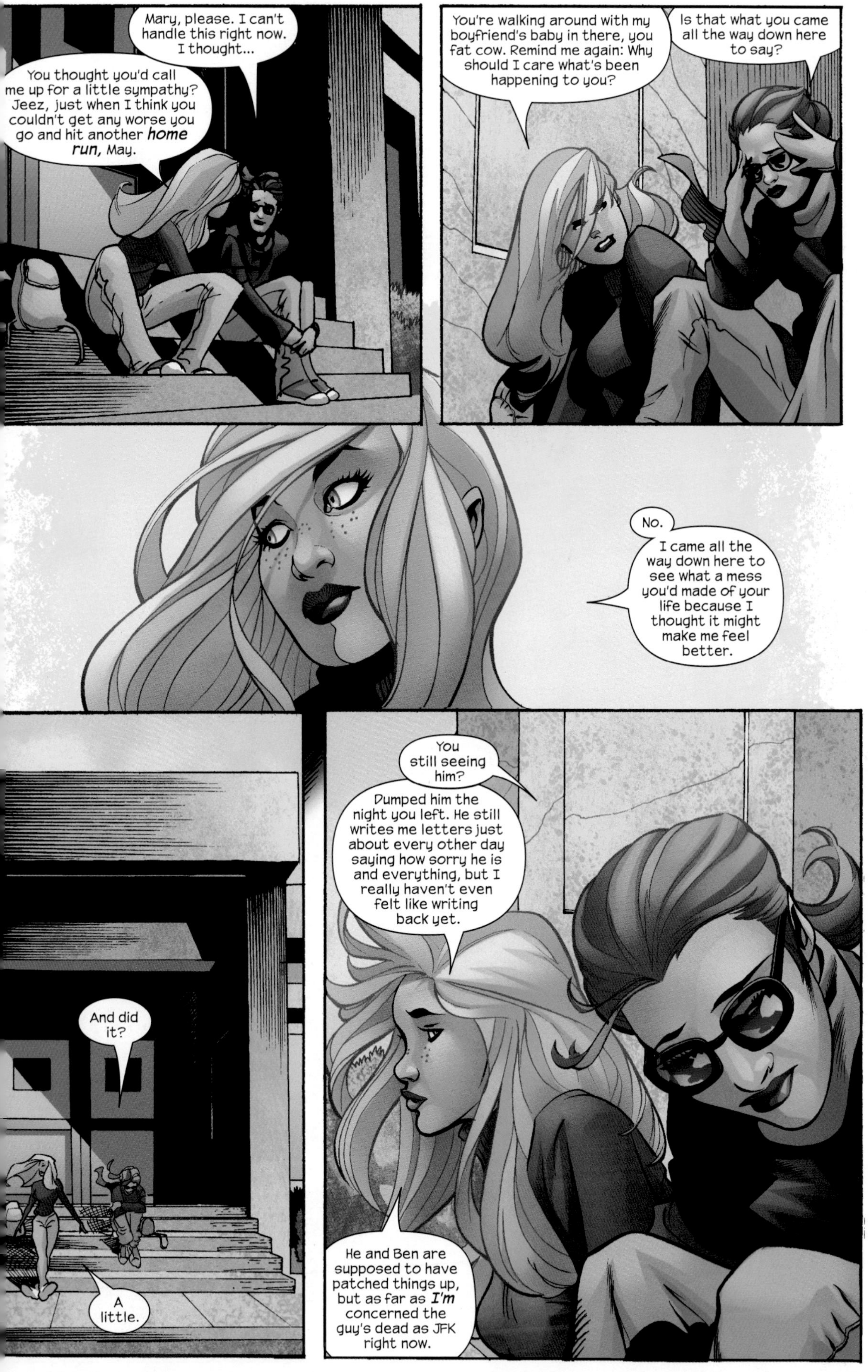
Mary, please. I can't handle this right now. I thought...
You thought you'd call me up for a little sympathy? Jeez, just when I think you couldn't get any worse you go and hit another *home run,* May.
You're walking around with my boyfriend's baby in there, you fat cow. Remind me again: Why should I care what's been happening to you?
Is that what you came all the way down here to say?
No.
I came all the way down here to see what a mess you'd made of your life because I thought it might make me feel better.
And did it?
A little.
You still seeing him?
Dumped him the night you left. He still writes me letters just about every other day saying how sorry he is and everything, but I really haven't even felt like writing back yet.
He and Ben are supposed to have patched things up, but as far as *I'm* concerned the guy's dead as JFK right now.

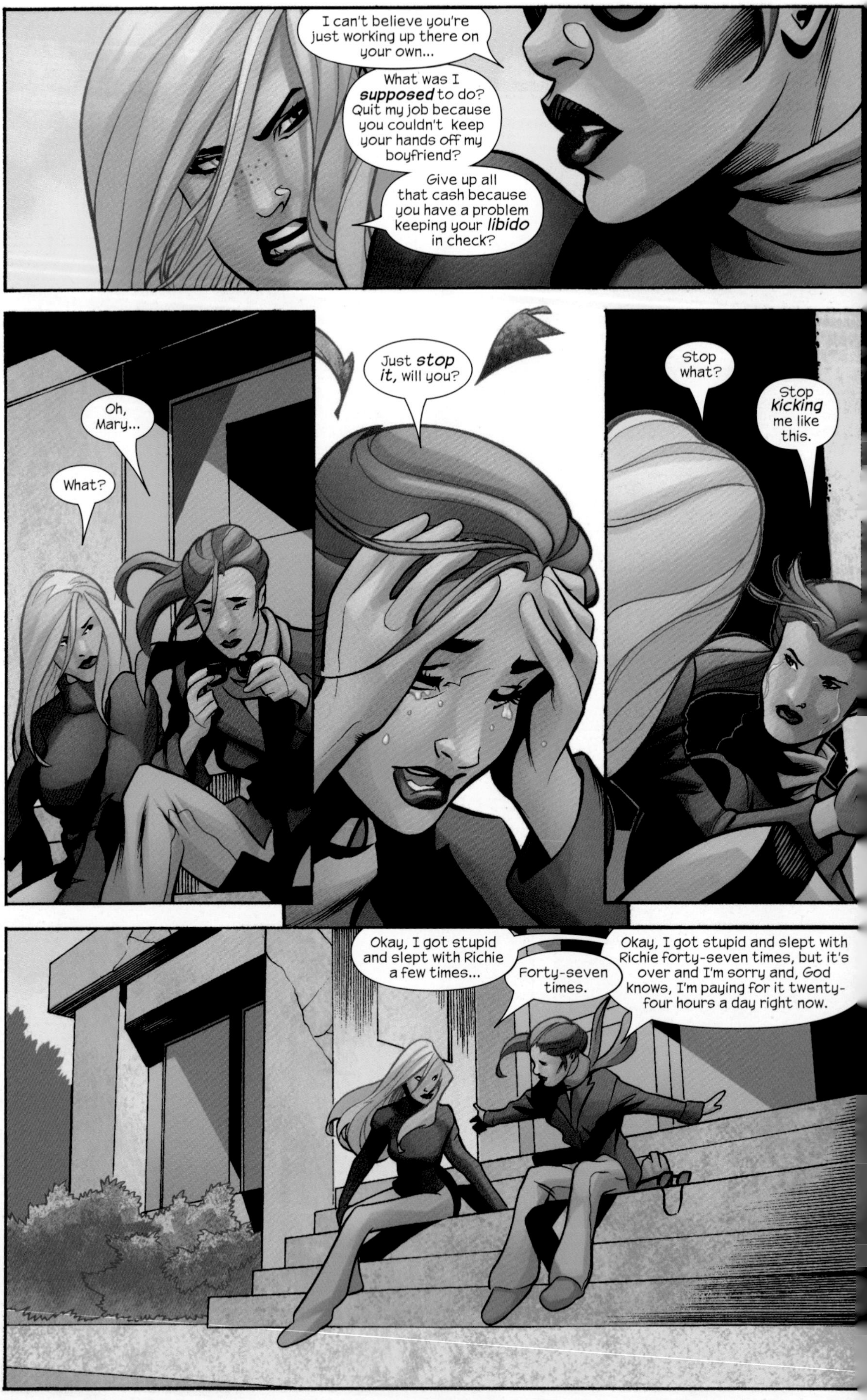
I can't believe you're just working up there on your own...
What was I *supposed* to do? Quit my job because you couldn't keep your hands off my boyfriend?
Give up all that cash because you have a problem keeping your *libido* in check?
Oh, Mary...
What?
Just *stop it,* will you?
Stop what?
Stop *kicking* me like this.
Okay, I got stupid and slept with Richie a few times...
Forty-seven times.
Okay, I got stupid and slept with Richie forty-seven times, but it's over and I'm sorry and, God knows, I'm paying for it twenty-four hours a day right now.

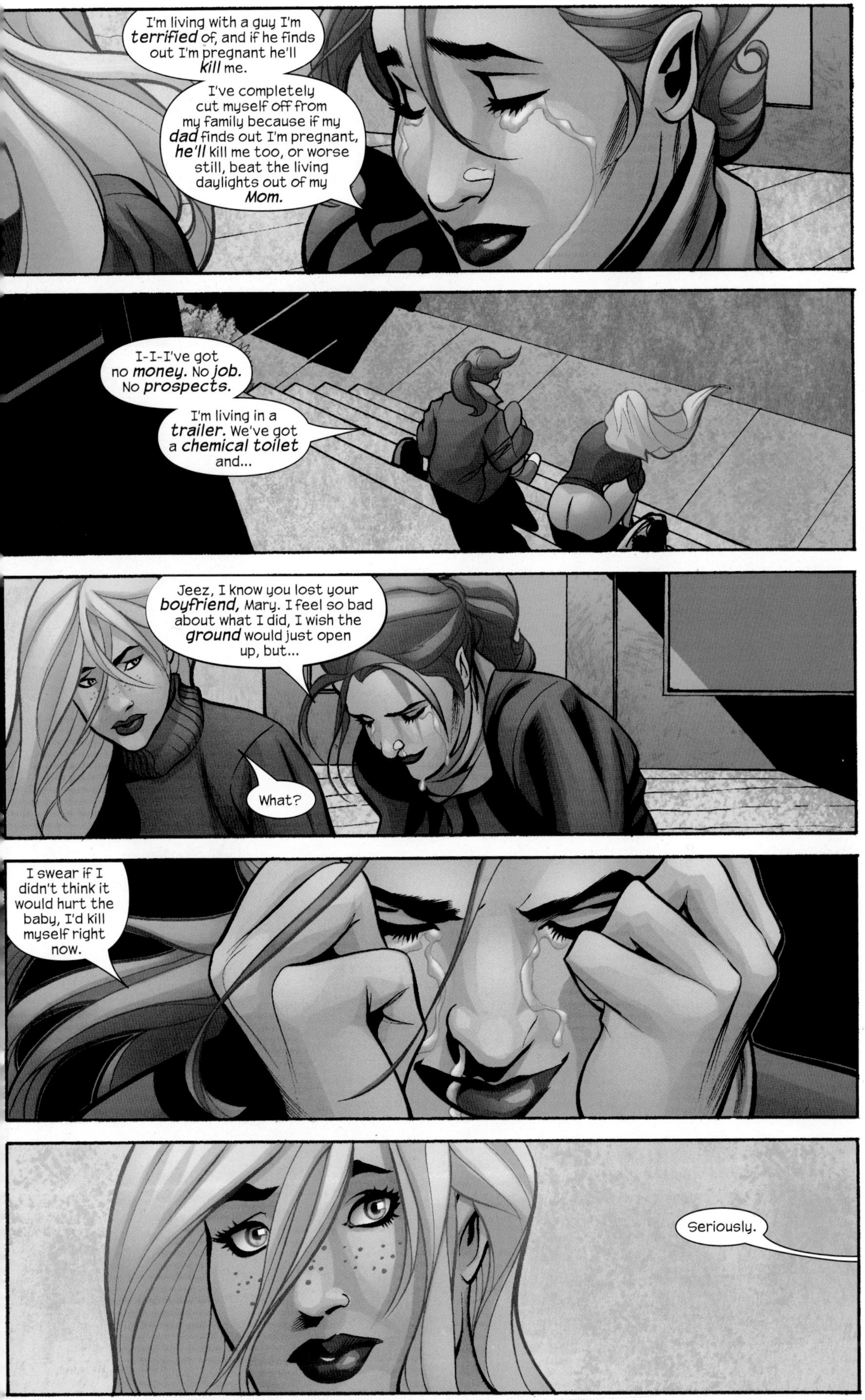

I'm living with a guy I'm *terrified* of, and if he finds out I'm pregnant he'll *kill* me.
I've completely cut myself off from my family because if my *dad* finds out I'm pregnant, *he'll* kill me too, or worse still, beat the living daylights out of my *Mom.*
I-I-I've got no *money.* No *job.* No *prospects.*
I'm living in a *trailer.* We've got a *chemical toilet* and...
Jeez, I know you lost your *boyfriend,* Mary. I feel so bad about what I did, I wish the *ground* would just open up, but...
What?
I swear if I didn't think it would hurt the baby, I'd kill myself right now.
Seriously.

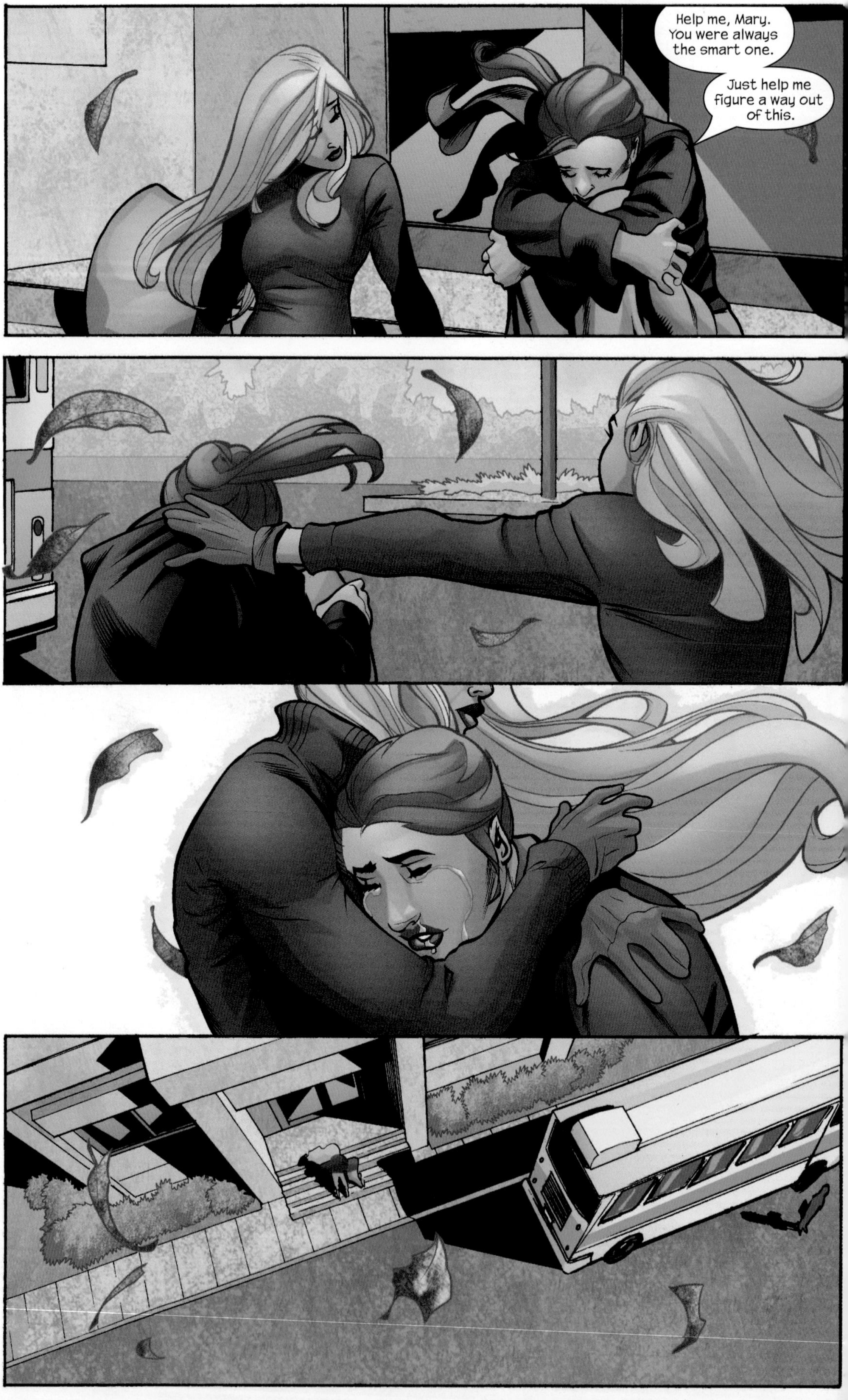
Help me, Mary. You were always the smart one.
Just help me figure a way out of this.

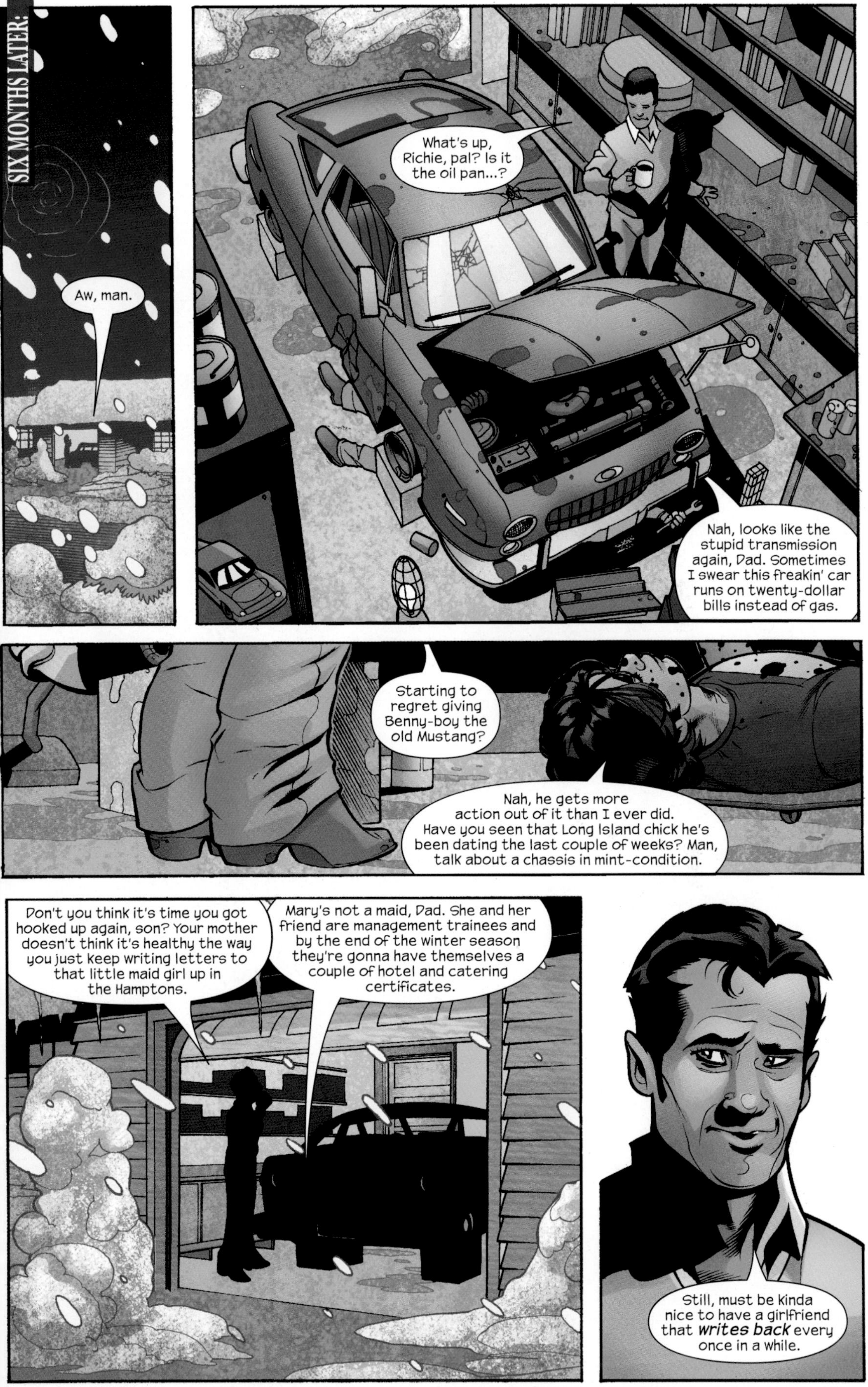
SIX MONTHS LATER:
Aw, man.
What's up, Richie, pal? Is it the oil pan...?
Nah, looks like the stupid transmission again, Dad. Sometimes I swear this freakin' car runs on twenty-dollar bills instead of gas.
Starting to regret giving Benny-boy the old Mustang?
Nah, he gets more action out of it than I ever did. Have you seen that Long Island chick he's been dating the last couple of weeks? Man, talk about a chassis in mint-condition.
Don't you think it's time you got hooked up again, son? Your mother doesn't think it's healthy the way you just keep writing letters to that little maid girl up in the Hamptons.
Mary's not a maid, Dad. She and her friend are management trainees and by the end of the winter season they're gonna have themselves a couple of hotel and catering certificates.
Still, must be kinda nice to have a girlfriend that *writes back* every once in a while.

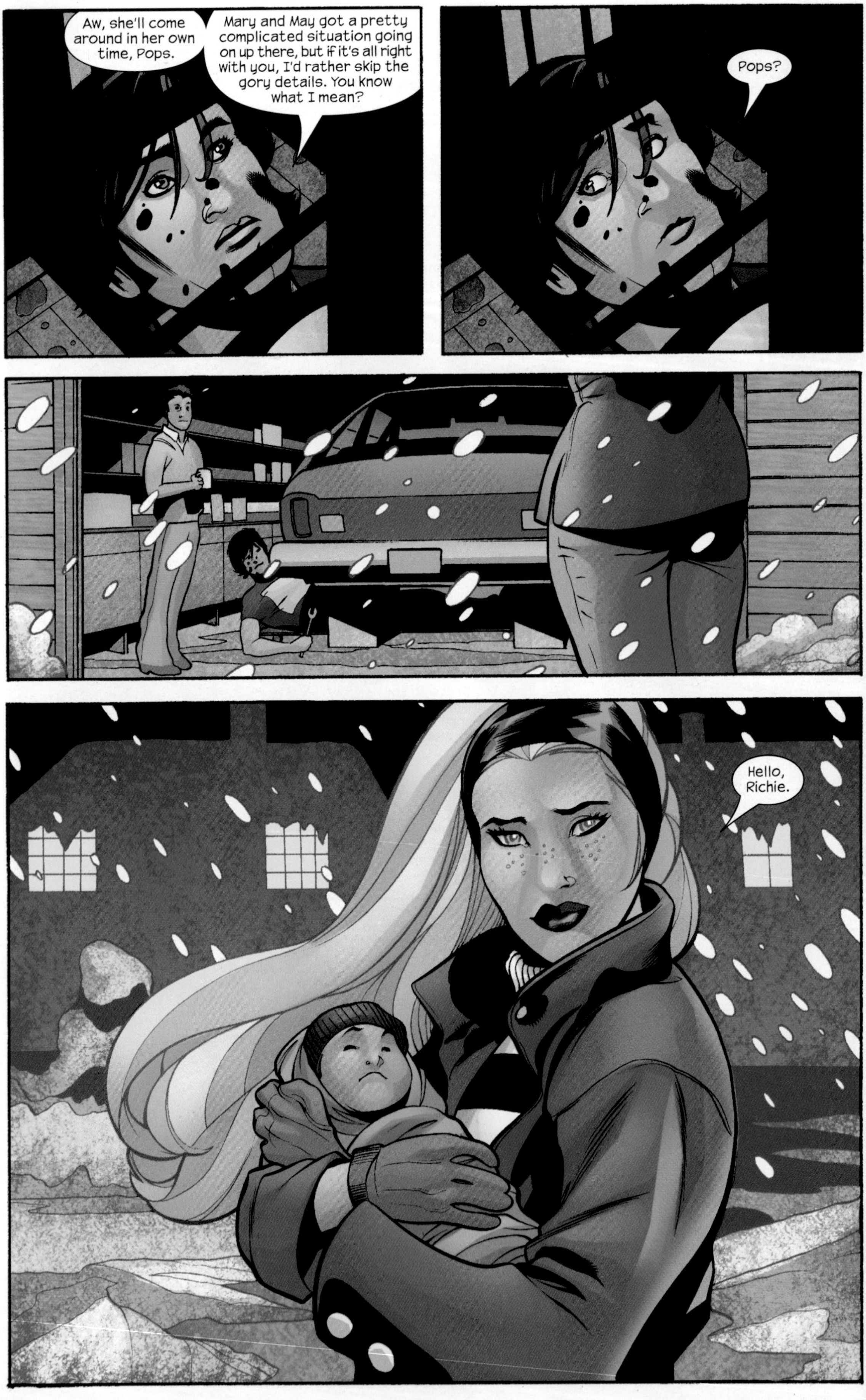
Aw, she'll come around in her own time, Pops.
Mary and May got a pretty complicated situation going on up there, but if it's all right with you, I'd rather skip the gory details. You know what I mean?
Pops?
Hello, Richie.

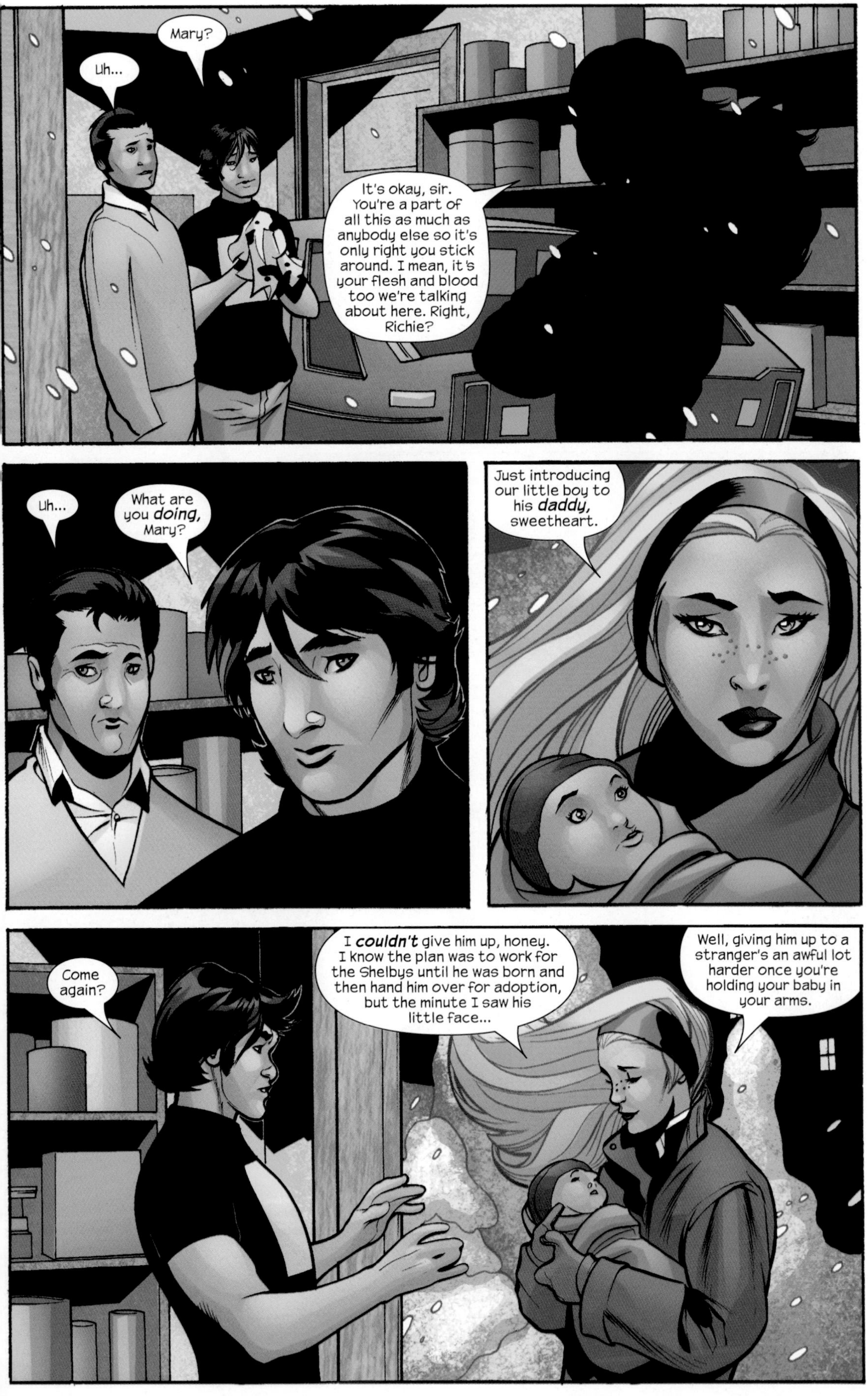
Uh...
Mary?
It's okay, sir. You're a part of all this as much as anybody else so it's only right you stick around. I mean, it's your flesh and blood too we're talking about here. Right, Richie?
Uh...
What are you *doing,* Mary?
Just introducing our little boy to his *daddy,* sweetheart.
Come again?
I *couldn't* give him up, honey. I know the plan was to work for the Shelbys until he was born and then hand him over for adoption, but the minute I saw his little face...
Well, giving him up to a stranger's an awful lot harder once you're holding your baby in your arms.

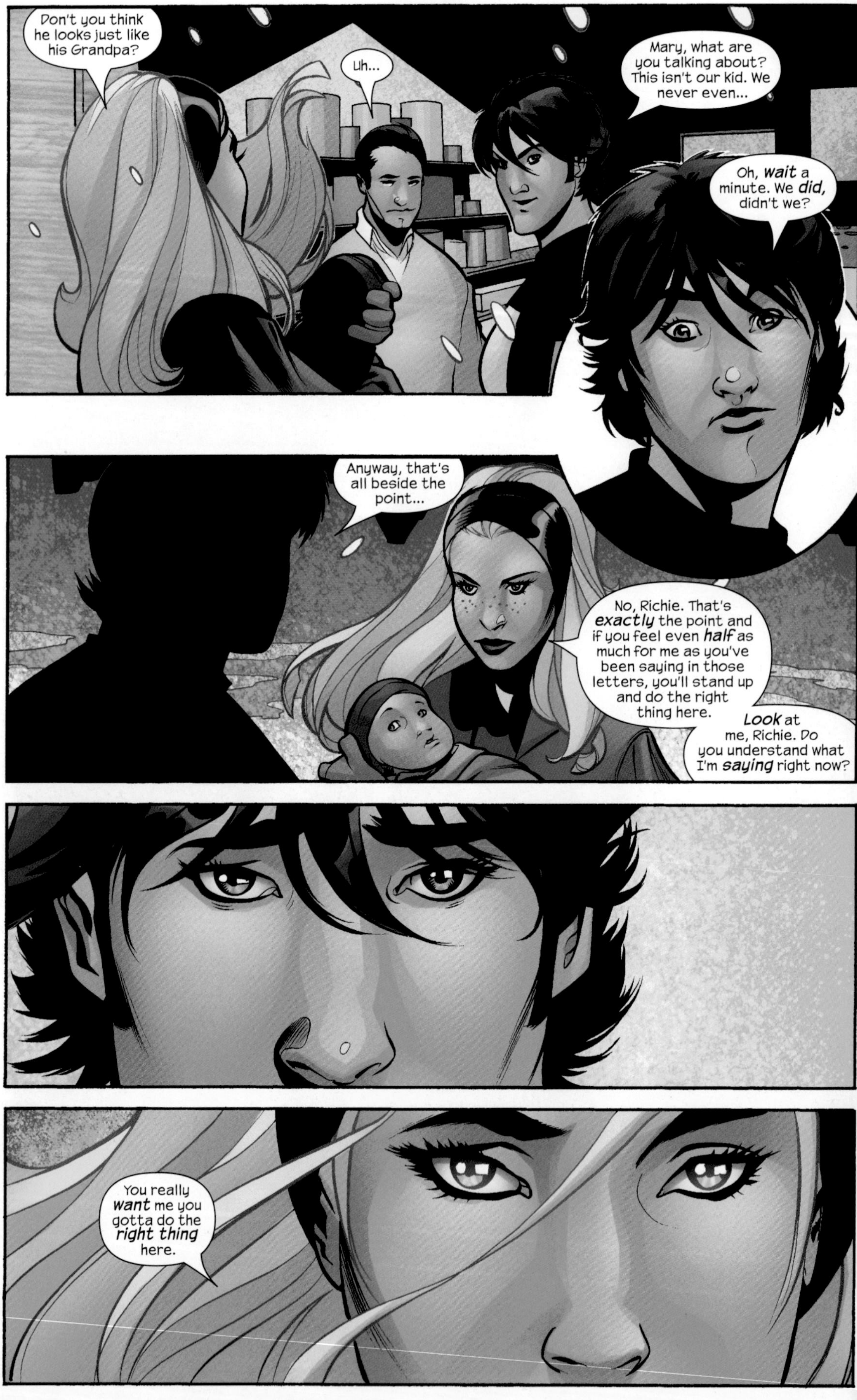
Don't you think he looks just like his Grandpa?
Uh...
Mary, what are you talking about? This isn't our kid. We never even...
Oh, *wait* a minute. We *did,* didn't we?
Anyway, that's all beside the point...
No, Richie. That's *exactly* the point and if you feel even *half* as much for me as you've been saying in those letters, you'll stand up and do the right thing here.
Look at me, Richie. Do you understand what I'm *saying* right now?
You really *want* me you gotta do the *right thing* here.

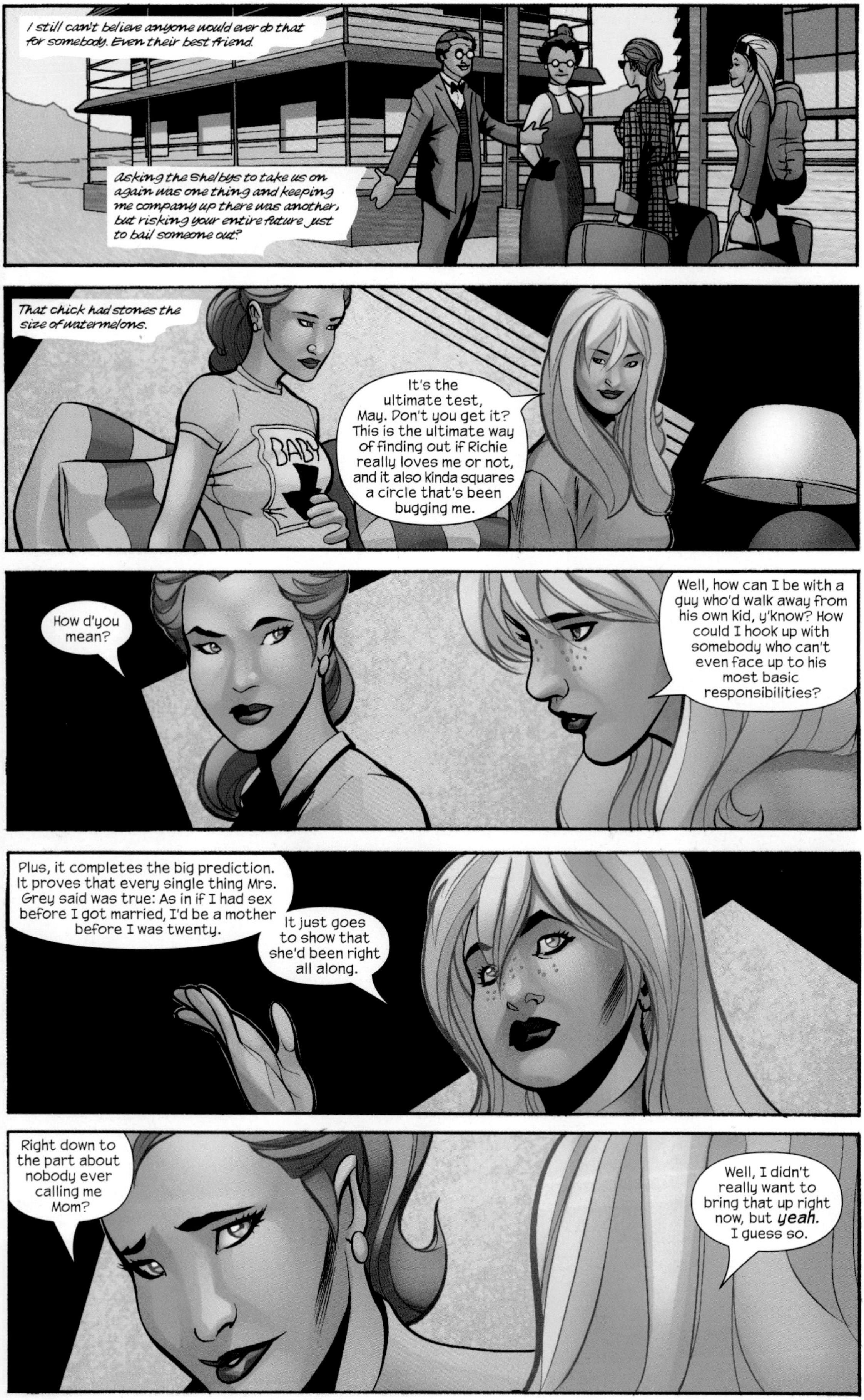

I still can't believe anyone would ever do that for somebody. Even their best friend.
Asking the Shelbys to take us on again was one thing and keeping me company up there was another, but risking your entire future just to bail someone out?
That chick had stones the size of watermelons.
It's the ultimate test, May. Don't you get it? This is the ultimate way of finding out if Richie really loves me or not, and it also kinda squares a circle that's been bugging me.
How d'you mean?
Well, how can I be with a guy who'd walk away from his own kid, y'know? How could I hook up with somebody who can't even face up to his most basic responsibilities?
Plus, it completes the big prediction. It proves that every single thing Mrs. Grey said was true: As in if I had sex before I got married, I'd be a mother before I was twenty.
It just goes to show that she'd been right all along.
Right down to the part about nobody ever calling me Mom?
Well, I didn't really want to bring that up right now, but *yeah.* I guess so.

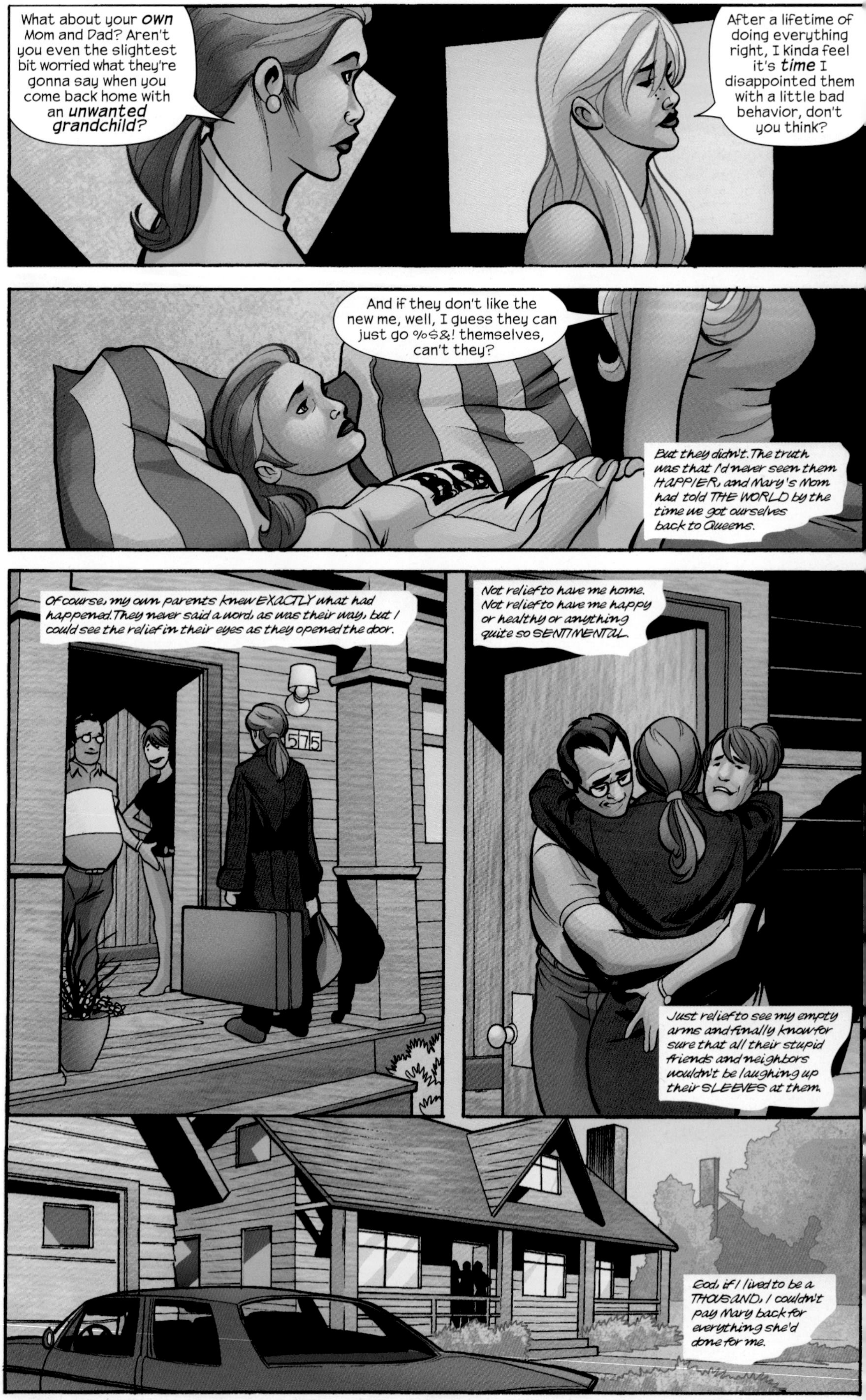
What about your OWN Mom and Dad? Aren't you even the slightest bit worried what they're gonna say when you come back home with an unwanted grandchild?
After a lifetime of doing everything right, I kinda feel it's time I disappointed them with a little bad behavior, don't you think?
And if they don't like the new me, well, I guess they can just go %$&! themselves, can't they?
But they didn't. The truth was that I'd never seen them HAPPIER, and Mary's Mom had told THE WORLD by the time we got ourselves back to Queens.
Of course, my own parents knew EXACTLY what had happened. They never said a word, as was their way, but I could see the relief in their eyes as they opened the door.
575
Not relief to have me home. Not relief to have me happy or healthy or anything quite so SENTIMENTAL.
Just relief to see my empty arms and finally know for sure that all their stupid friends and neighbors wouldn't be laughing up their SLEEVES at them.
God, if I lived to be a THOUSAND, I couldn't pay Mary back for everything she'd done for me.

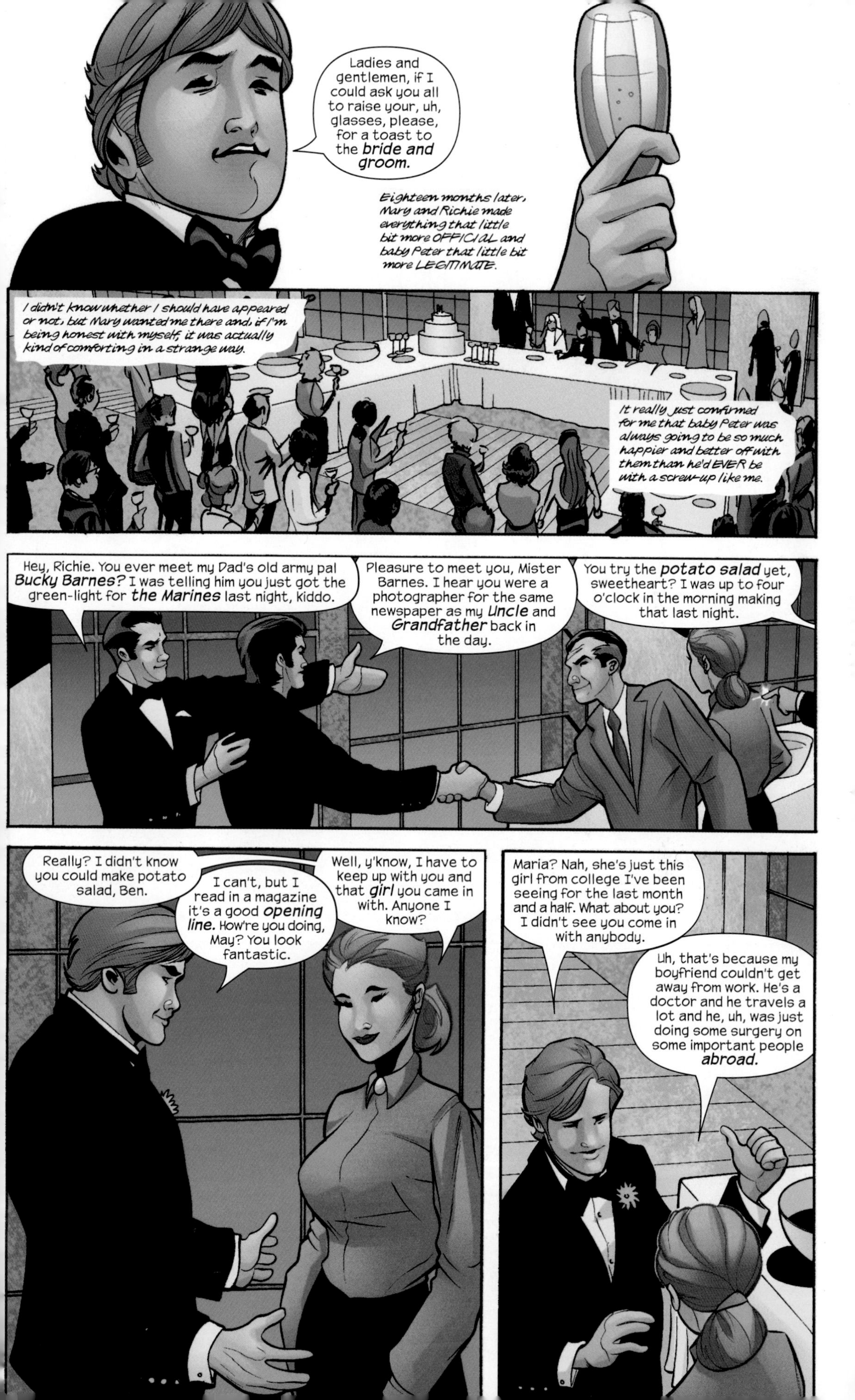
Ladies and gentlemen, if I could ask you all to raise your, uh, glasses, please, for a toast to the bride and groom.
Eighteen months later, Mary and Richie made everything that little bit more OFFICIAL and baby Peter that little bit more LEGITIMATE.
I didn't know whether I should have appeared or not, but Mary wanted me there and, if I'm being honest with myself, it was actually kind of comforting in a strange way.
It really just confirmed for me that baby Peter was always going to be so much happier and better off with them than he'd EVER be with a screw-up like me.
Hey, Richie. You ever meet my Dad's old army pal Bucky Barnes? I was telling him you just got the green-light for the Marines last night, kiddo.
Pleasure to meet you, Mister Barnes. I hear you were a photographer for the same newspaper as my Uncle and Grandfather back in the day.
You try the potato salad yet, sweetheart? I was up to four o'clock in the morning making that last night.
Really? I didn't know you could make potato salad, Ben.
I can't, but I read in a magazine it's a good opening line. How're you doing, May? You look fantastic.
Well, y'know, I have to keep up with you and that girl you came in with. Anyone I know?
Maria? Nah, she's just this girl from college I've been seeing for the last month and a half. What about you? I didn't see you come in with anybody.
Uh, that's because my boyfriend couldn't get away from work. He's a doctor and he travels a lot and he, uh, was just doing some surgery on some important people abroad.

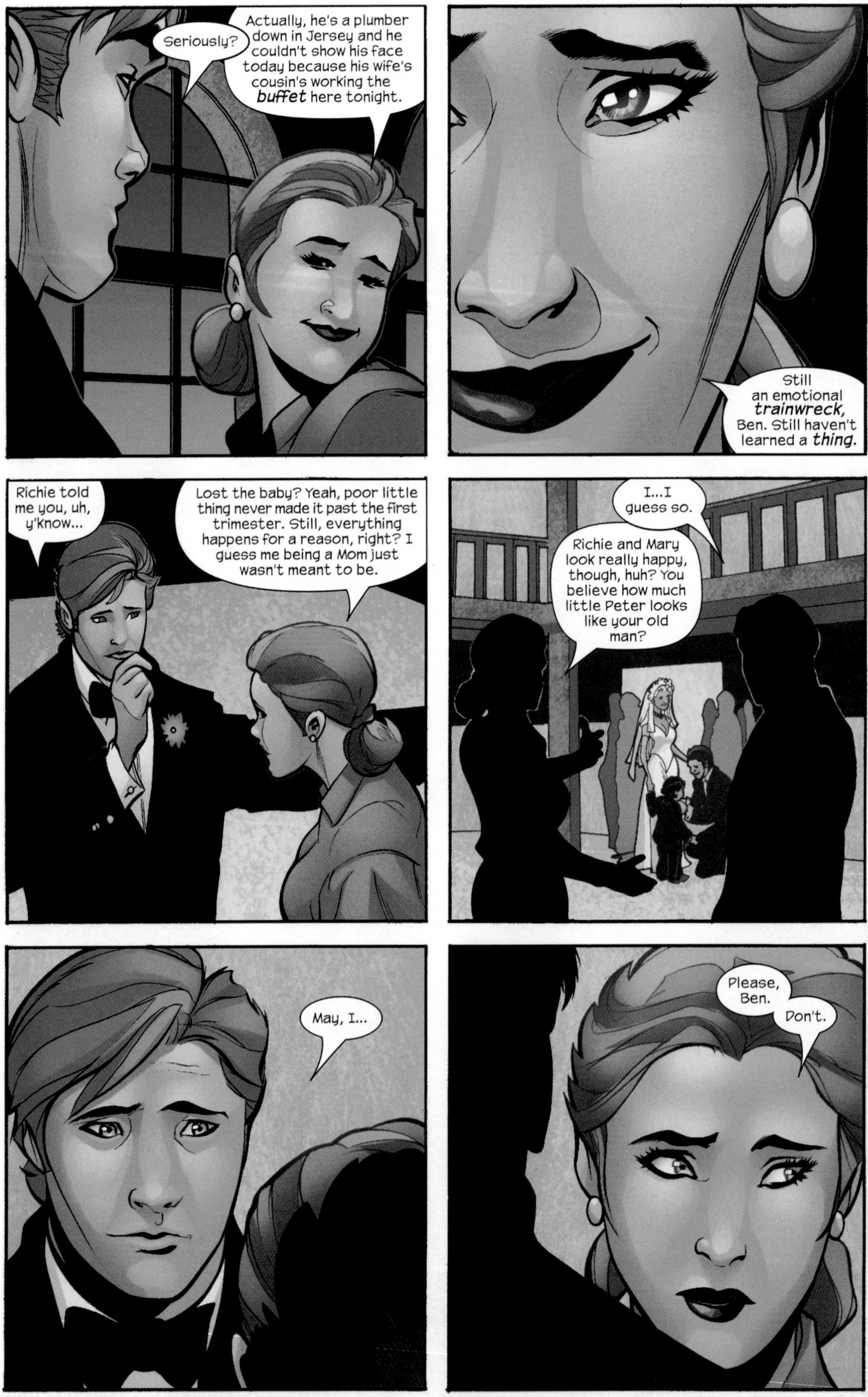
Seriously?
Actually, he's a plumber down in Jersey and he couldn't show his face today because his wife's cousin's working the buffet here tonight.
Still an emotional trainwreck, Ben. Still haven't learned a thing.
Richie told me you, uh, y'know...
Lost the baby? Yeah, poor little thing never made it past the first trimester. Still, everything happens for a reason, right? I guess me being a Mom just wasn't meant to be.
I...I guess so.
Richie and Mary look really happy, though, huh? You believe how much little Peter looks like your old man?
May, I...
Please, Ben.
Don't.

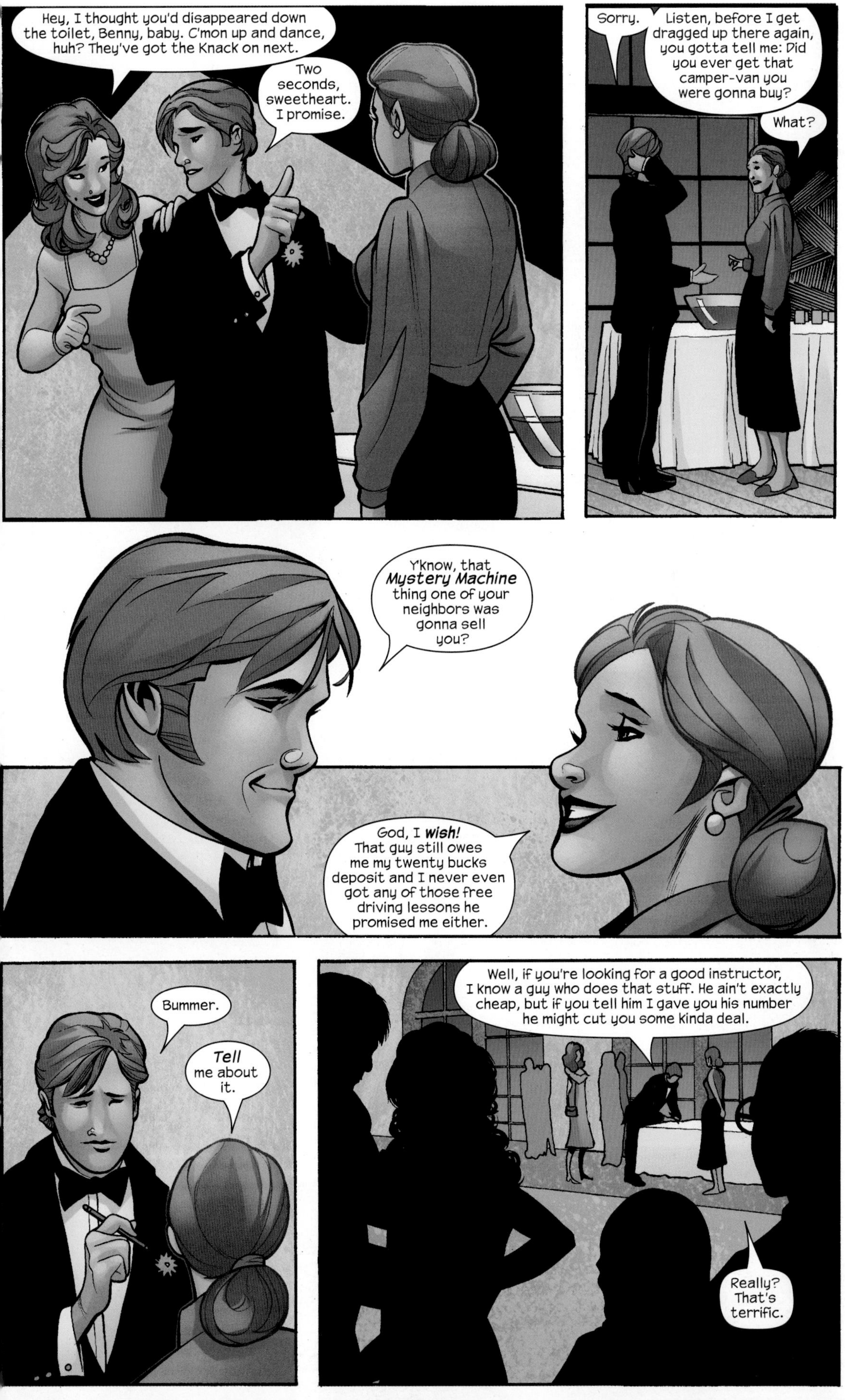

Hey, I thought you'd disappeared down the toilet, Benny, baby. C'mon up and dance, huh? They've got the Knack on next.
Two seconds, sweetheart. I promise.
Sorry.
Listen, before I get dragged up there again, you gotta tell me: Did you ever get that camper-van you were gonna buy?
What?
Y'know, that *Mystery Machine* thing one of your neighbors was gonna sell you?
God, I ***wish!*** That guy still owes me my twenty bucks deposit and I never even got any of those free driving lessons he promised me either.
Bummer.
Tell me about it.
Well, if you're looking for a good instructor, I know a guy who does that stuff. He ain't exactly cheap, but if you tell him I gave you his number he might cut you some kinda deal.
Really? That's terrific.

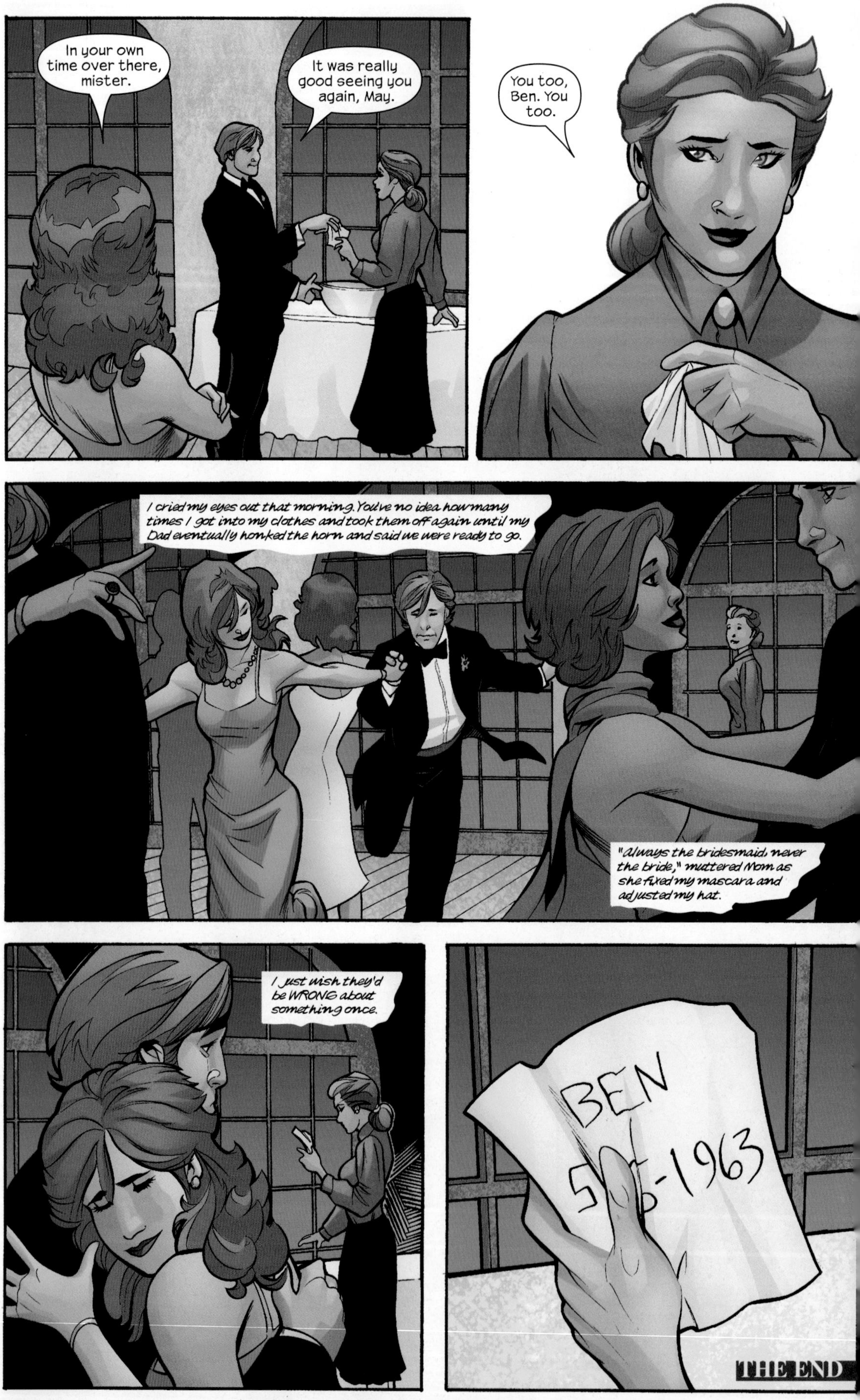
In your own time over there, mister.
It was really good seeing you again, May.
You too, Ben. You too.
I cried my eyes out that morning. You've no idea how many times I got into my clothes and took them off again until my Dad eventually honked the horn and said we were ready to go.
"Always the bridesmaid, never the bride," muttered Mom as she fixed my mascara and adjusted my hat.
I just wish they'd be WRONG about something once.
BEN
1963
THE END